Actions of a Few (Councillors) are felt by all

An environmentally friendly book printed and bound in England by
www.printondemand-worldwide.com

Actions of a Few

(Councillors)

Are Felt by All

•

Anthony Glanfield

FastPrint
Publishing

www.fast-print.net/store.php

Actions of a Few (Councillors) Are Felt by All
Copyright © Anthony Glanfield 2012

Revised Edition

ISBN 978-178035-533-7

First published 2012 by
FASTPRINT PUBLISHING
Peterborough, England.

Contents

*

Chapter 1 / Policy Background / 1
Chapter 2 / Choosing Where You Live / 5
Chapter 3 / No Trees, Just Concrete / 10
Chapter 4 / The Green / 16
Chapter 5 / Double Standards / 21
Chapter 6 / Taking on the Council / 24
Chapter 7 / Too Time Consuming / 29
Chapter 8 / Petition / 32
Chapter 9 / Super Grandmother Takes on Robbers / 36
Chapter 10 / Disabled Couple in Close / 43
Chapter 11 / Author's Start in Life / 47
Chapter 12 / Hoppy My Cat / 52
Chapter 13 / Claim on the Green / 60
Chapter 14 / My Close Family / 64
Chapter 15 / Power / 66
Chapter 16 / Accidently Cutting Down Three Trees / 70
Chapter 17 / Leaving Wealthy Areas Alone / 76
Chapter 18 / Section 106 Agreement / 81
Chapter 19 / Properties Seriously Devalued / 84
Chapter 20 / Petition to Reclaim Our Play Area / 91
Chapter 21 / Residents, Followed like Sheep / 95
Chapter 22 / Car Registration. It's all in a Name / 99
Chapter 23 / Committee Meeting / 102
Chapter 24 / Who Owns the Land? / 105
Chapter 25 / Can you speak at Committee Meeting? / 109
Chapter 26 / Three Questions Were Asked / 112
Chapter 27 / Development Proposal Notification / 116
Chapter 28 / My Old Neighbour / 120

Contents

*

Chapter 29 / Consideration for the Environment / 124
Chapter 30 / Removal of Two Cherry Trees / 128
Chapter 31 / Our Local Councillor Lost Her Seat / 132
Chapter 32 / Take a Wonderful New Journey / 136
Chapter 33 / Two of my Objections / 139
Chapter 34 / No Considerations for Disabled Couple / 144
Chapter 35 / Due to Unforeseen Circumstances / 148
Chapter 36 / Some of the Amazing True Costs So Far / 153
Chapter 37 / Democracy Gone Mad / 156
Chapter 38 / Children Can now Play in the Road / 163
Chapter 39 / Could Have Been Curtains for Me / 166
Chapter 40 / Rivers of Blood / 170
Chapter 41 / Who is in Charge? / 172
Chapter 42 / Too Late to Change your Mind / 176
Chapter 43 / Change Policy Background / 180
Chapter 44 / Our Close Neighbourhood /184
Chapter 45 / Mr Day's Knighthood / 187
Chapter 46 / Long Weekend Away with Hazel / 190
Chapter 47 / Hazel Preparing for the Olympics 2012 / 195
Chapter 48 / Our Other Neighbours in the Close / 198
Chapter 49 / Respect / 202
Chapter 50 / Early Days in the Army / 205
Chapter 51 / Court Appearance / 209
Chapter 52 / Settle a Score in the Ring / 212
Chapter 53 / Interesting Discussions / 216
Chapter 54 / I Cannot believe it / 220

Acknowledgements

*

To all my family who were extremely
Patient over the months spent
Researching material to
Complete this volume.

*

Hopefully this book may save some essential small greens.
For HRH Price William through his project, which
Has started in attempting to save 2,012 play areas
From the greedy developers by the year 2012,
To commemorate the Diamond Jubilee of
Queen Elizabeth II.

*

I wish to say a very warm thank you to Ian Hal for his grateful
Assistance, without your help with technical support
I would have struggled immeasurable.
Many thanks it was much appreciated.

Miserable Old Git.

CHAPTER ONE

*

Policy Background

Since the interest is kept consistent. The reader will try to anticipate ahead of the script therefore eager to see the next line, or paragraph. Then on to the next intriguing chapter, learning from the early part of each chapter as to which town.

The volume you are reading is mainly aimed at achieving just this interesting balance, which is not very pleasant for some. With the intention of encouraging others with promoting democracy, which I feel personally has been lost throughout Great Britain.

The balance, you must firstly consider. Has democracy in this country been thrown out of the proverbial window by local councils over the past years, with confrontational scant regard towards local resident's concerns or feelings, by intentionally removing all essential open spaces, that held the local communities together over many, many years in the past?

Council officials using unacceptable bullyboy tactics, an acceptable way to carry out business. Regardless of the utterly irresponsible outrageous scandals, with MPs parliamentary expenses claims, acting with extraordinary behaviour along with local council officials and councillors alike throughout this country.

Before even considering writing this book, my only intention was to write to our local councillor, to remind her that Shortmeadow Green had a policy background prohibiting any plans to build on this open space. Her immediate unexpected response, along with all other local councillors in this town, stating that all the open spaces without exemption, would eventually be built on to provide housing and objections would not be considered, this idea is crazy and absolute madness.

Disappointed, naturally with this inexplicable announcement, I personally wrote an extended letter, to our local MP for an explanation; unaware at the time she was extremely busy sorting out her own very important scandalous parliamentary expenses. Learning from her, the very same statement which our local councillor's had stated earlier, that all open spaces which were set-aside sensibly by the planners years ago, as designated play areas with very young children in mind, plus local residents.

Was indeed going to be taken from us showing obvious animosity towards the entire local resident's on both estates, which used to share this same green. The consequences of their actions would involve extremely serious devaluing of all the local properties sounding the green.

Now you see, and fully understand the reason for my actions in writing this book, to draw attention to this preposterous ridiculous way of thinking by MPs and councillors alike. Possibly dishing out, and planning the same treatment in the future in your town.

Soon after our local and general elections complete, a fundamental outcome with the result, our local councillor, who was self-assured carrying out her duties as mayor for a year, quite confidently just a couple of weeks before the local election, was shocked unexpectedly, to find she had lost her seat on the council. 'Why you might ask.'

Two elementary reasons, for her unexpected loss of her seat, initially she offered absolutely no support in trying to save our essential local green.

Second reason, which was equally as important, not listening or communicating, with the local resident's on her patch. Disregarding concerns with each of the surrounding properties being devalued, by the introduction of this new development proposed in our close neighbourhood.

The council sold the green on to the developer (section 106) agreement for approximately £20,000. (This was found using freedom of information).

On a separate secret committee meeting, held in private on 22nd September 2009 a further (section 106) agreement, involving the important area, where a huge number of garages were demolished, leaving only two garages on the initial working plans. Changing this garage area into a Brownfield site unlawfully soon after, into a freefall site which was only yards away from our essential green, used by all the local children/residents in the near neighbourhood.

It was found impossible, to source the exact amount the council received from the developers for this garage area. Even resorting to using (freedom of information act), through our local legal department in town, their solicitor remarkably was unable to reveal the true amount.

Which remains questionable, and a complete mystery why this was never truthfully revealed to the public? Of how much the council received from the developers to build seven houses that were shamefully changed sometime later to six, in this garage area. You will hear later why this was shockingly changed to six, involving a serious blunder by the local housing manager Mr Day.

Firstly no consultation, and respectable debate, or a meeting to discuss locally with many serious issues regarding this new development. One can only guess up to £800,000, the council may have received from the developers to demolish 47 garages locally in this area without justification. Furthermore, an extremely important say with changes disrupting our area, soon to affect all our lives.

Importantly, there has been an unacceptable and noticeable, exodus of eighteen families having sold their homes with others to follow, all of which have been seriously devalued with a naturally reduced rate, due to the foreseeable expected controversial changes, this development has caused. Which is unforgivable and of significant, profound concern for future developments in this town. 'Why are all these families being forced into extreme action, in selling their homes?'

Seriously, I will be next to leave because I cannot accept this enforced intrusion this development has caused, most of the houses locally are privately owned, no development should ever cause this exodus, plus ill feeling by the planning office, who couldn't not give a damn. An absolute shambles, affecting all the property values that the planning office considers not important enough consideration with the planning application. Where is democracy? The green was snatched from us, showing little or no sympathy with people's emotions, ignoring all local objections surrendered into the planning office, is a disgrace. Without showing any respect, or consideration or concerns regarding local issues.

This is extremely serious and dishonest treatment, which has been dished out and has to be challenged and changed for any future proposed developments, nevertheless it is not in their back garden, it's in ours. There is no rationalization for this treatment of refusing an important essential meeting with the local residents concerns, regarding this new proposed development. After exhaustive countless attempts at trying to arrange a meeting, to discuss these serious issues with the head of planning Mr Bent refusing this necessary important meeting, with offering a surprising response and explanation, from an official who is paid hugely by the ratepayer is outrageous, stating **'It is too time consuming, plus you are wasting our time.'** (You will hear more on this subject later).

How can this be acceptable leading into the 21st century, where has democracy gone, in this society? Back in 1983 the head of planning Mr Parry, who should have been put into a straight jacket, for his atrocious behaviour and cunning way he confidently went about, trying to take our very small open space, he was like a bulldog he would not let go. Continuing to show on each occasion his willingness to go out of his way, to unjustifiably upset as many residents as possible. You are not permitted to smile, or laugh throughout this whole volume! (Intriguingly it could be happening to you in your town, which is no laughing matter).This book was never meant to be pleasant reading, mainly to inform local residents in other towns, of how the local councillors are treating us citizens.

Please promise now. If you laugh then you appreciate a good joke, along with the 'planners and officials' who are paid huge salaries by us all, after making sure we are fastened to the ground unable to move, with duck tape placed across our mouths. Which is frustrating enough, knowing that the council officials are showing no respect what so ever, or sympathy towards the local residents in each neighbourhood?

To fully understand the above, you should firstly consider, the planners in the past had the tenacity and forethought to create, and provide essential small open spaces like 'Short meadow Green' at the bottom of our cul-de-sac, shared between two estates over many years, for the whole community to take advantage of and enjoy. With the local councils proving to be as corrupt, and dishonest as central Government has proved to be.

In retrospect, it was always, understood and assumed your right over time; you now have some serious claim as yours. One has to be extremely careful with this claim, it is not like in the bad old days, when the lord of the manor, would just take what he could get away with. Such as King Henry VIII in the past was well recorded in history. He would change at will any legislation to suit, plus laws, constantly changing to suit him and the very rich. The councils are just as guilty nowadays, with selling off land to the developers for a pittance, and then sold for a massive profit to the housing associations. With absolutely no consideration to the natural devaluing of all properties surrounding the new development, as mentioned earlier by anything up to £20,000/£30,000.

They could not care less. Like years ago as a fine example, when serving in the armed forces over a period of one week each year. Remembering us soldiers, were commandeered and requested, to stop any person entering onto MOD land, and explain politely that you are now entering onto land, owned by the government.

This example shows proof that all councils have an obligation to announce ownership of open land used by the public each day.

Allowing the public to use this common land continually, for recreational purpose without acknowledgment, it is the council's duty, to remind the residents of proof of ownership, remembering each year to secure this legal duty. Now this may not have been the best example. But what is understood by the subject above, you have to remind everybody who uses your land, that it belongs to that person or organisation, and you have a responsibility in having to remind all those who enter onto the land in question, of this fact! You only have to speak with any solicitor here up North, or down South, to find this is essential important information, and must be taken seriously.

That over time our open space, used both as play area, or for general use, belongs solely to the residents in the near neighbourhood who have enjoyed and used the play area constantly, (over many many years) without once being challenged with the fact of natural ownership. It becomes understandably quite clear to any English person, concerning democracy that common land is for all, to use without question, and certainly worth fighting for. There will always be contentious views on ownership, of much of the land in this country, we use commonly. With no notice locally as who owned 'Shortmeadow Green,' the land we spoke of above.

For the local resident to use and enjoy, not sold off for a considerable profit, where are the children going to play now, was never considered in their plans? Another contentious view would be to allow the council officials to continue snatching these small essential areas away from the children, and local residents of each town, and sold off to the greedy developers for a pittance. The reason for mentioning this preposterous statement above is to satisfy the majority in this country, who think that we should not bother, to save these special areas set aside for recreational use. The local children were never considered or consulted, when losing their essential local recreational area.

Although I feel extremely sorry, and sympathise with all those without homes in this country, but importantly the buildings must be placed sensibly with wisdom, in areas needing regeneration, not snatching open spaces already set-aside and dedicated for recreational use.

This is my main argument; they should not have developed on this green, when there are other plentiful areas in and around this town, which should have been chosen, not on this essential open space, which has been seriously affected by devaluation of all the properties in the local area predominantly because of this new development?

May I at this stage mention a wonderful quote from a true Englishman from the past? The right Honourable Edmund Burke:

"All that is necessary for evil to triumph is for good men to do nothing."

I can remember this quote when reading a history book as a young boy; you will soon comprehend its true meaning throughout this book, where many exceedingly good people do absolutely nothing against the corruption and deceit, both by the central government, and local council officials!!

Now with this more modern quote quite offend heard: "what can you do about it."

CHAPTER TWO

*

Choosing Where You Live

Triumphant and delighted that over 44 years ago, we had successfully accomplished a pleasant and suitable place to settle down, after getting married. Armed with the local knowledge, and reassurance with the above open space nearby, was protected with a policy background securing Shortmeadow Green would never be built on. We felt extremely confident and assured, it could not be better, we have landed on our feet, feeling well chuffed.

After four years of marriage, and problems encountered in London now in the distant past, leaving without a choice, we both decided to venture away, and settled down in a pleasant new town.

Now seriously contemplating and ready to start a family. Little did we realise what lay ahead some years later! (Do not get the hankies out yet, you will need them much later).

In their wisdom, our local council inappropriately suggested that the play area of ours, which the planners set aside some years previously for the very young children and local residents, should now be used to house the elderly and handicapped. An excellent idea, except this small play area is approximately. (Apologies for using imperial measurements) 500 yards away downhill from essential amenities, such as the bus connections and other indispensable local shops.

You can imagine the elderly or handicapped, attempting to carry their shopping, with a walking stick in one hand, and umbrella in the other, on a cold windy rainy day. The long walk home would be interesting, if of course you include the very small white dog in the party, and ice on the pavement.

Now stop the smiling, you were told this is serious! The choice of prefabricated bungalows seemed rather odd! When you firstly consider the location of these fragile bungalows. Even if the bungalows were made with bricks, or stone, or like the fairy tale story, of straw. There are many mature 50/60 feet trees on this site, and surrounding the whole of the green. Which did not make much sense?

If there was a storm, and the possibility with high winds, in these conditions we encounter from time to time, it could topple not one or two trees, but many more. For example the great storm in 1987 occurred on the night of 15-16 October, when an unusual weather condition hit much of southern England. With devastating consequences, which the councillors plus planners have not stopped to consider. Now let us first consider, the safety of the elderly or handicapped living surrounded by, and within close proximity of too many very large mature trees, is there any sense in that at all?

The tall mature trees have been there for many, many years well over 80years, possibly longer and a joy to experience each day. As the name suggests it was once a meadow area to play on, environmentally friendly, not as a building site but with a safeguarded policy background that no residential housing would ever be considered on our green.

These trees should, with respect for the environment never be cut down. How would you like to be cut down in your prime?

We locals already know that bats predominantly roost in both top & lower areas of the open space, as well as countless other wildlife and birds visiting constantly 24/7 throughout the year.

You will hear later of the enjoyment my three children and others watching the bats from the end of our terrace, each child prepared with a torch in hand smiling on their return, seeing who spots the bats first flying towards the trees in question.

Also knowing it is against the law of the land, to interfere in any way with bats location. Planners were aware of these facts with our open space, choosing to ignore the obvious, and refused to react or respond when objections were submitted into the planning office. However, I cannot believe for one moment of their concerns for the environment, just like the way children were unable to play on the open space, now forced to play in the street, all the trees will suffer the very same end, there in the way of progress, and regeneration! Without any real concern for the children's play areas, or resident's feelings or emotions locally.

Experience tells us from the past, that the councillors will surely approve the request, and the planning office will grant approval and turn a blind eye, with the removal of many of these trees. With this attitude and reputation, the planners have lost all credibility, plus respect, and cannot be trusted for the future. (More on this subject later). Of the council officials saying how important it is to care for the environment, then not caring a damn for the environment at all.

Amazingly with each new development, using rules of their own, and getting away with it, just to make lots of money, with each (Section 106 agreements) with new developments. To change this attitude, is extremely important, which urgently must be challenged now, for the future.

This may be the most challenging difficult question you will ever be asked, look around your town where you live, and I will bet you any money you cannot find a council official, or local dignitary you can really trust or rely on to consider supporting you, and importantly call upon. Who could help solve this similar scenario above successfully, with regards to the local environment?

The planners have been gifted with far too much power over the years. Furthermore, the councillors are always agreeing with the planners, like a flock of sheep, until like magic when it comes round to election time they will pretend for a very short while, to fall over backwards, and promise anything just to get your vote. You will find out later how many trees were shamefully cut down in total, it will amaze even the hardened campaigner; I can still hear the chainsaw in the background.

Today, December 2009 the first cherry tree has been cut down off site, and returning on 28th January 2010. To remove the second perfectly healthy pink mature cherry tree as mentioned off site, in close proximity to the green. With only two blossoms tree's standing in our small cul-de-sac, how did the council manage without any consultation with the local residents, to remove both trees, showing absolutely no concern for our local environment?

6

This action was primarily to achieve widening, the entrance towards the site, from three meters to five! You can see also from the following photo, how beautiful those two mature cherry trees were.

The white beautiful cherry tree in front had the most wonderful scent as you approached it on the early spring mornings, on my way down to the garage area. After waiting a full year, this is what I appreciate each year, when nature takes over with a delightful show and surprising us all with such beautiful expectation of blossom each year. Also this is what the bees and seriously, all the insects have waited for.

Now history; gone forever because a few inconsiderate naive mindless councillors, who decide at a committee meeting, that the development is more important than the local residents emotions.

You can see from the following photo background, the prefabricated bungalows sited on our green, which were clearly not in keeping with the local properties in the neighbourhood, for well over an extended 20 years.

Worse is still to come later, and this is nothing to do with cutting down of the trees. Involving huge very ugly unacceptable buildings, placed extremely close to the current resident's properties, which I will explain shortly in another chapter. In addition, the council have the cheek to say that the environment is important to them, what about us; it is our environment not theirs, what a joke.

We are aware of their exceptional expensive mistakes of the past. What the (MPs) council officials, and councillors also the planners are extremely clever at, is not listening.

Alternatively, when you consider our semi detached house is on the end- of- terrace, where both terraces merge the perfect location to witness from either direction.

Taking advantage of seeing the bats flying past our terrace from both directions, and great fun with all the children in the near neighbourhood with torches in hand, watching for their return repeatedly, catching moths, and many other insects.

Would a wise old owl, such as a learned, experienced, trained planning department, even consider this proposed scenario? Yes is the answer.

Along with the unappreciative councillors who haven't a clue, of how to maintain a healthy environment. Yes, they would allow, and successfully achieved destroying the environment in our local neighbourhood in such a short space of time.

The site manager Alex Talat was the first on site, stating quite categorically and promised that most of the trees were to be retained on site. This proved to be the first of many, many continuous lies to follow from the developers. As site manager, he managed get away with placing the expensive hoarding surrounding the complete site, six weeks before the council committee granted 'approval' for the development to proceed.

He then handed the baton onto 'Andy' to complete this development. Mr. Alex Talat as manager of this controversial development was never ever seen again vanished interestingly to undertake the start of another development in town, just three miles away by the same developer.

Our two beautiful cherry trees locally off site.

Astonishingly the removal of these two beautiful cherry trees, cut down outside the site without debate or consultation is unbelievable and absolute madness, the other large mature tree shown in the photograph, along with countless other mature trees also cut down in addition, without consultation and nowhere to turn for help in stopping the above.

Which held for numerous years, an abundance of goodies mainly for the bees and other insects alike? Shall I repeat, the only trees now gone in our small close that had beautiful blossom each year?

Astoundingly Mr Alex Talat the site manager who had secured a great number of other developments in this same town including a large development on the old school ground, where surprisingly the swimming pool was demolished soon after very expensive £178,000 refurbishments were carried out. (Which again we will cover later in another chapter involving unnecessary waste of ratepayer's money).

Amazingly it has to be mention at this stage, that most MPs in central government, along with local council officials throughout this country.

Have placed themselves in many very small rowing boats without oars, and are going round and round in circles heading in no particular direction.

Absolutely lost, each has been given a head between their shoulders with a brain inside, but have not realised that you are supposed to use it!!

CHAPTER THREE

*

No Trees, Just Concrete

Earlier, with the first plans submitted into the planning office, the developer had stated the removal of not one or two trees, their intention on the first plans was the removing of no less than eight mature trees. Very soon altered on the next set of working plans, with the removal of no less than 17 mature trees, including two cherry trees off site mentioned in an earlier chapter! Showing on the final working drawings, a staggering increase of many more trees to be removed, some unbelievably cut down (accidentally), without any concern for the local environment what so ever, or local resident's emotions or concerns.

Still not certain of the final total of trees cut down, still opportunity of further changes. Now this is madness even to consider or should I say, 'not consider' the outcome to the environment, with carrying out the above carnage! The head of planning along with other officials are paid a great deal of rate-payers money to damage the environment, to our amazement we were all witness over a period of 20 years, of this!

(Following later with more detailed explanation). Remembering these same council officials are willing to receive huge salaries from us ratepayers/taxpayers, a great deal of money to make these countless, substantial appalling very serious expensive mistakes.

For these nameless officials to achieve a silly award mentioned earlier, with each opportunity. Astonishingly all that was revealed by the planners when the developers, cut down a great number of mature trees accidentally, which should have been retained on site, instead of an expectant hefty fine, when you complain, it is stated that the trees will be replaced. What these very clever authorities did not realise, that I have the evidence on video, of the whole area, on and off site, and tree locations beforehand. To produce the video confirmation, showing after the development is complete, with convincing evidence of their deceit. This evidence would be found, difficult to disprove now captured on video. This is my proof to show after the destruction, of our local environment, to shame and blame any or all MPs, plus councillors who take on this risky destruction business, which seriously harms the healthy environment unnecessarily when aggressively '**land grabbing**' small essential greens.

Apparently for the sake of what is termed regeneration. With advantage of new available technology, of cameras such modern technicality of video evidence makes it so much easier to capture and gather verification instantly. Recording, and checking the stills, plus videos as confirmation, taking full superior advantage of this new technology on offer nowadays, of new techniques, and using instant technology, which is far in advanced now than acceptance years ago, and demonstrates in a professional manner.

An example, a few years ago all you could do was take photographs, then wait ages to use up the whole reel of let's say 24/32 films, then wait possibly a further 7/10 days, before you receive, and see the proofs. The quality of the photos was always questionable on each occasion, without instant checks. This is achievable in seconds nowadays, like with using the mobile phones as a device to communicate, and able to take photographs/video within seconds, also visit the internet, it's unbelievable how technology has progressed in just a couple of years. Making it extremely difficult to get my head round all of these new technologies, some we find impossible to live without nowadays.

A further fine example, years ago, you need to use the phone locally, look around; hopefully you would find a street phone which was working, or having to wait until you arrive back home. The mobile is on your person, and ready to use instantly within seconds taking a photo, or contacting and communicating with friends.

Including many other new technologies such as the sat-nave showing your position anywhere on the globe, within the location where you stand, improving our lives.

The very same cannot be said of the treatment the council officials are still dishing out, Showing absolutely no respect, this needs urgent attention as we proceed further into the 21st century. Already the local residents affected and concerned, with the loss of so many trees in the local area, disrupting our healthy environment in our close neighbourhood.

We are aware and have noticed with evidence that the wildlife have receded, in fact gone from this area, the proof if needed is so obvious. By removing a great number of trees, you remove the wildlife; the repercussion clearly involves the local environment. Furthermore without any chance of reproducing oxygen back into the environment, this is normally forgotten, how valuable trees are locally, could we possibly manage without them. The answer unmistakably is impossible; each tree essentially harbours its own biodiversity and natural environmental systems, with attracting different wildlife and insects to that particular tree. Again the answer is extremely simple firstly, if you have to build houses and carry out regeneration in an area like all excellent ideas, simply go to an area where no trees have to be removed, or unnecessarily cut down.

Furthermore look after the current residents, they will be here long after the developers have gone off to develop, or demolish trees on the next proposed development site. With the development complete, also the environment devastated, and the wildlife gone forever never to return.

Additionally be witness to this behaviour through to perpetuity, this disastrous aftermath, it makes your blood boil with anger at not being able to put a halt to this madness, which these foolish council officials cause with each proposed development.

Extremely important at this stage to highlight and explain this indispensable local recreational space and play area, which proved essential in maintaining the whole local community? As mentioned earlier which happens to be some 500 yards or more downhill from the nearest amenities, and local shops also bus connections?

Now for an athlete 500 yards is no distance at all, but for the elderly plus handicapped person, we must show some compassion and respect, with placing their apartments in close proximity to amenities and bus connections. Initial this serious problem was not even considered, as to the elderly plus handicapped person having to encounter, the distance of travelling from the play area to the aforementioned essential amenities!

Second and most significant problem with the safety of the occupancy, if these mature trees were to fall on the fragile prefabricated buildings, with tragic results in very high unexpected winds as mentioned previously.

11

However, the serious consequences encountered in the lightning storm we experience occasionally, with the possibility in experiencing the domino effect involving more than one tree is highly possible and their safety is not the councillor's or other officials concern.

'Who' would be responsible for their safety? Planners (No). Councillors (No). Local MP (No). It would be our fault, us local residents.

Us taxpayers/ratepayers (who pay our council tax), to keep them in employment, for not stating the obvious with our objections. Which were all ignored without appropriate response when sent into the planning office stating the above possible serious scenario?

After the planning application is submitted into the planning office by the developers, there should be no significant underhanded alterations to the working plans. As you can see later with some of the following objections submitted, how is it possible to ignore at your peril, these serious noteworthy objections with more trees cut down, which should have been retained.

These are some of the necessary changes, which must be made, legislation should state that all new developments should have much stricter rules, more in our favour with a transparent meeting being the first consideration. Always the council officials and planners make up the rules, as it suits them, liken to the arrangement King Henry VIII, and others continually change legislation to their advantage.

Councils have no regard to the amount of trees cut down, while turning a blind eye with each revised working plans. Safeguards must now be in place with strict boundaries, which are seriously followed with each (Section106 agreement). The planners have ignored the lot; have a close look at some of my objections submitted into the planning office, who take scant regards with people's lives, like this group of individuals on this council who haven't realised, who pays their salaries, ' for how much longer?' In the way, the elderly and handicapped are treated without compassion in this country, with little or no respect shown towards their safety for the end product, so called regeneration suggesting placing the elderly also the handicapped, into prefabricated bungalows in close proximity to many tall mature trees, is absolute madness, along with the serious mould inherent in these units.

Surprisingly no guarantees that the objections submitted regarding planning applications, are ever read by anybody, or even considered! Seriously why submit objections that produce no appropriate response, it does not make any sense what so ever.

Unbelievably six objections out of fifteen of mine, asked serious questions which I expected immediate response, without any reaction from the planning office, is 'highly questionable.' First and most important objection submitted, which was extremely urgent asking why no transparent meeting to discuss the new development? This was the most fundamental objection. Which needed an urgent immediate response? Submitting this objection early because of the 21 days restriction with all objections:

How was it possible that the eight foot wooden hoarding was erected some six weeks before the committee meeting, you cannot start the development until it has been approved. Which needs some explaining by the local council officials?

Fundamentally, we live in a democratic society, so we are led to believe, where all peoples, feeling plus emotions come first, when a development is proposed, in a residential area which involves the whole neighbourhood.

Planners must consider the possible changes this development may cause to all those current local residents living in the area.

Therefore, it is vital that a meeting is called in the first instance by law. In the more affluent areas in each town they are unaffected by the planners actions.

Importantly we are the taxpayers/ratepayers, and showing some respect as, 'we pay the very expensive bills' when it goes pear shaped, otherwise the cost could be sky high, to correct mistakes afterwards. It is unlawful not to allow a debate, and hold discussions with all concerned locally; this was their first of a many very serious unlawful mistakes so far, with this individual development.

When you flout the law, and unjustly ignore these rules and policies set down for good reason. Consequently cause unnecessary unrest using bullyboy tactics, and then you should be accountable and be put in your place, which could mean finding another job. Which does not involve using your brain?

Moreover, stop this unnecessary continuous situation in upsetting the local residents constantly, there is a limit on how many times, you can upset the residents in each town, now needing urgent action for the future, as we enter into the 21 Century.

Consultation, plus communication with the local residents as stated by the head of planners here on our council, 'that it is far too time consuming,' for them to hold a meeting. Its logic, they must consider a transparent open meeting firstly, before any foreword stages and financial commitment is decided upon, of any kind, especially financial responsibility, which could mean the taxpayer having to foot the bill after.

Our head of planning, Mr., Bent stated when asked about a meeting before development, his reply astonished us all, to hear that a meeting carried out before a development, I will repeat. **'(Is too time consuming)'** and he stated on a number of occasions. "It is not usual with any new development to hold a meeting" 'What hat did he pull that remark out of,' found possibly in a Christmas cracker?

They would much rather use tried and tested methods like, bullyboy tactics, which would most certainly be 'less time consuming?' Accordingly, not having to answer any questions which must be asked at this meeting, with regard to any new development in your area, is most certainly 'less time consuming.'

This sarcastic remark was mentioned on a number of occasions after many exhausted attempts, at requesting a meeting to fully cover all aspects of the new proposed development. (The deal had already been made that's obvious).

Fancy wasting the councillors, plus planner's time, they are very bossy and powerful important officials, who have lost all creditability and respect towards the people who pay their salaries. '(Please stop that smiling and laughing this is not a comedy)' possibly and almost certainly happening in your town in the future?

You may be interested to realise the sizes of this extremely important priceless essential recreational play area in question. Approximately 40yards wide, by 100yards in length with a gradual continuing slope; importantly the garage area was only 40yards by 10yards. (Besides, it would be interesting to remember these sizes for the exam later)! How many times at school did you hear that stated, as soon as the words, interesting to remember was mentioned, you know that in a test at the end of term would be a question on that exactly topic, so please pay attention.

The trees that were supposed to be retained on this site in total, shown on the early working site plans, top end of the green, with a gathering of about 15 large mature trees. Lower end some 12 of the same tall mature trees. Surrounding the whole site, was lined on each side with countless extremely large mature trees, with many other interesting unique features included.

Incidentally, with only three yards (approximately three meters) road entrance onto the site, as seen on the earlier photograph in (chapter two) of the site entrance, where two cherry trees were removed without consultation to achieve the necessary five metres width.

Keep this in mind for later you will find this of interest, how this local council can manage to get a (quart into a pint jar). Also several outrageous changes concerning retained trees on site, (or possibly not retained).

Even the famous magician Houdini could not solve this difficult magic trick. Nevertheless, the council here are magicians. Besides, have full control over the planning department working very closely alongside, actually sharing the same office in the town centre! With the environmental same group, also others were all sharing this very same office, which becomes very interesting with agreements plus arrangements.

You will hear more of this conspiracy and secret underhanded arrangements, nudge-nudge, wink-wink between the council officials, as they touch the side of their nose, after the completion of yet another successful deal (or fiddle).

What's more, the planning office meeting together over months, in close merger of secret meetings and sharing information, with the developers always in their favour, with very deep pockets ready to seal a deal without any paperwork?

Essential necessary important changes for the future must now be given, showing more transparency towards the residents for generations to come. An example on each arrangement will follow later; this is not very pleasant reading for any residents treated in this way, on the receiving end of these bullyboy tactics that all councils seem to be dishing out, and the local residents except willingly without complaining? They make it so obvious that someone is on the 'make' proving it is another thing!

We will now return to the situation of the council attempting to locate the elderly and handicapped surrounded with huge mature trees to contend with. Another member of the council probably with just a modicum of common sense must have reminded these nameless fools, that the elderly and handicapped would find extreme difficulty on occasions with this unnecessary hill to negotiate.

Moreover, the thoughtfulness of the distance of 500yards to walk before arriving at the bus connections was never consider with the type of weather we experience at times in this country. Altogether, an unnecessary hurdle, too much to attempt this ordeal maybe when travelling by bus, when attending hospital appointments, or do some shopping, maybe visit friends down town at the library.

Locally we residents needed congratulating we pointed out a flat area of grass, just behind the shops within yards of the bus connections, not being used currently. This area of green was an ideal area, and more suitable for the elderly, just yards away from the bus

14

connections, with a flat area of ground, and no hill to negotiate in the winter period, possibly with ice to contend with.

Considering the welfare and safety concerns, the bungalows placed in this safer area. The shops nearby were not surrounded by very large mature trees. Simple ah!

This was achieved, with common sense positive, communication, and consultation, plus in a positive democratic way. Proof that this approach will always work, without upsetting, or alienate anybody locally. Another small field close by within yards of this same area, was also suitable for the handicapped with no hill involved, flat as a snooker table. That's two small fields in close proximity, both successfully achieved with satisfactory outcome without upsetting any local residents.

How about that? 10 out of 10! For us sociable residents willing to guide and help the council officials at anytime, with no cost involved!

Our play area now left alone, what a relief we still have our essential local open recreational space, saved from the clutches of this thoughtless bunch of fools.

Alternatively, shall I say for how long before these nameless individuals, will once again try and take this essential recreational play area, down our very quiet cul-de-sac from the local residents.

Local small greens are so important in maintaining a healthy local community. It's about communities coming together for countless reasons throughout the years. By snatching these local essential greens the communities just disappear, proof is all around in each town with councils land grabbing:

It's the responsibility of the local authorities to hold onto, and maintain these open spaces for the future.

Shamefully this was just in remission.

CHAPTER FOUR

*

The Green

Village greens established over the years, have always been the central point where all of the local community meet and greet. It is the (hub) to hold fetes, the children to play all types of make-believe games. Starting with an all time favourite hide and seek! Then on to the obvious run and chase, followed closely by the girls, collecting small flowers, such as daisies and of course buttercups, and many more interesting flowers, all year. Not forgetting, the boys routing around trying to find snakes plus worms, and spiders also other nastiest, to frighten the girls. (Well I was guilty of that). Now regrettably and shamefully, all this is in the distant past!

Other extremely, memorable street parties were held throughout the year to celebrate birthdays, official or otherwise on every type of important occasions.

Local schools, where it was common with a whole, group of children, lead in columns of two, hand in hand with their teacher plus helper. The children chatting excitedly, all the way from school pleased to be out in the open, until arriving on the green to take advantage of the natural environmental finds! This is repeated throughout the whole country, it's the British way.

After having an enjoyable lunch on the green, the children would be taught about the environmental issues, starting with different types of trees, and flowers, then on to interesting wildlife found throughout the local area where the children live.

This is how our essential green used to be. Including November 5th when all the locals, for weeks talking excitedly, trying to comprehend with all the local parents/children eagerly waiting for the bonfire night each year. It was always a wonderful priceless week, equally as important as receiving a Christmas gift, with importantly a wonderful local community spirit with everybody involved.

I can recall, on many other occasions over the years, when the snow was on the ground, we had a natural gradual safe slope on the green, just perfect for the youngsters to slide safely down, at a controlled speed, made from anything that the children could sit on. Excitedly throwing snowballs at one another, this was enjoyment for all the local residents to join in, as a reason collectively in getting together as a close vibrant community on the green in wintertime.

Now only distant memories exist, to remind us all of this, with the kids now deprived of this pleasure forever. To a greedy planner and councillors alike, consideration only to wish, for the green looking like a building site where housing to them means revenue to the council.

It takes just a few moments at a confidential 'controlled' committee meeting, to sell the green on to the developer for a pittance, without any thought for the above particular effect on the local community. The councillor's sole interest is the value gained of the section 106 agreement? This greed, is there one and only aim, and will prove conclusively the incorrect route in the end. Conversely, when the ratepayer understands the true loss of this open space soon, that could have been saved from the developer.

Surprisingly the other day, but too late in stopping this development. A marvellous report by the 'mail-online' with HRH Prince William spearheading a project to create 2,012 playing fields for his grandmother's diamond jubilee in 2012. He spoke out with some meaning, in support that all councils throughout the country, should now leave small essential greens for the local children/people to use as playing fields and not build houses on. In this report, it states that an ambitious aim is to create 2,012 playing fields as a permanent memorial to Queen Elizabeth II fields programme, celebrating her diamond jubilee year.

Announcing his patronage of the Queen Elizabeth II, fields programme, the 27 year old, could not think of a more fitting tribute to his grandmother's 60 years on the throne, coinciding with the 2012 Olympics.

While carrying out research, an extremely important very late finding has become known after 11 months into this development, concerning the ownership of the play area in the hands of Guinness (Trust) Partnership. Ironically a senior housing organisation with funds of £863,124 from (HCA) Homes Communities Agency.

Shamefully, what puzzles me without calling a meeting with the local residents, who are about to lose this small recreational area, set aside for the local children, shows absolutely no respect or credibility whatsoever from the housing trust in question. This very same ignorance with ignoring the policy background, and aggressively snatching the recreational area from the local children.

The housing authorities from Guinness Trust must have visited the area, so are just as guilty as the local councillors who decided to ignore the local resident's feelings plus emotions. They too have also lost all credibility and trust, we have to live with the new arrangement when completed and the developers have left, to carry out this same destruction elsewhere.

Knowing full well, for the second time in the history of this small field, that all our properties surrounding our playing field, once again have been seriously devalued, quite considerably. By at least £20,000/£30,000, now the open space has been built on permanently, ironically with prefabricated cheap residential housing, would you believe it. However, the local residents have gained absolutely nothing over the years, so why should we accept nothing; we are losing everything from this new development.

HRH Prince William had an opportunity to save this green when I wrote to his father only last year 20th July 2009, expressing my deep felt concerns, with the loss of a perfectly healthy environment, and importantly the very small essential designated recreational play area. Prince William could have successfully spearheaded his project in this country, making our very small significant essential play area, his first of 2,012 for Queen Elizabeth II on her 60th diamond jubilee.

Ironically HRH Prince Charles, who by coincidence, is patron for the Guinness (Trust) Partnership the housing association in question, which has purchased this land from the developers, once the development is complete?

In my opinion, I find it difficult to comprehend why Prince Charles could not have at least looked into the seriousness of my letter and concerns, knowing of the 'field's programme' his son was involved with. Would have been apt as an example of what Prince William was trying to save further land grabbing from the grasp of the developers very soon to be activated by his son, Prince William.

Because of my very genuine sincere passion, for maintaining a healthy local environment that is equal to his, now been lost forever.

Councils are always on a win, win situation open to scandals also open fiddles, but extremely difficult to prove, with exceedingly clever ways to conceal from the truth.

With tunnel vision, wearing (blinkers) not to distract from their hypocritical attitude, stating we are providing for the needy. When taking this very essential play area from the local children, consideration for their 'needs' was absolutely necessary, and we must fight extremely hard against losing other play areas to the developers.

With the councils throughout Great Britain, years ago selling off many hundreds of thousands of rentable council houses, now highly embarrassed, with this substantially expensive mistake. With a deficiency of rentable houses locally, they just do not give a damn, who is upset in their quest to seize and secure, these are priceless local greens and recreational areas.

All the children plus adults locally, each family will record in their mind different stories and fond memories, of fun with their children on the green over the years. The green is everything, one moment a play area for the local children, next an educational environmental area, with a determined aim to open their minds and study the wonderful environment nearby. Also as stated earlier to maintain a close vibrant community.

With each find a valuable adventure along with all their friends, when routing around the bushes or looking up into the nearest tree, towards their next interesting find. Which would prove a learning opportunity, to ask more questions of us adults, recognising tree types from looking at the leaves?

The local residents to walk their dog on the green, and meet likeminded individuals with their dogs, to have a daily chat, also a place to walk and contemplate your thoughts. Being able, and possible to get out of the house to appreciate a well earned break, and inhale some fresh air.

To play with the children/grandchildren, while taking an opportunity also to meet other neighbours in the area, for a chat this is what holds a community together.

For us grandparents, to watch over the grandchildren close by on the green with the grandchildren enjoying playing with all their friends who live locally. At my age unable at times to walk a great distance like a mile and a half to the nearest park then return some time later, this is what a local green was intended to achieve.

You can see in their faces, they are pleased their grandparents are close by for a quick cuddle when they fall over, maybe there friends need a cuddle, an essential timely smile, of reassurances we know importantly they are safe; this holds a community together, and has proved collectively the catalyst of a happy vibrant community over the years, without this essential green in place.

18

Evidently proved shamefully over time, no meetings taking place with other close neighbours, shamefully there is no community what so ever, why? This is the evidence we have to live with now, each council in their local magazines stating how important the community issues are to them? (What a load of rubbish spoken in jest).

Remembering on countless occasions years ago on a cold day in winter, one of my three, or maybe another day all three children, would come bursting into the house after discovering some interesting find? Which they have never seen before. With a smile on their bright red faces while needing our attention, to explain what the find was. We surely miss this inquiring necessary interruption, and on that occasion, will explain to the kids that the snake found was an (European Viper) or 'common adder' found under a sheet of metal, so one would mention, saying when lifting the sheet it was lying there. (This was on numerous occasions over the years on our local green).

Along, with countless other finds, when I was a youngster, I handled the same type of snake with interest on a number of occasions.

Showing the kids, how to recognize the 'zing sagged black stripe, and light brown background,' this is how you will be able to recognize the adder next time. We returned the snake to where it was found. Then I would enjoy spending some valued time with the kids, busily looking for other interesting items.

That same afternoon, another find, a small kitten lost in the bushes, one of the younger kids knows the little girl who owns the kitten, I returned home leaving the children at play. Seriously, this is what a green is for. 'You cannot put a price on the value and loss of our local green remembering Guy Fawkes Night was always welcomed and enjoyed by all.'

Shamefully just the other day I was discussing the loss of our right of way, with a mature woman who lives on the other estate which used to share our green. I gave some assurances that it is now in the hands of the planners to sort out this unexpected serious problem urgently, because the development has only two weeks approximately left, then the new residents will be occupying the buildings. The planners stated that the developers were wrong to have taken liberties closing our right of way across what was our green; hopefully it will be sorted out soon.

The main disappointment and complete surprise, was that her son who was not born 20 years ago and had no experience with how essential the green was to the locals. Unforgivably, was not born when the green was first taken from us, surprisingly stating he was not in agreement with saving the green.

I was totally amazed and flabbergasted with his remark, and he has a very young child of approximately two years of age standing next to him. He has no idea of the importance, a local green has in holding a community together, he may regret soon when his young child has nowhere locally to play, unless of cause, he does not mind his children playing without a choice in the road. Has he stopped to considered, the remainder of the community and other children locally, obviously not?

Clearly, he has square type of thinking, while still inside this box thinking only of his own negative attitude, the term was used years ago for very good reason, and I am not certain he would understand this next section while still remaining inside this box!

19

The green was priceless to us all, noticeably all the local children looked healthy being out in the open enjoying themselves each day, and when called in for lunch would be extremely keen to explain their mornings activities, ready to eat up and out again, with the other local children for the afternoons busy schedule.

With further adventures, to enjoy in the afternoon, returning later for tea. This importantly used to give the children more confidence allowing them freedom to play quite naturally together with the other local children, is a positive collective community.

Nowadays most children are cocooned and never allowed this essential freedom, which is a crying shame. Those were the days, not horrible days with people being killed, but busy hurried times with everything happening. Those were the days, with no time to think, but extremely enjoyable times.

While busy working, I would always find time to play with my kids, which is what bringing up children is all about, and I truly loved every priceless moment. Now I have more to look forward too, with adventures out with all my lovely grandchildren in the future. They need to be taught about how to look after, and appreciate the environment, a great pity no green nearby. 'How is it possible now?'

Could I include an excellent example, which many would understand instantly, try to imagine children looking out of the window with a small-grassed open space in sight. With other local children already playing on this open space. I would bet my monthly pension or any money in the world, that the children would be eager to be outplaying, with the other children rather than stay in inside?

This shows the importance and the attraction of any open space, relating to keeping the children interested and active. Now when the development is complete, the children will now remain inside playing on the play stations or more presently, the mind blowing contagious gadget the (DS). My grandson Kai although quite bright, and I love him to bits, is already addicted, we have great difficulty in prised him away from the (DS) and (wii games) he could be encouraged to play on a green, if we still had it nearby.

Foolishly quoted by our local council in 2010 entered in our local chronicle, 'You are permitted also encouraged to play in the street as long as you use a soft ball.' (This will be covered in another Chapter later).

Having increased traffic now after the development completed, may concern some parents/grandparents. Possibly with one or two children injured into the bargain! This may interest the councillors who voted like sheep, that our green and others like it should be sold off for (30 pieces silver), or less to the developers.

Disappointingly Shortmeadow Green has now gone forever, a true English man would never, ever have allowed this to happen in the past. Additionally, with increased 'on street parking' should add further to the dangers of now having to play in the street:

A green as explained earlier, used to act like a magnet to entice all the children out into the fresh air, and enjoy playing to their hearts content. 'You're only young once.' The children were never considered or offered a choice.

This is unquestionably, the mistake of this 21st century by this council, also other councils who embark, down this very slippery slope just for greed, blinded by the revenue, which can be gained from this very foolish enterprise.

CHAPTER FIVE

*

Double Standards

Expectation of fairness, after all, we are only 12 years into the 21st century, so this is the council's plans for the future. Worryingly, never selecting wealthy areas in any town, disregarding the more affluent areas entirely on each occasion. Why? Evidently the more prosperous in each town are extremely sensitive of devaluation of 'their properties' and guard against any thought of devaluation in these wealthier areas.

Most residents in our area own their houses, and have paid colossal amounts over 30/40years or more, to achieve this commitment. Furthermore, when one looks anywhere near to the more affluent areas in each town concerning regeneration, their contacts in the town hall, would put a halt with consideration or proposal of any development, and refuse any thought of regeneration in their areas, which shows double standards are widespread throughout Great Britain.

Seriously what about our properties, well over 95% of the properties in our neighbourhood are privately owned, and for countless years, maintained by the local residents sacrificing their life saving over countless years in achieving this aim. Councils are not showing respect for the above commitment towards the local residents, by refusing a necessary transparent open meeting, when proposing a new development nearby, is the primary most important consideration, before using bullyboy tactics in taking over our essential open space.

By land grabbing, and selling the green off to developers secretly. 'Accept what you're given,' attitude in less affluent areas whether you like it or not, mindful of double standards which is prevalent, with absolutely no concern, with convincing evidence seen in all towns throughout the country. Consequently, the new development has caused devaluation up to a massive £20,000/£30,000 on all our properties locally, since the development was first proposed, with at least eighteen families having to sell their properties and move away, why?

This particular important true example which follows, be aware and remember the next short statement, this could be happening in your area keep vigilant, as to your near surroundings. This truly happened on our recreational area.

It was noticed that the grass was left uncut for more than four weeks; try to imagine how tall the grass was by early June. The usual expected schedule maintenance, was not been carried out, the length of grass was impossible for the children to play all types of ball games, such as football, or cricket for example, or even throwing and catching a ball was virtually impossible. You would be held back with the long grass, and possibly soaking wet with early morning dew or after it had been raining. Usually with this play area, the grass was kept short and maintained, at least every two weeks in the growing season, and manageable. Now the children were unable to play most other ball games especially when it was extremely wet.

21

Most of the residents also found great difficulties for the very same reason, in walking through the long and sometimes extremely wet grass, with short wet grass, it is sensible to wear decent waterproof shoes or wellington boots, when taking their dog for the morning and afternoon walks, but long grass is understandable unpleasant for all.

Astonishingly, the rubbish is never left lying around for weeks, the local residents plus council workmen normally kept the area clear, so this is **'obvious deliberate neglect,'** with the intention of making the play area looking rather like a 'tip,' our recreational area was normally kept clear of rubbish. This is why we pay our local council tax, for the expected scheduled, planned preventive maintenance (PPMs) to be carried out. **Something was not quite right!** After countless phone calls, by most of the residents over the weeks to the authorities responsible, asking for the above maintenance to be attended too.

Each phone call to the council, saying we are looking into the problem, which will be dealt with 'immediately.' This was stated and repeated with most calls, eager that the children could résumé playing on the green, the local residents continued on each occasion requesting for our area, to be maintained without much success, or any response from the council. We all know the reaction from the children, with inventing games, like adapting to the conditions playing hind and seek in the long grass was great fun.

On numerous occasions our three children would be hiding from me, when calling out teas ready, or that, it was bedtime, and they were trying to stay out a bit later. (Please no laughing this is serious). The maintenance to the grass was never carried out; also, the rubbish was left lying around for many more weeks. One would agree this as premeditated cunning ploy, to say that the area is in need of regenerating!

Quite spectacularly, back in 1991 later in August, only after the planning application was granted in record-breaking time, (breaking all the rules on the way, to a speedy completion), without any consultation or debate with the current local residents.

Now as if by magic, the hypocritical lying authority, quite spectacularly made certain the grass was eventually cut, also you guessed it, the rubbish disappeared in a flash. The green once again looking pristine and in perfect order, returned now to its former glory.

The council here do not ever hide their unlawful or despicable behaviour, it is done appallingly quite openly, as if to say, (what can you do about it) this is what is very upsetting with their sarcastic attitude.

Ironically, in our local darts team unbelievably, three very close friends of mine who used to cut the grass for the council. When asked why our green was left uncut, stated that the council's instructions were quite clear "Leave the maintenance on Shortmeadow Green alone, until further instructions are given to resume."

This is not uncommon, for all councils to leave grassed areas uncut for long periods intentionally, making these areas look as if in need of regeneration, by also deliberately leaving rubbish lying around.

Now that could not be clearer, there is an almighty fiddle going on, and they were caught out on this occasion because of the disclosure, the three lads from our darts team, who cut the grass after (scoring 180), had noted and spoke of, incidentally the whole world can now share this revelation, and judge, if this is fair, or a gigantic fiddle?

22

We had not encountered on the relentless attempts this council will go with countless lies, also cunning tricks with aggressively land grabbing our essential very small open recreational space. Over countless years, the council officials had set their mind on taking this small wonderful green of ours, as usual using unconventional rules with bullyboy tactics, **'and taking the gloves off.' Shamefully this is why I have also removed the gloves and unconventionally hit below the belt, exposing this deliberate deceit, if this is happenings here on only one isolated development in our town, astonishingly this is most likely replicated throughout Great Britain, with all councils carrying out this disgraceful land grabbing, to make considerable amounts of money on each occasion with (Section 106 agreements).**

The part that really hurts us residents locally, is the fact that all the properties have suffered immediate serious devaluation once again, and the council officials are turning a blind eye to those of us who have spent a small fortune over the years.

Please allow me to explain, with having to maintain our properties to a fairly high standard forced without option, to upgrade the old unacceptable wiring in these 60year old buildings, which cost us all a small fortune to carry out?

Then each of the windows and doors in these houses were changed to double-glazing a further serious huge cost.

Including without choice a separate necessary cost of the cavity wall insulation. Not forgetting the most important expensive responsibility, our initial financial commitment with paying our mortgages over 20/30 years, which works out with each property, to a colossal hundreds of thousands of pounds over this period, and was unbelievable never considered by the planning office as a serious objection with the planning of this controversial development.

Choosing this area years ago, because of the wonderful green and extremely light traffic down our quite Cul-de-Sac, which was supported by a policy background that no residential house would ever be considered on our local green.

This above important situation alone would have been kicked into touch, if this was suggested in the more affluent areas of this town, the wealthy are always insulated against this intrusion when consideration towards planned engagement and regeneration in their area is ever spoken of.

While I am still furious from what has just been covered above, enraged with the fact that a small fortune of mine has been spent in writing and publishing this book.

Hopefully it will not have been wasted and immediate important changes will successfully be carried out, to alter the way the citizens of this country are treated in a more democratic way, by the MPs plus local councillors for all future proposed developments.

23

CHAPTER SIX

*

Taking on the Council

Noticing by chance, one of my children indicated a small notice, which was placed on the lamppost in close proximity to the green. We all thought it was one of those advertising leaflets, something for sale locally, or possibly a lost cat/dog notice placed there for the last couple of days!

To our utter surprise and dismay, the contents stated that **'due to unforeseen circumstances'** and problems with concerns with the homeless. This play area on Shortmeadow Green was soon going to accommodate (unsightly) prefabricated bungalows, (suggested before, back in 1983, for the elderly and handicapped).

Stating on this notice, a minimum restricted 21days, to submit all objections regarding the proposed development which is so unfair, the council may have had months or possibly years in planning, and they offer the local residents only 21 days to contest against the development. Late in June 1991, the whole neighbourhood was unaware, that a housing trust was going to take over the green, on this occasion with no ifs or buts; it had already been decided and approved. Central government were paying a colossal £630,000, and the council were riding along with it, or lose a great deal of money involved, the true cost was kept secret why?

Overhearing this amount mentioned by a councillor discussing with another councillor at the time, that the government were financing the proposed development.

Astonishingly the planning office was ignoring the significant safeguards that our green had a **policy background, that under no circumstances, would any residential housing be built on our green.** This was in writing for all to see on the council database; with the last takeover attempted some years previously back in 1983. Moreover, continued to say in 1991, we had now, to repeat the previous attempt with fighting to campaign, even with this policy background, that residential housing would not be considered, and kept as a recreational area for the very young children.

Then low and behold, in 2009/2010 once again, the council will be taking the open space from us local residents, unbelievably for residential housing. With the policy background history in mind, let us start concentrating whether this book with the following example, will maybe explain the reason for creating this volume, hopefully to anybody brave enough in taking on your local council. 'YOU WILL NOT WIN, you do not stand a chance, you are wasting your time,' and many more astonishing outrageous comments that are more than surprising to hear. Said by the majority, of the local residents, when visiting the whole neighbourhood in campaigning against losing the open recreational space.

It seemed that most of the local residents could have secretly been indoctrinated, with something unexpectedly. 'Possibly in their water supply.' When campaigning you must accept on countless occasions, these very same remarks early on, in your quest to muster support for your challenge, and campaign.

With all these fruitless comments, and many more to encounter. Some comments will certainly surprise any campaigner. I will follow later with some classic remarks in the past, which should amaze and amuse most.

May I digress just for a moment to explain and show a fine example; this will enlighten most with imagination, when taking on any local council officials.

Incidentally I am surely, no expert with mushrooms; all I know is that they are sold in supermarkets, on shelves mainly in paper bags. Moreover, are quite tasty especially with omelettes or in the morning with my full English breakfast.

You may be puzzled, reaching to pull out your hair at this point, thinking what the dickens has mushrooms to do with the above interesting subject: 'you are now confused.' Well that is the intention, with all local councils who are very skilled at confusing people, be patient and all will become clear quite soon.

On entering a wooded area looking for mushrooms, only the experts have the confidence, and knowhow in picking out the edible, against the risky non edible type's of mushrooms. Would you blindly go into a wooded area, and select at random without the awareness? 'Seriously ask yourself have you the knowledge and confidence.' Not too many have this profound expertise. The risks are obvious if you have the knowledge, plus confidence and the skill just like gypsy families, all well and good. I am totally confused, and wonder in amazement, and marvel with the different varieties of mushrooms to choose from. Sympathising with all those in the past, who may have suffered illness, or worst still, many fatalities, in finding out and discovering which mushrooms are safe for us all to eat? You either become a hospital visitor, or smile with satisfaction after an excellent full English breakfast.

Hoping this example is sound advice and to the point. Fully explaining that when you take on a serious challenge. Have some knowledge and confidence plus expertise beforehand, plus the skills and tools, to take on this challenge. (Some of my own personal objections will follow).

Evidently all councils, will continually get you confused, this is the name of the game, also their aim. When there is a proposal involving the town or area where you live, control is their endeavour. They ask you kindly, please send all your objections into their planning office, you will consider this a very helpful suggestion, and of course go along with this very good obliging helpful advice of theirs. You have no choice but go along with their suggestion; otherwise, their comment would be that they did not receive any objections concerning the new proposed development.

Please also consider, another tried and tested route; (because it is a ploy by the planning office), there advice on submitting objections is not a favourable act to follow on your behalf, certainly not advisable; you are now in a very weak position.

Consider this next suggestion very closely, they have the opportunity, and may look at your objection or objections, but never, and I do mean never, ever consult with you on the subject of your objections offered into the planning office. When requesting an open meeting to discuss the proposed development it was mentioned by our council on countless occasions that a meeting. **'Is too time consuming.'**

Answering questions is not their speciality. It means that they may have to put themselves in a position in agreeing with your argument. Falling into a trap with having to answer, any of your interesting questions is not the plan, or their concern. This is totally the wrong way in handling a very experienced planning office. You have to be equally as clever as them; this next declaration is the most important statement to remember.

Instead of only sending one objection or objections hoping that your work has been completed. Proceed one particular important step further, involving your local councillors? (This could possibly be in the exam later).

Significantly, your next step is, to seek out your local councillors for that area. Then remind them your important vital significant vote got them winning the seat in the last election. Now you are calling on their support, with this new proposed development or whatever the council are proposing, maybe something primarily in your direct neighbourhood. Possibly to do with your local School, or community centre, but do not be afraid. Keep reminding your councillors they have secured your vote, play one off against the other, on more than one occasion about your continued support.

Worry the hell out of them; making sure that you get as many local councillors behind your appeal, the more the merrier.

You will never realize the importance of this last remark, until you have gained the experience on how the system works.

With your local councillor's support, you will remember who assisted, then next time the election comes round again, they can rely on your vote, it is assured. It is worth repeating the above.

As mention previously your local councillors are the most important contact in helping your campaign, they are called upon, and importantly the ones that put their hands up at the necessary planning committee meeting, to agree or disagree, with any planning application.

So please do not waste your time on protocol. The planners would go out of their way, to make sure you follow their planned instructions, laid down by them knowing the council would have the upper hand, and you will find it extremely difficult to regain a strong position. What we were unaware of at the time, that another area in town had also been selected to house the homeless, approximately three miles away from our open space, with eight of the same temporary prefabricated bungalow units.

On visiting this other site, sometime later, all eight very similar unsightly prefabricated bungalows were sighted, in this very quite area on the other side of town, interestingly with no tall mature trees nearby.

This area was ideal for this 'exceptional circumstances' development. With flat ground, no mature tall trees involved on or nearby the site. Therefore, the area of grass next to the site could have accommodated all the needs required. Counting all of our ten units, plus these eight, amounted to eighteen with ease, possibly 100 more could without difficulties be added to this site with room to spare.

Observing, that a play area was nearby within yards of the eight units, with no foreseeable inherent technical expensive problems to encounter, which our site has!

The planners sensibly, stated years ago in their planning manifesto that our open space down the bottom end of our quiet Cul-de-sac. If you recall earlier, which was unsuitable for residential housing, and must never even be considered under any circumstances, was now going to be unbelievably developed.

Besides, no objection was going to change their proposed plans, with all local councillors in agreement. Incidentally and equally important reason this other site in our town should have been considered, was also ideal because: Absolutely no foreseeable parking problems, also no demolishing of buildings such as garages.

No problems from local resident's objections. (Because there were no residents in the near vicinity). Also no significant serious technical problems what so ever. So why do these mindless bunch, of councillors also planners think that swimming against the tide is easier? How about this for an important fundamental fact.

Apparently no trees to cut down, not even one tree. That shows proof, that the environment could not possibly be altered significantly, with redevelopment especially on this other site. This location like our site was down a cul-de-sac, with very light traffic, leading to another extremely very large football playing field only yards away, years ago I have fond memories with scoring countless goals as a youngster, which is in the past now and enjoyable fond memories.

This has to be the perfect setting for any planning officer to handle, and architect office. So why try the impossible with just the opposite scenario to our open space? Which is now going to cost the taxpayers/ratepayers £millions to achieve realization with regeneration on our site is highly questionable, how can the developers afford this loss?

Back here at Shortmeadow Green, they would encounter all the technical difficulties in achieving success, with this new proposed development, and regeneration aims. Next year after the development is complete, at the council main meeting, to discuss where clearly all the taxpayers/ratepayers money has been wasted you can bet your bottom Dollar. Some councillors will go sick that evening, so that the blame can be pushed around in other directions. You may question also, 'what have the local residents gained' by placing this development on our doorstep 'Nothing.' So why I repeat do we accept? 'Nothing.'

This permanent new development has vastly more technical expensive arrangements to consider, the cost is huge at Shortmeadow Green, compared with the other site in town previously mentioned which could with easy accommodate over one hundred units at a fraction of the price. This is madness.

What compensation is there for the current local residents, (18) families have decided to sell their properties which were seriously devalued significantly, the new buildings are positively not in keeping with all other current residential buildings locally, how on earth did the planners get away with this arrangement against very strict planning regulations?

Amazingly agreeing to a placement of an unacceptable septic tank in close proximity to the current residents' properties, where was the planning and agreement and acceptance, of placing a septic tank in the 21st century, on the current resident back door. This tank is emptied by a tanker each month because the sump pump has failed on each occasion.

Each year one hears of many occasions with unnecessary deaths involving these septic tanks, I can recall in 2012 in Ireland an unfortunate serious incident, where a dog entered a septic tank, the owner an elderly gentleman went in after to save his dog and was unfortunately overcome with the dangerous gases emitting from the septic tank. Two of his sons without concern for their own safety, entered the tank and were also overcome by the same dangerous gases; these two were extremely strong rugby players who lost their lives in attempting to save their father.

And yet the planners plus developers have agreed and totally ignored these possibilities. On a fine day the very young children can be seen innocently sitting on top of this septic tank, naively busy playing with their hand held DS gadgets, also drinking and eating, should their welfare be considered or ignored, both by the parents plus Guinness Housing Thrust, along with the local authorities' involved. What would health and safety have to say on this matter would be extremely interesting, is it acceptable?

True to form, the local authorities have once more accepted placing a dangerous unacceptable septic tank, unpretentiously on site where very young children would be innocently playing.

The former temporary arrangement with the prefabricated bungalows over a 20year period, also had a septic tank situated in the middle of the site and was frequently emptied by a tanker each month throughout each year, you obviously knew when the septic tank needed emptying by the unacceptable recognisable awful stench locally? Once again, you don't need to attend the Routledge intuition of Bleeding Obvious.

CHAPTER SEVEN

*

Too Time Consuming

Altogether, this is the main reason why it was unsuitable for residential housing in the past. What with great difficulties with emergency vehicles having also to negotiate this narrow entrance onto the new development, these very same difficulties experienced each time while attempting to enter and exit the site in an emergency when the temporary ugly prefabricated bungalows were inappropriately placed on the green. With parked vehicles in the vicinities, would be near impossible at times to guarantee a clear passage for the emergency vehicles, subsequently unwise with selecting this site in the first place.

One has to remark where is the sense in carrying out this very difficult development, here when all of the eighteen units as I explained in an earlier chapter, would be accommodated on the other site across the town with relative ease, with a huge outstanding savings on costs, also with a magnificent playing field nearby? Without upsetting any local residents, (it is not like the old phase you often hear), 'not in my back yard' has any bearing with this situation.

With no residents locally to upset on this other site, the council officials will always swim as stated previously against the tide, why? It is evident, that all council officials plus elected councillors lack any common sense and show disrespect, to most residents in all towns throughout the country. Less and less respect each year is shown towards the local citizens, which now has to change for the future. Conversely, this is where the promotion of democracy must start which has been completely lost: To the council, the latter would not achieve their usual naturally unpleasant result.

Because as stated before on most senior council members (CV's). The intention of most council officials and councillor's alike throughout the entire country, when dealing with housing, and planning issues, their sole notable aim is to constantly keep upsetting the residents why? This evidence becomes obvious when listening to the news on the TV/Radio, plus reading local and national newspapers each day.

After all, a meeting is regarded by our local head of planning as being '(too time consuming),' and asking questions like what is your name, may be regarded as an extremely tiresome difficult question to answer, and not be tolerated!

The trouble is that the head of planning, 'Mr. Bent' here in our town, and probably 'Mr. Bent' in your planning office, has the very same attitude. Has quite forgotten who pays his salary, and for how much longer? If the residents do not receive some respect and transparency as a norm, with future dealings'.

Mps have recently learnt an extremely important lesson that you can only get away with treating the public disrespectfully for so long, before things had to change. Having subsequently learnt a huge lesson, when they forgot the rules, with their expenses scandal, and who was paying their huge salaries.

29

The Daily Telegraph newspaper here in the UK is a senior most important newspaper, considered by most as a well informative notable respected paper.

When each day is dedicated to proving you are worthy of a silly award, most members of parliament surely won 'top prize' going. (Absolutely no laughing out loud, you did promise.) 'Congratulations' we will never forget what you have achieved, well done to **'Daily Telegraph' Newspaper Team.** Your work has gone down in history, and will never ever be forgotten, 10 out of 10.

Exposing the expenses claims with not only one party, but also all Mps alike, was a good kick up the proverbial backside, which is what they all deserved, these bunch of thieves? Now the same kick in the same area, with all the seemingly clever local authorities, and elected councillors who are only one-step down from running the country.

This same situation of open fiddling, and mistreatment towards the local citizens will not be tolerated for very much longer.

Calling on the **'Daily Telegraph' Newspaper team,** (your services are urgently needed once more to sort out this unacceptable mess please). This outrageous statement mentioned by our head of planning Mr Bent. That a meeting regarding new developments in this town are unnecessary.

'AND FAR TOO TIME CONSUMING.

Especially when the council are anticipating a new proposed development, near where you live, affecting all the residents living in the neighbourhood close by.

We could not believe what he had said, it seriously left me speechless for some time afterwards, and this will be difficult to forget especially a statement as ridiculous as that, quoted by our head of planning.

(I naturally apologized to him for wasting his time, asking him a question). He thought I was taking the 'mike' what do you think! (You promised no smiling). One has to remark, as I have mention previously where is the sense in carrying out this development here on our extremely important designated recreational play area.

When all eighteen units, could have been accommodated with huge savings in cost, and offering further expansion without any difficulties, been placed on the other site.

Without upsetting any local residents and most importantly, no trees cut down, also no demolishing of any off street parking (garages) plus affecting the devaluing of all the properties locally. However, as you have witnessed earlier the council has a certain aim in life, how much money can we fiddle firstly?

Confident that nobody can do anything to stop those like with the MPs getting away with the outrageous expenses claims they think they are entitled too.

They continue with the latter to achieve the usual naturally unpleasant result, not just in this town. In the news each day, we hear that council's throughout the country seam to go out of their way with appalling behaviour to upset as many local citizens why?

The problem is nationwide, because as stated previously each council official like on their (CV) having to achieve this extremely 'silly' award thing each day after being consistent in upsetting their quote of discontented residents each day with a silly smile on their faces.

Now let us approach this handling of objections in a different way, by asking councillors we have elected, to balance the power towards our favour, instead of them dictating the parameters. We have given over an unacceptable amount of power, to the planners and elected councillors in the past.

Unfortunately the electorate has lost all control of any say regarding local issues. We are evidently dictated to, and have grown to accept this very strange undemocratic and disrespectful, treatment over many years. Making a stand now, is important for generations ahead, planning (excuse the pun) ourselves out of this mess?

For the citizens in the future would then appreciate our actions today, they would not thank us, if changes were not made now. Starting with a planned necessary transparent meeting, before any development is proposed, with the people who are locally affected by its serious local issues, and showing respect is so important.

The complete rubbish that our head of planning Mr. Bent must surely change his attitude that a meeting is unnecessary, inappropriate, plus time consuming.

Have you ever heard of anything as absurd as that, wasting whose time! (You can see, too much power has been handed over to the local officials).

This is a fine example just covered, which would alleviate unnecessary anger towards council's, with residents constantly been upset, when decision makers are not listening, and make huge substantial expensive mistakes, at the taxpayer/ratepayers expense.

Time to listen to us dissatisfied (taxpayers/ratepayers) is now!

CHAPTER EIGHT

*

Petition

Gathering signatures for the petition that follows, and submitted into the planning office was completely ignored, with our attempts at trying to save the play area, from the greedy councillors and developers. Stating it is necessary to take this very small piece of land unlawfully without good reason, for permanent residential housing? Knowing, and ignoring that it was secured with a policy background history, stating quite clearly that under no circumstances, would residential housing be considered on this open space.

The planners designated some 60 years ago play areas for the local children/residents to enjoy, recognising originally the green was found unsuitable with obvious inherent substantial expensive problems. Eventually after 20 extended years, the 'temporary homes' on our recreational play area on Shortmeadow Green are now empty and declared redundant, predominantly because of serious health and safety issues, encountered with these prefabricated bungalows.

Due to the constant mould problems associated with the inside areas of the ugly prefabricated bungalows over the years. With great difficulties and expensive attempts to eradicate this serious mould problem. The promise at the time was to return the open recreational space back to the local community, to enjoy and appreciate once again this very small priceless recreational area, which will naturally reunite the whole community for generations to come.

Our council have reneged on this promise. This claim is supported strongly by the knowledge, and assurance that the aforementioned had as stated previously a policy background, which mentions and (did) continue to say (until changed recently by the council). That other forms of residential development will not be accepted or even considered under any circumstances or conditions, because it was found to be unsuitable. With notable concerns to safety and several other extremely serious expensive issues, in 1983 and again in 1991 into 2010. That emergence vehicles had in the past encountered many problems and difficulties down this narrow quiet road. The local neighbourhood were unaware at the time that this land had already been secretly sold off by the council to the developers, then later purchased and handed over to Guinness (Trust) Partnership soon after completion.

Which is proud to have, and be supported by HRH Prince Charles, as their patron, is a surprise as he has always shown in the past, his appreciation and passionate concerns with all healthy environmental issues?

The developers have proved to ignore this fact, by having no awareness of the natural environment. By cutting down many mature trees, 'accidentally' and furthermore other trees 'intentionally seriously damaged,' and having to be removed later for safety reasons, which should have been retained on the development site.

32

With cutting many of these trees 'accidentally' which show on the last approved working plans to be retained, and not afforded an agreed normal official protection of 12 times the diameter of the tree trunk?

Shamefully less than two weeks after this incident, three more trees were 'accidentally' damaged, by removing the soil away from the tree bases. Consequently, the cowboy developers deliberately ripping away the roots using a digger, extremely close to the tree base, knowing and aware of the strict rules that apply with the retained trees, should have been given the affordable protection after securing planning approval. This shocking deliberate damage to these trees can be seen in (Chapter Thirty-Seven).

Uniquely, Guinness Partnership has only just surfaced after 11months since the start of the development. Why did they hide their interest until now?

Observing on a rather large notice board recently positioned at the bottom corner of the development, out of sight, half concealed behind a new three-metre wooden fence, the local residents cannot straightforwardly see this notice at this location. Interestingly enough the committee meeting was held on the 15th September 2009, it is now 10th May 2010. Why have they hidden their interest with this land until now, is questionable? What have they got to hide by not revealing this important information, half way through the development, makes you wonder what is going on, yet another twist, with this new controversial development;

Likewise, not knowing at the time of the committee meeting, the planning office kept this essential information from all the local residents.

Receiving, a huge grant from Homes & Communities Agency (HCA), backing of £863,124. With central government assistance, like the previous development involving the unsightly prefabricated bungalows, 20years ago was also backed by central governments of a further £630.000 powerful connection for the unsightly bungalows. The next statement is a fascinating fact and a puzzle worth investigating further.

Surprisingly, was never mentioned and kept secret, is the fact that the name (Shortmeadow Green) was never seen on any working plans. Only referring to the 'garage area', which is only a small fraction of the development, site overall. The majority of the buildings were placed on what was formally 'Shortmeadow Green recreational' area.

On visiting the 'Guinness Housing Trust' web page, again stating that the development took over a disused garage block, no mention of 'Shortmeadow Green' recreational area, shamefully unable to truthfully state that the development replaced the local children's essential play area why?

It's as if 'the recreational area' never existed, as if by magic disappeared, 'just like that,' As Tommy Cooper would say! While all councillors, including planners, constantly use power against the locals to achieve their success, neglecting to inform us residents, that Guinness (Trust) Partnership had anything to do with the development overall, only finding out 11months after the start of the development, is out of order, and highly deceitful. Councillors plus council officials have lost all or any respect over many years in each town, how can they possibly function, having lost all credibility and trustworthiness, shown with each opportunity?

In the centre of all this deceitfulness, we can only blame ourselves, for allowing this to get out of hand over the years, and ignoring these situations without challenging the officials before now. On your own, you do not stand a chance, against the council officials plus councillors. Please let me explain, with the following excellent example concerning this power in general.

When us youngsters, at school in (PE) lesson for example, or after school time, can you recall yourself and many others, gathered around in an area waiting to be picked by the captain of each football team.

If you were chosen early on, you felt on top of the world, and of course worthy of that selection, therefore felt rather 'smug' with not being left until the very last to be selected, mainly because you could be playing on the losing side possibly!

The very same situation also applied with the girls with basketball or hockey, or any other competitive games. Try to recall how that felt for you, being the very last to be selected! Possibly with (NHS) spectacles, or very thin legs, or unfortunately quite plump, with pale features who does not show much interest with games or sport in general? This I think, is how the council along with councillors and other officials, collectively forming a power group working together strongly, against the weak, and have successfully proved beneficial over the years, using bullyboy tactics to continue without change.

Now try to realise how this game of football would be played out.

Alarmingly each time the council propose a new plan or are involved with a new development, it is liken to an arranged 'football match' with obvious predictable result.

With the council officials in charge, also able to keep fully in control, manipulating right from the start of the match, even the arrangements of 'drinks or oranges' at half time would show their confidence.

Secured direct instructions, to all residents, making certain of a win-win situation, stating that you have 'only 21 days' to submit all your objections into the planning office, with encouragement to opponents on the other team. Offering helpful advice, on directions where the objections, against the new proposed development should be sent, safely into the planning office. Nicely tucked away showing that they have viewed all the documents '(or have they)' and placed them on the database for public viewing, without a personal response of any kind.

With the objections now safely in place, the 'friendly football match' can now commence. The councillors, and planners, and all other council officials on one side. Which looks unfair from the spectator's point of view, a very strong team to play against? Like playing against the top teams in the country, such as Arsenal, Chelsea, Man united. Now only 21 days to play the game, they start to smile with great satisfaction, knowing they have chosen importantly, the correct time of the year between June-July.

When most of the residents are looking forward to their first break of the year, with most people away enjoying their holidays. (Believe me this true and well calculated). With the players on this, other team predominately made up from all the local residents and other taxpayers/ratepayers, 'Who are tied down to stakes in the ground unable to move.'

The fans now all realizing this unfairness, simultaneously start to shout out boisterously to the Woman referee, who happens to be their local (MP). This is unfair, controversial, undemocratic, stop the game. This is not the democratic way to carry on. She takes absolutely no notice inadvertently too busy, shamelessly trying to sort out her 'own parliamentary expenses claim' for refereeing the match.

Each player on the resident's side is staked to the ground, with duck tape, placed across their mouths, not the nose, it would not seem 'fair' or appropriate if the other team were unable to breathe, as they are local taxpayers/ratepayers, and killing them is a rather bad choice, as the huge salaries are paid by us all, in each town.

Also paying for their huge expensive mistakes all councils make throughout Great Britain, and try very hard to hide under this very large magic carpet.

Now the match can go ahead with a predictable result! The first goal scored by the councillors also planners and other officials, 1-0. Hooray, some of the fans can be heard shouting; soon they score the next goal 2-0, more applause from the same council officials. Thereafter the next goal soon made it 3-0 for the council & officials, this continued for the next 21 days. How can they possibly lose, and this is how (excuse the pun) the plan each of the professional bodies have deliberately laid out in their favour. On each occasion over the years, in each town throughout the country.

Certainly, a (Win-win) situation all the way, and nobody yet is able or strong enough to challenge this situation and stop this ludicrous state of affairs continuing:

Please remember references to this football match, as an example on many occasions, referred too, the way councils mistreat their citizens throughout the book. (Could possibly be a question in the exam later)?

Rather like this new recent arrangement, a coalition government between the Conservatives and liberals constantly changing legislation to suit themselves.

This is somewhat like in an earlier chapter which stated; that all MPs and council officials are all back in very small rowing boats without oars, you cannot help laughing at this situation there in. Heading in no particular direction, stating a policy today, and tomorrow heading in the opposite direction to follow, a completely unexpected policy, just dreamed up, to suite the situation of the day, significantly heading for absolute destruction.

CHAPTER NINE

*

Super Grandmother Takes on Robbers

Excluding this incident in February would be wholeheartedly shameful, when you consider this wonderful brave lady Ann Timson, who took on six men who were attempting to break into a jewellery shop armed with heavy sledgehammers, in broad daylight at 9.30am, 8th February 2011 in Northampton shopping area.

They had not bargained, or taken into account how harmful a handbag is as a weapon, in the hands of a woman over 70 years old, who was determined enthusiastically to clobber the raiders and stop their activities, at a stroke or several stokes.

Proof that they were no match, and had to run for their lives, she was fearless plus reckless, but extremely brave! It was fantastic to watch this video; taken by freelance camera operator Ben Jacobson who acknowledged, that this did involve a clear element of risk to her life, her bravery and courage was shown around the world within an hour of the raid, she was a true British hero;

It will truly surprise me, if this wonderful reckless brave woman does not receive from the Queen the Victoria Cross medal for her bravery, she was the only person representing us elderly citizens, brave enough in taking on these thieves without considering her own safety first. Afterwards stating, 'I'm no hero, someone had to do it.' When shamefully others in the near vicinity of the jewellery shop did nothing, until after the incident.

Anyone thinking of raiding any jewellery shop in the future had better watch out! For a red headed woman, with a white scarf, and red coat, armed only with a black HANDBAG, and bags of guts, thieves throughout the country, you have been warned, 'supergran' will certainly not be hanging around.

Just like Ann Timson, I am taking on these local council officials single-handed; this inspirational woman of my same generation, carrying out or bringing to light, the thieving local council officials, who are getting away with stealing unlawfully, in broad daylight, land grabbing this recreational area from the very young children and local residents.

These council officials are clearly showing absolutely no respect towards the local citizens. I feel rather like our young hero, Ann Timson (without a black handbag) that writing this book, could be the only way changes can come about. It is similar to when someone is putting their hands into your pockets, thieving. Arrangements must be changed to a fairer open transparent meeting with each new development, to debate, discuss, and have full consultation concerning local issues.

For example, can you drive extremely large 21meter length vehicles on and off the site safely? The answer clearly is no. Because each time a vehicle of this nature attempted this manoeuvre, all parked cars had to be moved out of the way which was extremely intolerable and unacceptable, with lots of swearing by the delivery drivers at times?

With site vehicles taking up all available parking spaces locally all day for over 14 months, until the development was completed, is what they call excellent planning?

Also if one can guarantee that these vehicles will not damage resident's cars and property, if you cannot give any assurance of this and many other serious issues, then the development will not go ahead. Already a number of cars were scratched along with a great deal of wing mirrors damaged, by these extremely large Lorries manoeuvring up/down this very narrow quiet Cal de sac.

Blocked by all the stationary residential vehicles, and site vehicles parked in the road each day, which has proved chaotic over this extended period of time. All councillors, especially planners find questions need answers, and answers mean they are speaking; this is what they are trying to avoid 'communication.'

You may be wondering why the duck tape is necessary across the mouth earlier, (in the football match).This astonishingly is very easy to answer, and is the main problem. (You will find out later), that when invited to attend a committee meeting, the very same 'duck tape' plus seriously controlled rules apply.

(Not permitted to ask any questions). 'Duck tape.' Only permitting three minutes to speak at a committee meeting, is totally out of order. If they speak to the public, the residents may be able to argue in turn, persuading the planners that the development should not go ahead, for whatever serious sound reasons. This should never be allowed to get to this 'intolerable' situation, as far as the planners are concerned.

This fundamentally is why the 'duck tape' is necessary. Would you believe, on reading in our local newspaper, covering this part of the country, stating on average the councils are mostly performing quite well and giving good value for money to residents. According to a government report recently published, if of course this can be believed.

It's the first time that auditors and inspectors have assessments on all six organizations in this part of the country, their findings and consequences are designed to highlight whether the services provided, offer good value for money.

And highlight where they could be improved, or only performing adequately and not consistently well, allowing for a great deal of exaggeration (the elastic movement) and falsification of the books, on most of the reports and findings in the country were acceptable. What the auditors and inspectors say about each town seems to concern the senior council officials to a greater degree.

So much so, the officials take it out on us residents, when their performances are found inadequate, and not up to scratch, and then make huge unnecessary expensive mistakes, which are kept rather quite, then covered up paid for out of the local council tax? This is well hidden (under a huge magic carpet) from the audit and inspectors visit.

If they were to seriously analysis truthfully, the cost so far of this open space over the years, each council official involved would be down the employment exchange after a less taxing position. It would not be an exaggeration to mention in the £millions the waste of taxpayer's /ratepayers money, and that is not a joke, a lot of that money is yours and mine, and could have been spent more wisely locally.

If this regeneration was carried out elsewhere, let us say just three miles away as mentioned earlier on this other site in town, the same development would amount to approximately £1Million. Possibly a quarter of the true cost, now that is understandably a worthwhile intelligent savings.

You will hear later of examples we council ratepayers have tirelessly reached into our pockets without batting an eye, and then the council just sweep their expensive mistakes, under this very same large magic carpet, and then threaten you with duck tape if you try to utter a word. This is very difficult to estimate, because of the huge waste of council taxpayer's/ratepayers money, which has mounted up over the years and is still being hidden away, ashamed to say compounding with each expensive mistake on this same site.

To set a further fine significant example, this has been described in more detail elsewhere in this book. Would you believe it, only last year early in 2008 a German company extensively carried out repairs and refurbishments' to all the prefabricated bungalows on both sites, Shortmeadow Green site costing £107,000, followed by another eight prefabricated bungalow units three miles away approximate cost of £100,000.

With its workforce of at least eight workers who carried out extensive repairs, because health and safety condemned the buildings on a number of occasions, since 2002, with serious 'mould' problems. The repairs plus refurbishments carried out, took weeks to complete over this period of time, to have completed all ten prefabricated bungalows, and also add together eight other units on the other site in town, with the very same serious mould problems, approximate cost totalling £207,000.

All these units were made redundant soon after completion, the council were as quiet as a mouse about these costs, and as usual just brushed this huge costs under this same huge magic carpet, and expect the local council taxpayers/ratepayers, to foot this unnecessary bill, without knowing the reason why, this is our money we are fully entitled with the truth.

How on earth, can they justifier this huge mistake. 'Here comes the punch line you promised not to laugh.' May I repeat in case you could not believe what I have just said above, less than six months later all the units are now redundant on both sites, in this town and have been taken off site and demolished?

We all paid with our local council taxes, so this makes us fully entitled in knowing why this money was wasted. Soon after this while attending another council meeting, gave me the opportunity to ask about this unnecessary waste, and who was responsible.

Resulting in the councillor's usual response, saying that they will look into the facts urgently, and come back to me later, which they never did. The question was far too difficult for them plus extremely embarrassing.

My local councillor was the very first contact without success, then onto our local (MP). 'Who was still very busy fiddling her expenses' it seems likely all the rest of the money shamefully wasted over the years, without ever finding out who is responsible. The true final cost was never disclosed! This is only one example there were many, many more examples, which should also be taken into consideration in this same town, showing a lack of concern as to where the money comes from in the first place?

Only this week, I happen to be speaking with a trusted council official, who has informed me that very soon all council decisions with regards to expenditure over £500, will need justification and to be acknowledged, should be much smaller amounts declared, because this still leaves it open to constant fiddling.

The councils will get round this, by offering many £499.00 bills in stages, so that the public are unable to see these, because the bills are less than £500.00, and unlikely to be seen by the public, they would not be declared.

Moreover, these checks should slow down some of the waste of taxpayer's money; this legislation is years to late being introduced, but is certainly necessary, and will make all councils more accountable in spending our money in a more controlled reasonable manner in the future. Pointing out for a moment, and remembering this brilliant example, which comes to mind, but well covered up shamefully and is mentioned in more detail later in this book. **(Swimming pool closure in our town why)?**

Approximately four months before closing down the training Centre in our town, the swimming pool on the old school grounds site was closed for **'planned extensive necessary repairs and refurbishments'** for well over three months, included with the cost of repairs, was new filtering equipment, new boiler, chlorination unit, and many other expensive new items of equipment. Also to our amazement the walls inside the pool area was attended to, repainting the changing rooms both male/female, new showers.

Then just weeks after reopening, we were given two weeks' notice before the whole site was closed indefinitely, unbelievably for the development for residential housing. The very same developers 'Slope partners' demolished the swimming pool, after all those expensive 'unnecessary repairs plus refurbishments' carried out, (Serious misuse of council tax). Amazingly, only a very small percentage of these proposed houses out of 174 apartments were designated for affordable housings, (not council housing any more).

In total all these houses built on, former school ground, were for sale on the open market, for anyone throughout the country to purchase not primarily for the locals. Now this again, is more evidence that taxpayer's money has been totally wasted, and the officials are still employed to carry on regardless.

All of these houses should have been for 'council housing only' for the local residents on this extremely long waiting list, particularly with the development carried out on the old school grounds. Because of the so-called shortage of rentable houses, the central government are always quoting, that they need to provide, this land was acquired very cheaply by the developer with the largest 'brown envelope' in the back pocked with lots of money. Meetings with the council officials, plus other attempts would not reveal the true cost of the swimming pool repairs, stating that it was impossible to source, which I find highly questionable! Writing a letter to the local MP still no response, said the very same feeble excuses, still busy fiddling her expenses no doubt.

Our local councillor, still no response same difficulty with the question, (how much money wasted)? After all the expensive repairs carried out, the swimming pool was to close directly after all these expensive repairs and refurbishment completed. Then unbelievably the swimming pool was demolished within two weeks without any explanation or justification, I am still waiting for an answer, as mentioned previously, as to who was responsible for this waste of taxpayer's money. After two years of searching, it is now 25/05/2010. A trusted close friend of mine has just revealed the true cost, of the above repairs and refurbishments, a staggering £178,000 wasted without any justification.

39

Now you see what we are faced with, and again the main reason which pushed, and inspired me further into writing this book, to assist and encourage others in campaigning successfully, if faced with the same situation with waste of taxpayer's money or (local council ratepayers money) throughout this country.

Who's fault, and who is responsible for this wastage, it is our money we are perfectly entitled and furious with the way ratepayer's/taxpayer's money is wasted. They would still be upsetting the residents if this book had not been published, with the majority of the local residents, resigned to the fact that you cannot do anything to change the way the council officials, treat local voters, with using far too much power.

If they had not taken our small play area, depriving the youngsters, of this priceless open space. This book would never have been started; publishing this book is justification, proving evidence of yet another huge expensive mistake placed under this same huge magic carpet. Compounding one mistake after another by our local council, possibly all councils throughout the country are just as guilty, and on behalf of all those responsible throughout Great Britain, this problem needs re-addressing urgently!

Examine please both letters, which follow, first letter by a lovely couple who I have admired over the years, this wonderful couple have lived a quiet life in our close over many years, please appreciate this letter, it is written truly from the heart. Try to imagine sending this same letter yourself into the planning office, which paid absolutely no attention as to its contents, or concerns for their age, both Ann and Charles are over 80 years. How would you have felt? This next photo offered is there view now what do you think, is it acceptable?

The quality of their letter I felt, deserves an entry into this book, because shamefully it should have been a fine example to inspire others emotionally, in this unique neighbourhood. Those individuals locally who could not care less or be bothered, on how to compose a quality 'objection.' Until it was far too late, subsequently these same local individuals all regret not acting sooner.

Contemptuous attitude shown by the planning office, with completely ignoring their letter without a personal response, when you first consider respectfully, both are into their eighties. Without a special personal letter in reply, sent to this wonderful couple in acknowledgement, would have shown a great deal of respect for the most senior members of our local community. Both have lived in the very same house for well over 45 years, and like ourselves, choose this location for a number of very sound reasons, which were never considered by the planning office.

A few noteworthy reasons to follow:

(1) Importantly next to a very small wonderful green, where it was extremely safe area for all the very young children to play.
(2) Down a quiet cul-de-sac with very light traffic.
(3) With a number of rentable garages very, close to their property.
(4) Without serious parking problems in the area.
(5) Secured and also supported with a policy background, stating quite clearly that no residential housing would ever be considered on our green.

Anna's rear garden view now.

The couple's view of the horrendous new building from their rear garden, which I will leave you to comment on, is this acceptable or totally unacceptable? The building has now replaced their vista of our wonderful local green.

41

In addition, all of the council officials should be ashamed of themselves, with the way this letter was ignored. The planning office sent the very same standard, repeat letter, which we all received with each correspondence, and objection, entered into the planning office with regards to the aforementioned controversial planning application.

Dear Mr. Bent: Head of Planning & Regeneration. Thank you for your letter regarding the proposed building on our small play area.

When I moved here some Forty-five years ago I chose this particular house because there were lots of green areas around for children to play on. Gradually over the years all the green open spaces were built on except for our "back field" as it was called in those days. All the children from the neighbourhood gathered there to play football and cricket in safety away from the traffic, and where we could keep an eye on them.

Sadly, in spite of our protests the 'temporary' Bungalows were built, but we were led to believe that one day the area would be put back as it once was. There is much publicity these days about many children becoming Obese because they are indoors playing computer games, play stations etc. instead of getting exercise outdoors but where are they to play now? The local park is too far away to allow young children to go on their own.

We are already concerned about the safety of small children playing out in the streets around here, and the dangers will be greatly increased with the extra volume of traffic, which will be going up and down what used to be a Very quiet cul-de-sac.

The small playing area is at the moment a haven for wildlife. We are able to watch the Squirrels chasing each other, and many species of birds, including lately to our delight Jays and Great Spotted Woodpeckers with their young, in addition bats in this same area, over the years. We also hear the Owls hooting in the night. Although we understand some of the trees will be retained, the building work will surely drive the birds away, which will be a great shame. I appreciate that there is a need for more housing these days, and it is current practice to build as many houses as possible on as small an area possible but surely there is more suitable site than our Green.

However, if this project goes ahead it will obviously devalue our property significantly. Will we be offered compensation? One thing, which concerns me greatly, is that if the plans have not been passed at the committee meeting yet, why has the site already being fenced off, and the residents have been given notice to vacate all their garages. It does make me wonder if the whole project is a fait accompli!! I do hope this is not the case, and that the many objections I know you have received will be given proper consideration.

My husband is eighty-one years of age and in poor health, and we had hoped to spend our remaining years in a peaceful environment, which will obviously not be the case if this building work goes ahead. I look forward to your reply.

Yours sincerely.

(Mrs) Anne Dawkins.

Sadly, since this letter was sent into the Planning Office for their consideration. Unfortunately Charles, Anne's husband has peacefully passed away on the 15th June 2010, after considerable period fighting health problems.

We all feel extremely sorry for Anna's loss in our close.

CHAPTER TEN

*

Disabled Couple in Close

Time now for another unbelievable letter, addressed to the housing manager from a disabled couple. Some time ago sir, I filled in a questionnaire regarding the use of my garage, stating both my wife and I are disabled keeping our mobility car in garage number (10). Looking at the bottom of your letter it says 'Positive about disabled people.' Well you certainly are if you think taking away our garage and offering one way beyond our capability to walk, to be positive. I would say positively cold-hearted.

You say 'due to unforeseen circumstances,' which is untrue. The fact that it is known that you plan to build seven houses on the site of the garage block, could not have been unforeseen circumstance.

You also mention, if no reply is received within 7 days of this letter, paragraph 'C' overleaf will be assumed, this paragraph states I do not require a garage. 'Please remove my name from the waiting list'

What if I was on holiday or in hospital? The date of your letter is 18th of June 2009. I received your letter on Saturday 20th of June there is no post tomorrow. So affectively, given that any letter from me would take at least 2 days to reach you, I have approximately 3 days in which to say (yes or no).

In the meantime, I have lost the tenancy of my garage. I think this totally unacceptable and I think your method of dealing with a loyal council tenant of 44 years is reprehensible, and I will be signing the petition currently going around opposing the restoration of the green, as promised by you nearly 20years ago.

My wife and I have always maintained our council house to the highest standard, and we have beautifully kept both front & rear gardens despite our disabilities.

I noticed that two of the garages on the block, are not being demolished. Why? I know one is privately owned. I wait your reply. This letter is going to be passed to the local newspaper as you already know they are taking an interest in the controversy concerning the green which was on the front page last Thursday.

Yours unhappily G&M Steal.20/06/2009.

My letter follows to a government office. Shaming all local council officials using undemocratic methods widespread, while attempting to achieve regeneration, and establish some support in carrying out this regeneration in a reasonable fairer democratic manner.

In addition, to highlight, whether it was customary for the local residents in receiving this type of treatment leading into the 21st century, see if they could offer any sound advice or judgement with this diabolical treatment, the local people are receiving which is unacceptable, by the local council officials.

With refusing on a number of occasions an open transparent meeting regarding the proposed development, using predominantly, bullyboy tactics, which were found prevalent with their dealings. There is a need urgently in promoting democracy.

43

Please try to imagine, when reading the following letter, as if you had sent it to the planning office for their reaction. These mindless, ridiculous councillors, when voting blindly at a committee meeting, do not consider the consequences of their own actions towards the treatment dished out to the members of the public. 'Who secure their huge salaries' and should read the following out loud before all council Meetings.

'ACTIONS OF A FEW (Councillors) ARE FELT BY ALL.'
(Before any council meeting the under mentioned should
be read out quite clearly as a reminder to all councillors).

A small amount of knowledge is helpful.
Lots of knowledge is of great use.
However no knowledge is useless.

To explain the above, means that a small handful of councillors without any regards to the cost of what they are deciding on. Vote blindly without firstly taking stock of the outcome of their decisions. Having already approached our local MP she is still far too busy fiddling her expenses. Then thrashing it out with this local council, plus councillors, was found to be a total waste of time, with nobody on the council listening!

HRH Prince Charles. Whom we now understand after 11 months into the development is the patron of Guinness Partnership Housing Association, responsible for taking the open space from our community, showing in the past, his sympathy for healthy environment issues in general. Not forgetting that we all live in a supposed true democracy, all the land in England was once owned by the crown, possibly still owns this land. Whether we are unjustly treated should matter if your sole duty is running the country. The result of his letter would be interesting, it will be the standard letter sent to all his obedient subjects.

Stating in the headed letter, that engagements he has will not allow him time to kindly look into such serious undemocratic behaviour, or unjust issues dished out by these local council officials. (This is part of the letter sent).

This question is extremely difficult for me to ask. Nevertheless, I feel I have no choice and absolutely nowhere else to turn. There is no labour councillor here in town that can be trusted anymore, they have lost all credibility with land gabbing this play area from the local children, is overstepping the boundaries beyond what is acceptable without wisdom.

Approaching central government through our local (M.P) to bring awareness, is also out of the question. She is currently extremely busy, outrageously sorting out her own parliamentary expenses claims. Is certainly more important, than assisting residents in giving support when needed; it seems that all decisions in this town, concerning our essential significant play area in the past, and present were totally ignored.

For well over 44years I have lived here in Judgement over this unnecessary carnage, which was arrived at without democratic consultation, debate or consideration for the local environment and current residents concerns nearby in a sensible just and fair manner. This wholly unacceptable and ridiculous situation which urgently needs sorting before dare I say it, before anarchy is involved, it is well out of control now. (Calling themselves councillors is a joke). We are in urgent need of 'judgement'.

44

By someone from your office who could look sympathetically into the proposed development involved, with a sensible intelligent approach. The planning application has extremely serious expensive issues for this new development to be successful, here on what was the children's play area. Has now been handed into the planner's office this week and we all know the result, a resounding win for the local officials.

Who are rubbing their hands together knowing we were firmly fixed to the ground, and have no chance of a win? You will find enclosed various objections offered some 20years ago concerning these extremely ugly temporary fragile prefabricated bungalows placed on our very small green. In close proximity to extremely large mature trees which one would find great difficulty in understanding that an experience planning officer cannot see the obvious consequences which could happen, with the possibilities of fatalities on a wild stormy day or night, is not their concern.

What troubles me is with the poor retched councillors' who haven't a clue or the necessary skills in deciding whether the history of this play area should go indefinitely.

Also the off street parking problems for the future has not been considered, they cannot see the obvious dangers that normal people can foresee, and these councillors, jointly will vote at the committee meeting shortly on 15th September 2009, just to please the leader of the party, plus planning office, and break this underlining promise, (in returning this open recreational space as promised).

This promise, importantly at the time was stated that when the prefabricate bungalows become vacant and redundant and not used for housing the homeless, then the play area would be handed back as open space for the local community and residents to use collectively as before.

When looking through the policy background in 1983 and again 1991. It states quite clearly in black and white, for all to see that other forms of residential development would not be considered on the open space:

It seems that the temporary homes have set precedence for further building on the green. This shows clearly, how underhanded the intentions by this council.

Where is this so-called democracy in this county? With this in mind, the council cannot be trusted ever again. With losing all credibility and trust, and have been granted far too much 'power' in the past.

This latest revelation and passion, that the council leader plus many councillors locally have stated their intention on a number of occasions, their building for the future, on all other open small areas of grass in this town. Is equal to mine, in saving this very small play area for the next generation. Once the permanent buildings are secured to the ground, in a short while, the playing field would have been forgotten, and this is what the councillors are banking on, knowing from past history. Then immediately on to the next green to carry out the very same unchecked!

Now you will appreciate the difficulty in my request, in asking the second most important person in the country. To step in and act as judge. Moreover, look on both sides; to see who has been cheated, out of this important and significant very small open space, secured for the local children/residents for the future, which must be saved, for the next generation to use, or lose.

This letter was a cry for help, and should not have been ignored by your office, the council locally have overstepped the line where common sense starts, by placing these horrendously ugly unacceptable buildings compromising a number of neighbours vista, of our wonderful green, plus many mature trees cut down 'accidentally' which should have been retained.

The local residents have everything to lose and absolutely nothing to gain from this new development. The (COUNCILLORS, PLANNERS PLUS LOCAL AUTHORITIES) are showing no fairness what so ever! We wait in anticipation for your reply.

When this letter was sent last year in June 2009, we were unaware that Guinness (Trust) Partnership, had any connection with this open space, unfortunately it seems quite intentionally that this information was kept from us.

Consequently was not included in this letter sent to HRH Prince Charles to draw his attention to this extremely serious environmental situation.

Prince Charles ironically happens to be the patron of Guinness Trust? Their interest was shown on the notice board approximately 11months into the development, 10/05/2010. The committee meeting was on 15/09/2009.

Consequently no mention of Guinness Trust Partnership involvement, which is highly controversial and highly embarrassing with the amount of mature trees that have been cut down 'accidentally' which should have been retained, who is responsible for the removal of this many mature trees?

All the remaining the trees on site were not afforded the approved protection, which the planning office should have been aware of, but totally ignored and turned a blind eye to this scandalous situation?

CHAPTER ELEVEN

*

Author's Start in Life

Offering my sincere apologies for not introducing myself to you earlier, may I start by stating that I am now a very rare interesting breed, with an exceptionally worthwhile long awaited award which has been granted to only a very few people qualified. After waiting for years patiently to be a member of the 'OLD GITS CLUB' with a smile from ear to hear. When presented a short while ago for my diligent work, being a grumpy old git, and very proud to have been recognised as such. Apparently even HRH, Prince Charles has not qualified, or been granted with 'THE OLD GITS' award, but has come extremely close on a number of occasions in the past.

With the way, he has been outspoken, calling a building a 'carbuncle' some years ago as an example with many other following fine examples over the years. What would he say about these rubbish buildings, built on this development site in question would be of great interest to me. These surprising comments he gets from his father HRH, Prince Philip, and many unexpected amusing observations, when called upon to open a new building or development, and can always be relied upon to utter the 'unexpected' with his recognisable smile. He would feel rather awkward opening this current new development when completed, here at what was for countless years as an open recreational space.

Used as play area for all the local young children, and residents to enjoy. What would his comments be with the loss of all these mature trees, 'accidentally' cut down and others damaged, and now having to be removed for safety concerns?

Seemingly unaware of the mindless councillors and developers who have robbed us all, on what was a wonderful priceless essential play area for the local children, without firstly smiling in his usual familiar Prince Charles way? (I think he has that same notable smile from his Nan the late Queen Mother, a wonderful woman who shared my birthday each year, on 4th August).

Prince Charles saying, just before cutting the ribbon on this new controversial development, to those same local councillors presently lined up and smiling. Soon to drop that same smile, when Prince Charles states this very true sincere statement. "Why did you not build elsewhere, Where are the local children going to play now, fancy depriving the young children of a very small essential play area, ironically did you ever think to ask them." His son HRH Prince William as I have mentioned earlier, has spearheaded a project in early June 2010, to save as many as 2,012 playing fields, missing this perfect opportunity from the hands of the developers, in admiration of Queen Elizabeth II diamond jubilee in 2012.

His Nan 'Queen Mother' always had a smile because as just mentioned, she shared my birthday on the 4th August each year. Try to image to your delight on this day in August each year it is your birthday and you are the only boy in the boarding school of let us say between 400-500 children celebrating a birthday on that particular day each year.

Now look up and around you, all you see is flags and lots of them, even a very large flag on top of the main school building. Wouldn't you feel on top of the world because later that day, it gets even better?

You cannot top the next experience, the bunting is brought out the long tables are laid with all conceivable goodies, any child could ever wish for jellies, all different types of cakes, and orange & lemonade plus ginger beer, and lots more.

What a fantastic party on my behalf. (Do not spoil it for me we know it is not only my birthday) but nobody has told me that. Not forgetting this happened each year. What with my cat 'Hoppy' and all my mates all enjoying themselves what could be better, presents cannot top the above feeling because I never received any that I can truly recall.

Knowing I can't wait until next year, thanks to a lovely old lady who I claimed as my 'Nan' who choose to share my day, with that lovely recognisable beautiful smile of hers.

Although it is awkward allowing others to know of your past, regrettably not recommended, remembering past incidents such as the abuse, and unconventional start in life, was extremely unpleasant on many occasions in my early upbringing. Without having a father, is a backward way to bring up any child. All kids need a level playing field; with each given the same opportunity with both parents it's natural. Not recommended is the placement into an institution, of a child, who will know nothing of life experiences, until released from this institutional way of life, some 15 years later.

Born in Harlesden, North West London in 1942. Apparently, I cannot remember the pain of the actual birth, but remember the smack on the bum afterwards and recall it hurt horrendously so I complained.

Surely, I did not deserve this unfair start in life, astonishingly it went downhill from there on, I doubt if life could get much worse for us lads in the orphanage.

Right from the start I cannot even recall any cuddles unfortunately, or comments like isn't he gorgeous who does he remind you of, his dad appears to have a nose remarkable like his, well I am pleased, nice size, would not dream of altering it. With this ludicrous situation my mother and father, playing Russian roulette, what did they expect when playing this type of game, leaving me the problem to sort things out later in life?

In those days if you have a child out of wedlock, the baby (that's myself) was taken from its mother and placed into an institution not the mother, the 'Baby'. She would be sent to the workhouse, for her punishment.

It has always mystified me, how it can ever be classified as a 'home' institution is correct but surely never a home, also called a boarding school. Even the title School, I would question what they taught us, was nothing. With excellent teachers, this confinement would be the perfect setting, to educate children to the highest level possible, because you are starting from a clear canvas.

After all those years serving my sentence, discharged shamefully without the appropriate education for life, shockingly without recognising that I was unable to spell, being dyslectic. When shared with more than 400-500 underprivileged boys, should have been half girls & boys that would have been lots more fun?

Nevertheless, possible problems because girls chat, and horrendously very bitchy, plus we would have to kiss them, that would be fantastic for the Girls.

48

Try to contemplate being housed in a boarding school in close proximity from birth with this amount of kids. Mercifully, not too many people nowadays will be given the opportunity to experience this type of lifestyle, thank God! Anyone who is given a preference of this type of existence please, refuse at the earliest, if you have the opportunity, and offered an alternative.

Tragically, for me this was bad planning by my absent irresponsible insensitive parents. Their concern or welfare of this poor little 'mite' did not enter their way of thinking; I was never consulted, with this arrangement, right from the start!

'Now is that fair for any child?

Apparently and shamefully, they had the fun then, and I struggle to see the funny side of serving this extraordinary long sentence, which was not very pleasant!

Consequently serving a sentence of let's, say fifteen years for doing nothing wrong, an unacceptable arrangement and unnecessary punishment for me or any of the other lads at the orphanage.

The boarding school at Mill Hill was only approximately a couple miles, from Inglis Barracks where I joined the army some years later in 1960, serving with the 1st Btn Middlesex Regiment called (The Die-Hards) I will describe later of some very interesting experiences in the army.

Throughout life, one has to keep setting challenges even the impossible challenge like successfully writing this book for instance, delighted after having completed this impossible task. When you consider the fact that spelling is my number one worst skill in my life, and writing this book was completely out of my comfort zone. Nevertheless, I must admit I'm rather enjoying this challenge, and using this opportunity in getting a couple of things off my chest:

It is very true, that anyone given the motivation, could complete this same wonderful experience, but dedication is the key word, set yourself targets and complete each stage in turn, there is light at the end of the tunnel. While attempting writing, this book, it has certainly challenged me to the limit, and hopefully as promised, in keeping the interest alive and to the point.

Constant annoyance throughout life is the fact I was with an age group who had very poor educational opportunities, most including myself where unconventionally accepted levels of education was found inadequate and common place, towards the end of the War years. Given the opportunity with choice, undoubtedly in having the ability and skill of spelling words, is an exceedingly powerful recognisable tool, and must be used with extreme care.

These Nuns were very strict, you dare not cross them with their traditional disciplinarian's attitude, but shamefully missed the perfect opportunity with educating us lads to an extremely very high standard. Their strict teaching of the catholic religion morning, noon, and night, has I supposed put me off following that strict catholic faith.

I'm on the left with my mate Chris at the Orphanage.

They should have concentrated on teaching worthwhile subjects, like the three (Rs) Reading, writing, and arithmetic plus grammar and sentence structure, to a very high degree. Like in the very posh boarding schools throughout the country, where the extremely rich children are sent, experiencing this very same discipline, if offered the same opportunity on equal terms with them and excellent teachers.

I'm in the front, with some of the lads at the orphanage.

Some of the lads at the orphanage, not sure whether any of the lads are still alive when you consider they would all be into their 70s I hope some have survived and in good health. I remember that day when this photograph was taken, we were all frozen.

CHAPTER TWELVE

*

Hoppy My Cat

While growing up, one has to experience as an orphan, all types of abuse and exploitation accordingly. My first of three boarding schools, supposed homes, was at St Mary's in Mill Hill in north London.

Hoppy my cat.

Which was run by Nuns with a few memorable occasions, some pleasurable occasions, others not so pleasant? It surprises me, why out of all those kids should 'Hoppy' my cat choose me as a very best friend? He was a stray cat, I found him down the bottom end of the playing field, while we were out busily playing during playtime. Hoppy was meowing and making an awful din, I am pleased he did, while justifiably stuck fast in the hedge area, unable to move from his location, with lots of bramble present.

After his release, which took some time without hurting him? He was purring loudly, we had a cuddle on the way back to School. Placing him down on the ground he followed me back to school, the Nuns were accommodating and satisfied with hoppy staying, well at least he will keep the rats and mice at bay.

From thereon we were glued together, best of friends for quite some years. The name Hoppy, I gave him because of the way my cat first hopped out of the hedge, after being released. One of the Nuns asked when we got back to the main hall, "Have you decided what name you are going to call your cat," 'Hoppy' it seemed appropriate; she was delighted that Hoppy was to remain. He was beautiful, pure black all over, except for his white chest and belly, along with the tips of his paws, which were also white. Each night, after successfully catching whatever outside, I would feel that same reassuring weight, of Hoppy resting on my legs, as he decided his sleeping arrangement each evening.

Each morning Hoppy would be found still curled up on the end of my bed in the dormitory; he never once paid any rent. How did he always find my bed I'll never understand. You could hear his purring with contentment from a mile away, 'you knew he was extremely happy' where he was. I can still hear that same sound sometimes even now after all these years, probably caused my Tinnitus in my right ear, which I currently suffer from. Remarkably, there were times remembering back, when one of my pals was a bit low and unhappy, about something or another. After handing Hoppy over for a quick cuddle amazingly, that same lad effectively had a smile like a Cheshire cat across his face, (excuse the pun). Always shared him with anyone who needed a cuddle, I did not care nor did my best friend: This must be the best feeling for any child, while at boarding school, on many occasions Hoppy would saunter through the door leading into my classroom, which was occasionally left ajar; We would all laugh and snigger, then he would jump up onto my school-desk interrupting the lesson, checking on my school work to see if I got all my sums correct, not sure how the door was found ajar; Someone could have been guilty sometimes with leaving the door as such, but was never brave enough to own up.

While playing football, maybe the odd stray ball, you would not underestimate the Sisters ability, their speed and skills you had a job in catching them, also keeping up with them they held up their black cassock which almost touched the ground and ran. Arsenal would be encouraged and keen to have signed a few. The great goals I witnessed over the years were somewhat first class even for a girl. To compare let us say Ryan Giggs, with one of his memorable runs on my team Arsenal a few years ago.

Nothing would have stopped old Giggs scoring that wonderful goal. This is what the sisters showed at times surprising runs with skills to match. Such dexterity added, we used to tackle them as if they were other lads.

Our football team, I'm sitting second on the left.

While playing Cricket If they took the bat, it was so difficult to get them out, sometimes it could be said we had some quite good times throughout playtime. Also on the plus side which has come out of my stay at St Mary's, is that on my CV, could always be added among my many other skills, which would secure a job for the future as a tailor of being able to include sowing, and other needlework, including how to knit, a woollen tie, or socks. Amazingly, a jumper was quite difficult, and I think the most complicated item of them all and my greatest challenge while at this school, was knitting a pair of woollen gloves. Which I admit was an extremely difficult task and achievement, but worthwhile experiment to undertake?

54

I should have continued these skills, which could have been a completely new chapter in my life, furthermore, turned out as a professional tailor. But was never encouraged further, these same skills were called upon in the army on countless occasions, in helping blokes with seams needing mending, or adjustments to the uniforms that needed sorting out from time to time, using our 'housewives' issued as necessary equipment to all those serving throughout armed forces.

Inappropriate, and astonishing treatment by the Nuns on occasions was totally unacceptable, we were very young boys exposed, and surely should not be touching us improperly. On occasions they over stepped the mark. Their room was in the middle of two corridors leading from the dormitories, if during the night; you were selected and quietly lead away.

It was hardly for getting a beating or any type of punishment, as long as others, meaning the other boys, did not see what was going on, we did not know any different. Shamefully we were extremely vulnerable to this exploitation, open to extraordinary range of abuse; we were all very much innocence of what was going to happen on each occasion, if it was your very first time, you could put it down as sex education I suppose nothing less than charming, the start of new experiences in growing up.

This same appalling treatment although at the time felt new experience, please remember this whole volume is (nun fiction), and actually did happen, accordingly needed a mention: Maybe other lads in this same orphanages went through the very same experience's but were encouraged like myself in keeping it undercover.

Which was out of the ordinary, very strange and unpleasant on immeasurable encounters, which took place in secret at these orphanages, even at other boarding schools later, it was the same hidden agenda, but very much worse in later days at these orphanages, which are best kept under wrap. With blatantly stepping over the mark by these disciplinarians, was outrageous to say the least, we were all vulnerable young children, open to most unpleasant demanding experiences. This is now out, and that is all I am prepared to say on this weird disagreeable subject.

With my first addition of this book, I had found a number faults, and had to be withdrawn from sale, this revised addition has offered me an opportunity to update one or two very interesting stories, with a fantastic example of camouflage which many who have suffered these abuses as young children, would clearly understand including us lads who were without choice placed into orphanages from a very young age.

Jimmy Savile a former BBC radio Disc Jockey and well known for presenting (Top of the pops), plus many other TV shows, shamefully suspected of child abuse mainly involving very young girls and a great deal of vulnerable patients in hospitals throughout Great Britain. This astonishing disgusting behaviour has emerged since his death in 2011 last year. He was knighted for his charitable work over countless years, a perfect concealment with being a nasty manipulator, in disguise to gain advantage with extremely young victims of saviles sexual abuse.

A paedophile masquerading as a Disc Jockey with investigations now into his activities,' possibly over 60 years. He must now attract rumours, because he was single and travelled throughout Great Britain.

55

Allegations as a predatory sex offender will now surface, because of his powerful position as a great charitable worker is now blown into particular dramatic explosion, which nobody expected or foreseen. Now starting a long inquiry over many years to come, which may reveal inordinate problems on how he managed to cover his tracks over many years. This was a brilliant example to demonstrate someone famous who was so powerfully situated, that everybody in authority was frightened to act in defence, of the extremely young children being openly abused by an exceptionally clever manipulator?

Unbelievable findings while looking through the lottery results from 1994.

Another amazing aspect which could prove worthy of serious investigation, and nothing to do with our local green situation, is the unacceptable results recorded with the national lottery which has been running in Great Britain since November 1994.

As from 15th October 2012 after a staggering 1,754 lottery draws, on only one occasion has there been 133 winners on Saturday 14th January 1995, also on two other occasions recorded (57) and (46) winners. On very rare occasions since the start of the lottery has there been any more than 12/15 winners with each draw, which makes you wonder, is it being firmly controlled by the lottery system, or the machines used?

To explain further since the start of the lottery, there has been 13 machines used, each machine is given a number from one to eight, if you add this total together you arrive at a grand total of 104 machines, if you are in the least bit interested they are as follows: Arthur, Amethyst, Guinevere, Galahad, Garnet, Lancelot, Merlin, Moonstone, Opel, Pearl, Sapphire, Topaz, and finely Vyvyan. This absolutely amazes me why so many machines have been produced, just to select a handful of balls with numbers on?

When all that is necessary is a rather cheap plastic see-through container like the one used when drawing out the football teams, playing against each other, which is as cheap as chips and obviously 100% fairer and obviously more transparent. These balls can be drawn out by members of the public, chosen at random off the street. You don't have to be a member of the Routledge intuition of 'Bleeding Obvious' to work that out, do you?

So why you might ask, is all this money spent on all these 104 machines which are totally unnecessary, the reason can only be described in a couple of words, mainly to confuse everybody, and camouflage what is really going on in the background.

Once all of the numbers have been selected by the punters, the system has within seconds decided which numbers are going to be selected on that particular draw. The proof if needed is in the results after each draw, with a controlled amount of winners, or no winners at all. For instants no winners, for a number of draws to build up a huge amount of money, by allowing many rollovers to accumulate. There should be no rollovers at all; it should be shared amongst the punters who have five numbers, somehow everybody has accepted this way blinded by the thought that if they won this would change their lives, not realising the system that Camelot has set is full proof in their favour, like Jimmy Savile.

They mention on countless occasions about how much they give to charity, and sports activities throughout Great Britain, which is a fantastic camouflage, but surprisingly can be withdrawn at any moment, they are a business. Once the machines have gone, and draws are drawn in a fairer more transparent way such as described earlier.

Then you would see a great deal more constant jackpot winner's straightaway it's 'Bleeding Obvious,' you do not need to be member of Routledge institute of Bleeding Obvious to realise there is a gigantic fiddle going on.

Take for instants the thunderball draw with only one machine called 'Excalibur' which has any number of machines numbered from one-seven, has been running from Saturday 12th June 1999. The highest amount of winners ever drawn on record from a single draw is (6), most of the remainder are no winners, or a controlled amount which questions how is this fair? Astonishingly with no rollovers involved with the 'thunderball draws,' why?

To make it more difficult to win, some time ago the numbers of thunderball numbers were increased to 39 from 34. Which is clearly in Camelot's favour, certainly not the person purchasing the ticket? If no (5 number) winner, then (4 plus thunderball) and so on down, immediately the less well of who buy these tickets would be down the shops after each 'draw' spending their winnings thus the economy would recover in a flash!!

If people would take the trouble to look back on the recorded results (Try visiting web page UK Lottery results) you would be horrified with your findings, witnessing a fully controlled system with only a small number of jackpot winners, I would again question what is going on? I only say what is recorded; it would be difficult in making this up.

Also if you look towards the Euro draws, both draws take place on the Tuesday and Friday, the first Euro draw took place on Friday 13th February 2004, since then on one occasion there were 20 winners also 5 winners in one draw in 2006, and again 5 winners in one draw in 2011, all the rest of the draws since 2004 have a noticeable extremely tight control on how many winners on each draw if any?

When one takes the trouble to examine these recorded results be prepared for a shock, currently on Friday 9th November 2012, as I am writing this, with an amazing string of (12 rollovers) from 2nd October accumulating an astonishing well over £122.6milion Given the opportunity and looking back through this extremely long list of results has certainly opened my eyes, between 22nd June and 7[th]August 2012 there were 14 draws without a jackpot winner, again looking back over these same results on other occasions with a noticeable 8/9/10/ or even 12 draws accumulating countless £millions on different occasions to attract punters to purchase more and more tickets.

When you firstly consider how many more millions of punters included with each draw. Not forgetting this is the whole of Europe, along with all the millions of tickets bought in the UK.

Which indicates that an extremely very powerful computer must be selecting which balls to select, which will only produce a small amount of winners or none? As mentioned earlier there should not be any rollovers, not a single rollover it is so unfair. Now if the selection of the balls was drawn instead of using these unnecessary expensive machines, they were picked out of a see through drum like described earlier, it's the British way and had stood for generations at fares and community halls, completely at random and clearly a fairer transparency with each draw?

With absolutely no need for these machines, the result of this way of selection I am certain would simultaneously produce many more winners and worth an experiment, and dissolve or dispel this uncertainty of any form of corruption or fiddling going on?

In the government there is nobody prepared to help the less well off? The more affluent and wealth can look after themselves, they obviously don't need help.

Let me firstly explain my true feeling on this amazing subject. If I was the designer of this machine and I wished to control the amount of winners with each draw, two small tubes with the orifice the sizes of the ball would be placed near the exit of the machine and well camouflaged, one tube holding six balls already selected beforehand by the computer.

Which would either offer no jackpot winners, or a very limited amount of jackpot winners with each draw, the other tube would take the balls not selected out of the way, extremely fast without anybody seeing how this fiddle is carried out?

Not forgetting this would be 'my way' of securing control, not Camelot's.

Waking up at 3am one morning, sweating like hell with this idea in mind, and has puzzled me ever since, it's not like me to think in this corrupt way, but it is highly possible that it would work, as long as the machine was not examined to closely by an expert.

With not being new to bright ideas, for countless years I have invented lots of possible worthwhile viable ideas, which I believe would have made me a fortune, but unfortunately and shamefully never metalized, maybe one day a great idea will surface?

Also Camelot has totally secured its future with selling these multitudes of scratch cards in nearly every sweat shop and supermarket throughout Great Britain. Ranging from, £1, £2, £5, £10, and I have heard £20 mention. Some have the same value but different face on the ticket, constantly changing the tickets faces plus values to confuse the punters.

Which have hooked and targeted millions of extremely poor people, who have very little amount of money. But with an expectation and gullibility that buying these tickets is a way of making a fortune, instead of getting richer, evidence proves they stay poor.

Wealthy people would never consider purchasing these scratch card tickets, knowing the odds are not in their favour.

Most people forget that Camelot have also a 'draw' each day organised just to accumulate even more money from the poor who are naturally naive thinking their next big win is just round the corner: Firstly with central government allowing and accepting this as normal way of living, without being accountable or questioning their true motives, in making as much money as possible?

The camouflage as stated earlier, that we give lots of money over to charities. Secondly it is significant that the government have not realised or aware that we are all in a economic crises, and the very poor are spending a great percentage of their income on purchasing lottery tickets and scratch cards, placing themselves in an impossible situation and cannot possibly avoid a complete disaster.

May I explain with a fine example with each lottery draw, now drawn in a more transparent way, and not under strict control with the amount of winners, with no rollovers or a questionable bonus balls.

Importantly if no winner with six balls, the payment would be given to the ticket with five balls and so on. Immediately the amount of possible winners would be significantly increased, it would not surprise me with hundreds of winners on occasions, each sharing the jackpot prize, considering most winners would be the less well off?

Depending on the total amount each winner receives the economic situation in Great Britain is noticeably improved instantly with hundreds of the less wealthy, spending their money in the shops after 'each lotto or Thunderball draw.'

The government are truly to blame, ignoring these possibilities with the economic crises we are currently experiencing. It's the poor that generate these huge amounts by continuing purchasing these lottery tickets. A responsible government would never allow any rollovers to occur; subsequently the economy would recover overnight with the winners spending their money importantly after 'each draw.'

All the MPs have been given a brain, but still haven't realised you are supposed to use it? You may question what has this serious awe-inspiring topic to do with councillors' mistreatment of its citizens; it has all the contents of absolute control, with making as much money as possible, and nobody is prepared to do anything about it. When you consider, if the council had not snatched our small play area from the young children, this book importantly would never have been published.

Could I remind you about the title of this book: 'Actions of a few (Councillors) are felt by all'?

CHAPTER THIRTEEN

*

Claim on Green

Necessary changes need to be carried out for the future, when taking notice on this, and other occasions throughout this book, are statements apparently intended to be controversial at times as you have just read. Referring possibly to countless other towns in this country, where most of the local citizens are unjustly treated, with disrespect by their local council officials.

Amazingly most council officials are acting in the very same disagreeable manner as in our town; they have no reason or justification to act in this way towards the local people who continually secure their significantly large salaries' each year.

Our very small recreational play area should never have been taken from us, we had this rightful claim and privilege also enjoyment for well over 60years, and they should have asked, not taken without a word of explanation, along with a refusal of an open transparent meeting to discuss serious local issues at the time, truthfully this is nothing less than bullyboy tactics plus open greed.

Having enough money, I would present a strong excellent case, and be willing to take those responsible to the high court, and explain themselves for unjustly breaking a promise of 20years ago, with an agreed temporary arrangement that this open common land designated for recreational use should have been returned to its rightful owners, the local residents/young children. Our local authorities had as mention broken a fundamental promise to hand back our green.

Satisfactory result quite straightforwardly and fair for all, would have been to halt the development load all the inappropriate unsightly prefabricated buildings, and wood/bricks, and other materials on to Lorries, and develop elsewhere. Selecting an area where no trees have to be cut down, and develop an area 'in need' of regeneration. Not on this open space designated, and set aside with a specific function and purpose by the former planning office, as a planned local recreational play area.

Experiencing all the unlawful ways with intolerable treatment, including all those blatant lies, by so-called professional bodies, over the years. Concerning this open recreational space, which has consciously, turned me into a fighter, rather than yes man.

If possible I intend showing, and helping others through some of the pitfalls, and hurdles when taking on their council. Which I am enjoying immensely, and would feel some of the power described previously, that the planners and council officials use against the local residents.

This next quote is ideal, as example of the way local authority commonly treat the residents in our town. While looking through our local paper I came across this wonderful true story, which I feel must be entered into this book, as proof of my own findings, as evidence when attending a fully controlled and a restricted friendly committee meeting.

We will call this young woman 'Karen.' "Yesterday I attended my very first council planning committee meeting as a member of the public. There were a significant number of people attending this meeting; the chair of the meeting had to explain the 'simple rules and regulations,' but excluding 'emotions' and feelings of the members of the public, which does not seem fair.

The applications were then explained, and surprisingly not even debated. Grouping all of the objections together so that only one spokesperson who was restricted too just **'three minutes'** to speak on behalf of everyone, objecting to the proposed development which I find absolutely ludicrous, plus impossible.

"My personal issues with the process are firstly, why ask for comments/objections to an application since I would guess that 99% are 'emotional' and so do not count. Secondly, most opposition comes from ordinary lay people who do not know the planning laws and consequently cannot compete in three minutes, with developers who do this kind of thing regularly." Finally, "why do we need a planning committee? It seemed to me on last night's evidence that the whole process last night was a waste of everyone's time, except the developer, who gets to build 100 dwellings on yet another green in our town."

"It all leaves rather a sour taste, and the councillors would perhaps do well to remember that many people, who vote for them do so using emotions."

The above development committee meeting which this young woman attended are the very same developers (Slope partnership ltd), this is their next development after our Shortmeadow Green is completed. What 'Karen' had experienced that evening was just the very same unfairness, with 'duck tape' applied so that she or many others attending this meeting were unable to discuss any issues regarding the development, and soon to be built close by where she lives. Important necessary changes must be offered for the future with regard to fairness, when one attends committee meetings.

This is the same unfairness, mentioned throughout this book. I would like to have a wild guess as too this young women's occupation, either a librarian, or possible a teacher, or could she be a police officer, the way it has been written I must compliment her excellent letter, it mentions people's 'emotions' which were not ever considered with planning applications.

Outstanding satisfaction, for me when successfully completing this book, unlike a weekly local newspaper above, this book should be around for many years and not easily discarded at any moment. If you remember just 50% of this advice, that should stand you in good stint with any future challenges in life so good luck and enjoy.

No challenge is impossible if you take on this challenge and campaign with an open mind, you now have some of the tools; now learn how to use them skilfully. Tragically, power with respect of running this country successfully, depends solely on the endeavours and actions of the MPs, who are still in these very small rowing boats without oars, going in no particular direction. They should have all be schooled as you will encounter shortly, in Mr. Fat Smelly Henderson's classroom, to keep them in line with what is best for all, not feathering their own nests. While concentrating solely on parliamentary expenses, and holding seats with very large companies to gain, even greater power is the wrong plan.

They forget like all local council officials the basics, with learning to listen, and taught how to keep the citizens happy also content. Starting with showing a great deal of respect towards the citizens who have supported them at election time, not continually upsetting the local residents in each town, completely forgetting who voted them into power and like our local councillor who lost her seat recently chiefly, because of no support with saving our green, plus importantly she was not listening.

Please allow me to explain with this fine example, decreasing standards in teaching in the proper manner, could be the sole reason for my inability and difficulty with spelling, and subsequently delayed my progress accordingly, with the traditional disciplinarian type of teacher we had at School, such as Mr, Henderson.

Word delivery, was aimed towards one particular incident in the classroom many years ago, which I can still recall quite vividly. Being summoned up to the blackboard, by the teacher in front of the whole class, and asked to write the word 'because.'

Carried out with confidence, and how all words are constructed with each letter, in front of the letter previous. Shamefully I was never taught grammar, or structure in any way on how to spell, reading any book at the time that I could get my hands on, helped remembering word structure as such, if a word was spelt correctly I could relate to that. Nevertheless, find spelling a nightmare even to this day, it should be made much simpler to understand. For example take the word "yacht" should been spelt 'Yot' also the word listens, why has it got a (t) also doubt why the (b) should be (d), another classic word specific, why the (s) clearly sounds as if it would start with a (p)

Alternatively (lead or lead) which is soft metal, and which is a dogs lead, both spelt the same. This fine example could have (led) anyone up the garden path, is spelt without the letter (a) but sounds the same. (There or their) is another fine example, remembering to use person /place. Couldn't give a damn, why the (n) on the end. To/Too/Two. Are words that sound exactly the same? Words like treacherous, with countless other words 'obvious' as an example, with silent letters which always catch me out.

I feel extremely sorry for others like myself, who suffer from being dyslexic, it is not as if intelligence is involved. Having the same difficulty, with countless other examples throughout the dictionary.

The words sounding the same but knowing where and when to use them is extremely difficult to remember, unless schooled in the correct manner. Recognizing in certain circumstances the child has dyslexia, (Impaired ability to understand written language) which places any child at a disadvantaged to others in the same class. (I digress).

let us return to Mr Henderson's classroom, immediately, after writing the word 'because' correctly on the blackboard. Mr. Henderson my teacher bellowed out very loudly, (as if in the Army, the Sergeant major would like everyone to pay attention). "Are you sure that is correct, would you like to try again, and this time, spell it correctly".

After a few seconds looking back at the blackboard and a second check, my reply was "that the spelling was correct," now the mistake was not with the spelling. It was the fact I had answered back. Now out loudly, knowing I was already in serious trouble, bravely said with (quite amusement) pausing hesitantly between each letter. 'B-E-C-A-U-S-E.'

With a cheeky smile while (writing the letters as you see them spaced out across the whole length of the blackboard). Mr. Almighty Fat smelly Henderson must have thought that I was being sarcastic as you can assume from the twist on name calling, that he was extremely large in stature, to my very small skinny attire.

Likened to the Oliver Twist film humbly saying "more gruel pleases Sir" Attitude. He could hit a fly from thirty yards off the end of your nose, on a good day with a piece of chalk, before you could blink an eye.

On a bad day your nose would be bleeding and bruised for several days, and possibly a visit to the Matron at the surgery, especially after he considered a few 'drinks' the previously night. Like possibly last night you could smell the strong whisky on his breath, when he got up close enough. Not even superman would dare take on old fat smelly Henderson. You can have only one guess, as to who was braver than Superman was on that fateful day. OK I gave you too much of a clue! All BECAUSE some clever person took on Fat smelly Henderson and lost.

The result of that encounter was that I could not sit for at least a week. What gave it away was the name which he was unfamiliar with, which I called him!!! It is before Nine o'clock and small children might see so I'll leave it to your imagination: 'I dread to think what punishment I would have received for getting the word wrong.' Nothing less than the gallows I expect? Life in an orphanage can be summed, up in just a few words, well three words, you either conform, or you conform nothing in between, you do not have too many choices, it is a closed shop where power is used against all.

The incidents like the above evidently did not happen too often, approximately once a day. Inwardly, you were starved, of a good sound education; nothing gets the brain cells going, if they are not being used. With no inspiration, to aspire, or champion to follow, and learn from. This is where the father figure comes into play if I had a dad, things would have been completely different and evidently more fun. Maybe later I will get a chance to explain in more detail, with the way us lads suffered in the past you either laugh or cry. What with the entire abuses, personal and physical, we all had to endure, and with the disadvantages for life ahead.

Deprived of a decent Education would come first on my exceedingly long list, a father figure is next, on that same list to guide me through the difficulties he would have felt when he was a small kid like me. Going to a football match sitting astride his very strong shoulders, bounding along the road shouting abuse at the opposition, possibly 'Chelsea or Spurs fans,' knowing that my dad would protect me at all times.

Showing how to fix things like the bike needing repairing, or going fishing, I supposed he would be keeping me on the straight and narrow, which would have been hurtful sometimes for me, but necessary, and a whole string of other things. Smiling when he gets the better of me, I would have loved that, always in competition with plenty of light-hearted or teasing amusing remarks and banter. Yearning, to be as skilled and as good as him, and learning all the time. Asking questions and eventually a good education, a natural follow on. Swimming faster, dribbling the football past him, as he got older, and he slowed down, would have been a wonderful challenge or exchange to have experienced.

CHAPTER FOURTEEN

*

My Close Family

Positive decision years ago like many other couples, when choosing to marry, unlike many partners today who do not favour a marriage relationship. The very best day of my life, was when my wife and I first got married. She was extremely gorgeous then and still looks as beautiful, however she would have preferred Cliff Richard but had to settle for second best? It was four years before we decided to start a family, our plans were to allow approximately four years between each child.

We have two great lads, and one gorgeous girl, as a father I found great pleasure in guiding my three lovely children through the straight and narrow, also found on countless occasions reason in grounding them all when necessary, that always used to give me great pleasure, sorry kids. They have unfortunately not turned out as good looking as me, nevertheless, they are OK.

Remembering some small but significant times like, Scott my eldest retreated to the loo, and all that was heard from down stairs was, "Bugger, Bugger" he was learning the English language after being told off by me, and grounded yet again. Another memorable occasion to my horror, a line of children arranged shoulder to shoulder outside our house lying down on the pavement.

Approximately eight of the brave neighbourhood children, along with my young daughter Beverley situated in the middle of the group, on the firing end, was young Craig positioned right on the end. This was at a very late stage, in attempting stopping the proceedings, with Scott hurtling at 90 miles an hour towards the ramp, in front of this group on the ground. With closed eyes waiting for the expectant inevitable screams from Craig, I heard the bike landing successfully with an almighty crash, and with screeching breaks, plus avoidable skid towards the wall in front, some three yards away.

Success on this occasion, I congratulated Scott, and then asked Scott 'if he could take up the position Craig had been laying and I was now on the bike.' Disappointedly, he refused my request immediately, I wonder why? Shortly after that incident. The boys had put poor little Beverley, up one of the crab-apple tree's outside our house, some eight feet into the tree to collect a Frisbee.

Both vanished immediately over to 'our local playing field.' Leaving Poor Bev, wondering how she was ever going to get down. On my return from work shortly after, I was inquisitive; there were a number of girls below one of the crab-apple trees.

Our poor Beverley she was found up the tree asking to be retrieved, I very nearly left her up there, but could see she was upset, I reached up let her down, gave her a cuddle and kiss and off she went over on the field with the other kids. With two older brothers, she was a tom girl at heart.

Curiously, the two boys were found over on the field with many other lads from the street, how could you possible tell them off, well on this occasion I had a word.

With countless other wonderful memorable situations over the years, great fun on each occasions all involving our small essential local green.

After all those years of carefully, looking after my children, they are now already looking around for a nursing home for me, not sure which one has been chosen and decide upon! They keep dropping hints like, "where would you like to live dad". As if it was imminent, which had me worried for a while?

'Remain here nearby to where the children plus grandchildren are living would be nice: Truthfully, with a choice I would not refuse a seaside area, thank you.' Now we are looking forward to enjoyment with all our five grandchildren.

While talking of grandchildren, my daughter has a boy called 'Kai,' and recent arrival of a beautiful baby girl another granddaughter called 'Ruby' born in late April 2010. Beverley's partner Darren is over the moon and I think these two will be married soon, because he has asked me quite surprisingly, in the traditional way for my Daughters hand in marriage which was extremely nice of him to take her of my hands?

I very nearly refused! With good reason, he is a 'Chelsea supporter,' his only weakness but someone has to support them I suppose.

My eldest boy Scott with partner, has a lovely granddaughter 'Amelia' she has a wonderful character and we all love her to bits, just started speaking. Incidentally she is rather bossy, just like my wife, but marvellous with it.

They have recently surprised us both by announcing we will soon be grandparents to yet another grandson 'Charlie' in March 2012 that's fantastic news, our Scott will be well chuffed now with a boy!

Latest great news as I speak, our younger son Craig & partner has produced a grandson called 'Finley' he is fantastic. I wish the kids would slow down now; this is rather expensive with all these wonderful grandchildren. Moreover, looking forward to all the baby-sitting and confrontational sleepovers, plus compensation they will either keep me younger or finish me off, proverbially the latter?

We are extremely pleased the children still arrive each Sunday for lunch, although it is exhausting for us both, we would miss them if the grandchildren could not come round to see us, it's marvellous seeing them growing up.

Returning to a much earlier period, I have a brother Paddy here in England who is four years my senior. Also with an extended larger family, across the water in Ireland.

I was going to ask Paddy, whether he could assist with this book, placing the dots in the correct position, and check with the grammar, he has all the academic skills retiring from Reuters, the printers in London, but changed my mind.

Nevertheless, I am very proud at having attempted the impossible myself, with great success and enjoyment so far with this surprising challenge, which was defiantly out of my comfort zone but successfully accomplished.

CHAPTER FIFTEEN

*

Power

Everybody with a choice would avoid politics, how can you possible preclude this topic. Now I will apologise for my next subject that at this stage has to be included dare I say it, bureaucracy. There I have said it, now try and explain anything remotely involved with politics or bureaucracy, and everyone including myself would run a mile, but it must be included in this book without a choice.

For those of you who may be too young to remember as fast as Roger Banister the first person on record ever to run a mile in fewer than four minutes, and would not remain the least bit interested with the bureaucracy.

You are trying now to anticipate what I am about to say next, before closing the book. Besides saying something like the statement, my lovely daughter comes out with, after successfully receiving once again the usual £5 permanent loan out of me on each attempt.

Saying "You're boring me now" and walk off with an achievable smile on her gorgeous face. With a sense of personal pride, using her usual devious tactics, which she learnt from her mum, which I allow on each occasion, then she asks if I could taxi home a group of her friends later that night, and on numerous occasions in the past.

Let us now get serious just before you do decide or think of closing this book, just when new interesting revelations are about to be revealed.

We all do it and nobody can say otherwise, just as you start a meal, the doorbell chimes. In anticipation, it could be the man from the Pools, or premium bonds, ready to hand, you that long awaited exceedingly large cheque. Stating that you have at last won the pools, or your long awaited massive premium bond has arrived, you dash to open the front door. To your annoyance you are confronted with neither, with huge disappointment you recognise whom the caller turns out to be, that very same councillor, only three weeks previous when you ask that very same person for her help and support, in saving our very small recreational open space.

From the clutches of the planning office and developers, including at this very late stage, Guinness (Trust) Partnership showing now on a notice board in May 2010, some 11 months after the development had started, with being the main backers with this controversial development. Increasingly faced with the councils unpopular decisions, throughout the country showing they are insensitive towards local issues, with being successful in building houses on our very small indispensable Green.

Ignoring planners previous wise decision years ago, who felt these open spaces squeezed between two houses estates, which are extremely essential 'common ground' for the local community to use and enjoy, not just for the past, but also with the future in mind to benefit the whole community.

'The councillor' states on her open address, "could I rely on your support with the local elections next Thursday."

With fish & chips spurting from your mouth while attempting to eat and speak at the same time, emitting fish &chips all over the front of her nice red suit. Tomato sauce on them would have been her next statement, which she prefers with chips.

Without a mouth full of Fish & Chips, now able to speak, you gave her a piece of your mind, as well as that free portion of fish & chips, which she hasn't paid for yet, about her refusal in helping to save the play area previously some three weeks ago.

'It's payback time'. "Why on earth should you expect our support when you need it for next Thursday's local elections? You will not get my vote, or any votes around here, now go away and think about your next move, until we are assured of your support with saving our local play area for the very young children?"

All of a sudden, it's 'Checkmate' the councillors have absolutely no power, looking in dismay as a quick exit was carried out, and she was never ever seen or heard of again, after the inevitability of losing her seat on the council. A rude awakening, she never learnt 'how to listen,' to the needs of the local residents, being the main reason for losing her seat on the council, I felt rather sorry for her, after having had fish & chip supper together briefly; it was brief, but nice! This sudden announcement of checkmate situation, characterized how this book can accumulate, and subsequently examine the evidence, on who actually holds this power.

The local Authorities, seam unable to operate without overall power, like the example if you remember in an earlier chapter, with the noticeable unfair (football match) we held.

Where if you recall, the residents encountered problems staked to the ground, attached to posts with shackles, and were unable to speak with duck tape placed across their mouths. While the other team consisting of councillors, planners, and other local authorities who were able to score as many goals at will, without any confrontation from the apposing team.

Running rings, round the residents who were left speechless, also frustrated and unable to say or do anything about this deplorable situation. Which understandably, is undemocratic, with absolutely no opportunity for a chance to debate on serious local issues, with any authorities locally?

Learning recently, from reading in our local newspaper, reminds me of a classic situation, of who holds the unexpected power, the labour leader in our town, was extremely upset when our local football team was promoted into the football league, without firstly consulting her, or anyone else in the council, changed part of the name of the football club. By dropping the name 'Borough' the football team management, are not obliged to consult with the council or anyone other than the fans concerning their business.

If she felt disappointed as the article mentions, by not being 'consulted' with this name change, it was just a fraction of the disappointment we felt personally, when our small green was taken from us for the second time in history, without consultation, or debate, by our local corrupt councillors or party leader who apparently couldn't care less about the community. This was another occasion in the same town where our local councillor has received a rude awakening, should have held a meeting now having lost her seat on the council, may have taught her this extremely important lesson.

Towards respect for the future, by not listening to us local residents who had not received any respect or help from our local councillor. Alternatively, any support when attempting to save our open space. 'Is like throwing stones inside a greenhouse without expecting the glass to break.'

Without consultation, with the residents, went ahead and demolished, all but four, 'off street parking' (this is local garages to rent). Amazingly out of (51) garages originally, only four remain, with a total of at least fifteen currently in serious demand locally. As I am filling in this line, in December 2009, the demolishing of the garages has now started, this is ludicrous, should have been stopped, in fairness to the current local residents demands. Now the clever council officials have created an extremely new amazing policy, called. 'ON STREET PARKING.' Which other councils may adopt in future if this proves successful, by demolishing as many rentable garages locally to build more prefabricated cheap houses? The work is being carried out with the sound of the JCB in the background, with only two more garages to demolish out of (51), their task is complete, and in one month in early 2010, the new development starts in earnest, leaving as mention earlier only four garages in total.

Let me explain the arrangements regarding the four remaining garages. Firstly, one local resident bought one-garage years ago from the Council. Secondly, another resident is currently renting two of the garages, one for this car, and the other as house storage. However, the last garage goes deservingly to the handicapped couple with justification that their garage should be in close proximity to their house.

BECAUSE I am not very bright, could someone please help me out? The dozy insensitive twits, in the housing office have agreed, with the rest of these very dumb council officials, plus an arrangement of councillors who turn up at the committee meeting, to decide on important matters.

To demolish unbelievable all but four, of the local garages, and dismiss any opportunity of existing residents, the prospect locally of renting 'off street parking,' is of extremely serious concern with policy planning, just to achieve changing from a brown field site to a free fall site.

By unlawfully demolishing 47 garages in total, where there is a strict limitation on the amount of building you are permitted to demolish on a 'free fall site,' which is why we have laws, and legislation in this country. Approximately fifteen, very frustrated residents demands for garages in the vicinity, how can anybody in their right mind ignore the demands of the current residents.

Very soon, when the 'muck' hits the fan Mr Day from housing, is likely to be in extremely serious trouble over the shortage of 'off street parking,' in this area, which never had a serious problem previously. In hindsight I cannot comprehend, how they are still employed, there is nowhere now possibly to park our vehicles safely off the street. Which would alleviate greatly, the serious parking situation currently, we find ourselves in, or keep the car safely away from possible thieves. Look up in the sky, possibly Houdini the great magician is just around the corner, ready to solve this particular difficult impossible problem. Perhaps wave a magic wand making the garages reappear from somewhere.

Consequently, the councillors, when voting to demolish all of these essential garages must have surely considered this scenario, or did they over look this at the planning stage? In addition, taken into account, as to where we could possibly park our cars safely now?

'**In the street,**' 'now why didn't I think of that?'

(The arrangement of councillors) is the most important entry into this book at committee meetings, where decisions are finalised, by most councillors who are voting beforehand according to the party leader's prearrangement in secrecy, and decided on privately with no intention or concern with 'fairness,' or residents emotions. This fundamental serious situation is impossible to solve, with demand for local garages in the area. Soon the councillors are going to realise their huge confrontational mistake, which will surely affect all the current residents in the neighbourhood?

Replaced, controversially with six ugly fabricated houses built on, what is classed as a free fall site, where the former garages used to stand, looking more like a 'prison/warehouse' not six wonderful houses which the senior councillors are convince of? (Please look at photo in Chapter Nineteen for your personal opinion).

Also having to provide 12 parking spaces must of course be considered, for the new occupiers of these 6 houses, (two cars per house) with a quick easy sum that is 12 parking spaces correctly sorted for the new residents in the garage area alone, 32 in total overall, provided for the remainder of the new development, on what used to be our 'Shortmeadow Green.' 'What about the current residents needs?'

Nevertheless, the council have been effectively, extremely silly on this occasion, in forgetting that we live in a free society, with strict necessary rules, and policy laid down in concrete, not (quick sand) for very good reason.

Councillors when carrying out their duty at counselling should take careful control of this power, with sensible fair calculated, decisions, mindful of democracy. This above situation is not fair, not sensible, and most certainly not democratic, with using bullyboy tactics against the local residents. We all felt completely devastated and cheated, with most of the residents quoting that wonderful remarkable quote, **"what can you do about it."**

Firstly, the new residents concerns and welfare have been considered and settled, by taking away 'off street parking' from the current residents, with no garages now to place our cars off the road safely. They have created a very severe parking problem with extremely serious concerns, that this problem cannot possible be resolved, without applying magic:

Importantly this is the reason you have procedure and policy laid down, so this cannot possibly happen, by ignoring the system, you now create this very serious unavoidable problem with existing evidence! And the planners stating on the planning application that there would not be a significant increase with traffic in our street? Which is a direct lie, there is a constant flow of traffic 24/7 now?

Disrespect shown from these councillors actions above, carries though for us not to return any respect, they have damaged any credibility and natural exchange. Could possibly lose their seats in the next election?

(Cannot wait to see what comes off the fan shortly).

CHAPTER SIXTEEN

*

Accidentally Cutting Down Three Trees

Therefore attention is now drawn to this next interesting situation, which will most likely upset those of you like myself, who are interested seriously and also passionate with maintaining a healthy environment. Look out for these important significant or slight changes to the initial plans by the developer, which are always extremely cleverly camouflaged. (Not behind the trees). Importantly the very first plans submitted which can be considered as a decoy into the planning office.

Accordingly, will never ever be used as working plans by the developer, with many more calculated changes to follow later before the development starts; 'Like the five major changes with this current development on our Shortmeadow Green.' Inevitably, changes to the plans will be altered a number of times as expected, and resubmitted to the planning office. With these important hidden alterations from the public, unless you frequently visit the planning office and familiarise yourself with the system, by constantly viewing the latest working plans, you would not be aware of these alterations.

Amazingly, many more trees were 'accidentally' cut down on site, stating that they were in an unhealthy condition, (another direct lie). When perfectly sound; as an example, three trees like on our current proposed development, cut down quite by 'accident by the developer.' Furthermore, others not accidentally cut down, but clearly deliberately damage with a digger close to the tree base.

Deliberately damaging the roots system, plus the removing of the soil, did not improve the stability for these trees. We witnessed damage to a number of other tree bases that were to be retained, found in an unstable situation without a doubt, had to be removed for safety reasons. This was the developer's intention all along, to remove as many mature trees as possible. You can see from the photos offered in (chapter 37), which show quite clearly, by the removal of the soil, and cutting the roots, how is it possible for the trees to stand?

With countless witnesses observing each day, also photos & video evidence saved and recorded, of this destruction of all these trees on a single site, has to be of some serious concern for future developments, by this same developer 'Guinness Housing Trust' possibly authorize this destruction one can reasonably assume, because they were not hiding this destruction, carried out quite openly.

Below a few comments from our local newspaper, who were kind enough in entering our appeal against this controversial development, with regard to saving our green? "The property developer has apologised to the planning office, after cutting down 'accidentally' a number of mature trees in error." Stating that workers belonging to the developers removed the trees at what has become a contentious development on our green.

Interestingly, the cutting down of any trees, is always carried out safely by the council arboriculture workers, so it seems highly unlikely, and I cannot believe for one moment it was carried out by the development workers. I am almost certain of this fact. "So the cutting down of all these trees is most certainly not cut down 'accidentally.'

In fact, a deliberate premeditated act, stated by the local resident, who drew attention to the policy background also?" 'Mr Glanfield mentioned that no residential houses could ever be considered on the open space, residents opposed the plans in the local newspaper for flats and houses two years ago, saying the green should have been returned to the resident, for recreational use after the unsightly so called temporary prefabricated bungalows had been removed.'

Besides this opposition from the residents, the council sold the land secretly to the developers, who are currently building 15 houses and 6 flats on this land that cost a pittance to the developer. Most of the residents are now extremely upset with the loss of the green, along with many mature trees cut down 'accidentally' which should have been retained. Worryingly a great number of residents have expressed their annoyance, and decided to sell up and move away because of the controversial development, the council have turned a blind eye and could not give a damn.

"Eleven trees were scheduled on the working plans to be retained in an area at the lower part of the site; he spotted only four trees were left standing, and reported his finding to the council planning office for their reaction."

"Stating that the developers are out of order and the council should have kept an eye on this project. I am certain without a doubt; many more trees have been damage at the roots, without affording them the official approved protection of 12 times the diameter width of tree trunk." "When you realise and witness how close the diggers were excavating nearby each tree, with having now to wait until the growing season to see how healthy the trees are," stated Mr Glanfield. Without any concern for the local environment, or the residents feelings. A spokesperson for the council said jokingly with tongue in cheek. "The developers have apologised for 'accidentally' felling of the trees as a result of discussions between the council and the developers, they have agreed to replace the trees and will be planting new hornbeam trees in November."

It is now halfway through January 2011, still no hornbeam trees. They may have promised to plant these trees but it would take years for them to reach maturity, now that the green has been scarred forever.

In addition, to the damage caused by the previous temporary development 20 years ago. These trees, which were aggressively removed intentionally, by the cowboy developers as, described above with no justification for their actions, 'not accidentally' like reported by the developers, and accepted by the planning office as acceptable course of action. Without considering any punishment, what so ever, (this is one of two areas) where the bats were seen roosting over many years. Ironically, on the initial drawings as stated earlier for this development, submitted into planning office for their approval, the public were assured that all eleven mature trees in that same area were to be retained; Over time it has be reduced surprisingly to only four trees in this same group. Which proves conclusively the point on intentionally spoiling our local environment?

When I contacted the planning officer, to visit the site, and check on these fundamental facts, also drawing attention to the fact, that the cowboy developers, had dug deep trenches very close to other mature trees, throughout the site not affording the necessary protection, and legal distance required.

71

Pointing out quite clearly to the planning officer, damage to three retained tree roots structures, he was not even surprised or amazed they were left in an unstable condition needing urgent action. Besides, unavoidable choice in having to remove these seriously damaged trees, safely out of harm's way, with families living within yards, worried with the amount of damaged mature trees nearby.

These precise instructions were totally ignored by the cowboy developer, when granted planning consent. The planning office has lost any 'credibility;' also, trust has been lost, with allowing this developer to further obliterate the limited environment left.

The letter that follows, is the same letter received from the planning office on the above serious incident which the same local newspaper covered in support with attempting to save our green. Showing a very serious breach of planning regulations but without any punishment what so ever? This has got to be a first; 'an apology from the planning office,' their letter in response, with above incident follows.

Referring to our meeting of last week in respect of the trees at the above site at Shortmeadow Green. Following our conversation, I inspected the site and noted firstly that three trees, which were indentified to be, retained on the approved layout plans. (Drawing C-j00-001Rev E). Had in fact, as reported by yourself been removed. These trees formed part of the group of 12 trees located on the landscaped area to the Southeast of units 8-12 and to the west of units 2-7. I have written to the developers requesting an explanation as to why these trees have been removed and what action they intend to take to remedy the situation. Also noticed, that none of the remaining trees on site, were not afforded any form of protection as you mentioned.

As required by our granting of planning permission, making the site supervisor, aware of these requirements at the time of my visit. Who has given a verbal undertaking to provide the necessary tree protection measures as a matter of urgency? It is my intention to revisit the site again on the week commencing 22nd March 2010, to see if these works have been undertaken. I trust this clarifies my findings, following my site inspection. Once I have heard from the developers in respect of the loss of trees, and the tree protection measures. I will again write to you and advise how the council intends to proceed with the matters above. Yours Sincerely planning officer.

This is the reply from planning office later. I refer to my letter of the 15th March in respect of the above. I have now received a response from the developer who has confirmed that the three trees were unavoidably cut down **'accidentally.'**(Is this possible)? They have apologised for this, and the concern it may have caused for the local residents. In order to rectify the situation, the developer's landscape advisor has contracted the council's arboriculture officer and agreement has been reached, that a further number of hornbeam trees, will be planted approximately in this same area. These are to be root balled 20-24cms/in size and be planted in November (the next available planting season). With regard to their current tree protection, I have visited the site, and confirm that those remaining trees have now all been afforded the approved protection. I trust this now clarifies the situation, and how the loss of the trees at the site is to be remedied. Yours sincerely planning officer.

Look out for these calculated and intentional deliberate actions with your developments, with absolutely no concern for maintaining a healthy environment.

Each approved working plans submitted would predictably change quite considerably in the very earliest, after planning approval has been agreed by the committee, this is certain evidently proved so on this site, and others.

All further approved plans regarding the development, will true to form, constantly change a few more times guaranteed, with directly confusing the residents, who were expecting a fair transparent arrangement. Proved inconclusively with evidence, showing alterations had been carried out when viewing each new plan submitted for planning office approval. This same developer will most likely, if not with assurance with the above evidence. Carry out the very same damage to the environment on the next site, with absolutely no punishment from the planning office!

As you have witnessed the developers are guilty of cutting down a huge amount of the trees which should have been protected also retained on site.

Proving quite clearly, that double standards are prevalent, if any member of the public was to carry out this type of action, the planning office would come down extremely heavy on that person, and a fine would have to be paid at the very least. What follows is extremely difficult to believe.

The development was completed in early March 2011, with all the new residents now settled into the new houses and flats. Some five months later, it was decided that more mature trees along with others in the lane, are now to be cut down adjacent to the development site. Is this reverse planning, and quite astonishing reasons for the removal of all these tall mature trees five months after the development complete is unbelievable, plus unacceptable.

(1) First serious concern by the Guinness Housing Trust was that the tall mature trees could possible fall on the new houses, being their main obvious reason for their removal.

(2) Followed by the fact that the trees were interfering with the reception of the TV signals.

(3) Amazingly stating also at this late stage, that the trees were blocking the light emitting into each of the buildings. (Proof absolutely no planning).

(4) Furthermore complaints that the mature trees were spoiling the new resident vista.

(5) Saving the best until last, while removing these tall mature trees, the council arboriculture workers obviously failed to carry out an important necessary risk assessment, in their haste with attempting to cut down all these tall mature trees in close proximity to resident's properties, unimpressively the inevitable happened.

The outcome as you can see from the following photograph was that one of the trees felled, came down embarrassingly across the fence into the resident's rear garden, missing the house by inches. Speaking with this neighbour after the incident, he has four dogs, which use the garden constantly 24/7. Worryingly and finding out through our discussion, that he has amazingly eighteen grandchildren who visit on most days of the week. Need I state the obvious scenario with their safety in mind!!

Tree felled, damaged to neighbour's fence.

Many trees cut down in the lane, five months after the development.

Deliberate wonton vandalism in our lane. Why?

Is it (fair), when planning any development, should the planners have allowed many more trees to be removed unjustifiably, five months after the development is complete, for whatever reason? A senior councillor was astonished, and commented on this wonton vandalism. These instructions to remove even more trees from our close environment, are they coming directly from Guinness Housing Trust?

Who have shown all along, scant regard so far with the cutting down of all our mature beautiful trees in the close neighbourhood. Since shamefully purchasing this land from the developer, knowing that it used to be a play area for the local children/residents to use, and was promised years ago to be returned to its former glory. Surprisingly with HRH Prince Charles as there patron?

CHAPTER SEVENTEEN

*

Leaving Wealthy Areas Alone

Evidently nearly all towns throughout Great Britain, seem to be run by inconsiderate council officials, who discriminate openly against less prosperous parts of each town throughout the country, using this same power they hold over us which is completely out of control. Curiously, we are met with this intriguing astonishing remark, mentioned earlier by Mr Bent. Head of planning office.

That a meeting is too time consuming which sounds rather 'Bandy' to me, (excuse the pun) stating quite categorically, without compassion, and sounds insensitive towards the local resident's feelings. Maybe you will find surprisingly the very same statement mentioned by your planning office in your town, however never ever in the more affluent areas of each town. So listen out in your town for this same unique quote, a meeting to discuss extremely serious issues, and the near total demolishing of all nearby garages, (off street parking) of which at least fifteen are truly in demand locally, Is too time consuming.

Shall I repeat?'TOO TIME CONSUMING' certainly not for us residents. The fact that we pay their huge salaries, and all other local authorities pay, which come out of local council tax. Should someone tell them this? There lost, in another world of their own, and have to return to earth some time! A short lesson in Mr. Henderson's class would indeed sort this lot out. BECAUSE warning them to protect their noses they would not hear, BECAUSE they would not be listening, BECAUSE they are not accustomed to listening.

This paralysing power, and situation with local authorities, always upsetting and treating the people who have voted for them, in a disrespectful manner, must now urgently and permanently, change with introducing legislation. With regards to major improvements and an accepted fairer playing field, with residents released from their shackles. Additionally a say in development serious issues, involving there area the sooner the better for all concerned, and for democracy.

When one listens to the radio, and watches TV news each day, also headlines in the local, plus national newspapers, it continually covers stories where the local councils, using this unnecessary bullyboy tactics, and are repeatedly upsetting the residents in each and every town throughout this country, and nobody is doing anything to alter this situation. The evidence undoubtedly felt by all, 'but never ever inevitably in the more affluent areas of each town.' Incidentally, nobody seems to be doing anything to change this power arrangement. It seems an acceptable thing nowadays by the majority of local residents, that once the council propose a new development in any area, **'everybody shrugged both shoulders and show both palms towards you, stating what can you do about it,'** are they all frightened of their council officials.'

These wealthy areas true to form in each town astonishingly are left alone; on extremely rare occasions are these residents ever upset, because it is kicked into touch if mentioned at any local council meeting.

Additionally, its current use would be associated or envisage, with very serious future possibilities, concerning serious parking problems, along with increased traffic. Added to the loss of 'off street parking' (garages) could only greatly decrease the value, with the nearby properties in our whole neighbourhood.

Down a once extremely quiet cul-de-sac, was another sound reason mentioned by the estate agent, including visualising a greater increase in traffic 24/7.

The loss of a great deal of garages, which was recognised immediately, it's like rubbing salt into an open wound, with at least fifteen other residents including myself refused the possibility to rent the garages locally, by the housing department who stated that all but four garages would be demolished, their representative was Mr, DAY the housing manager, who expressed that the demolishing of the garages were due to unforeseen circumstances. Which is yet another direct lie?

Furthermore, he should be brought forward along with the council officials to explain these lies. He may have to return anyway, and justify his actions when the parking problems become even more serious or extremely critical.

Also a number of neighbours disputing their outlook, now compromised with 40ft horrendous buildings blocking their vista, where the distant view of the green plus the important loss of early morning sun shining first thing from the east in the morning, with no official meeting with the residents, is a combination of madness or stupidity?

Accepting, 75 new residential users, squeezed into 6 flats plus 15 private houses (21 units in total) in such a small area of one hundred yards by thirty yards, together without any space between each building, does not seem a very sensible plan for future planning.

That within a very small open space, the Guinness Trust decided without taking into account the current resident emotions, and personal feelings with placing 21 mixed flats and houses into an impossible compacted area, like packaging 'sardines' into a can on our recreational area.

Without apprehension, with the devaluing of all the properties surrounding this area. With the outcome that the new development has already, and will further reduce the value of existing properties in the vicinity. To the point of confrontation, with the new/current residents in the near future is obvious and inevitable, it only needs one incident. Already the new development has caused 18 residents to sell their houses, and now have left the area, why should they be forced to leave?

This is unbelievable, to lose this priceless small field, which had far too many technical problems for the new development to succeed. Without spending £millions to overcome these many serious technical problems, with this highly controversial development having unbelievably placed a permanent dangerous septic tank a (cesspit) holding human waste in the 21 century, within yards from the local residents properties, which is the main reason that 18 families had decided to leave the area.

The stench when this tank is full each month is awful. (Seen in the following photograph). Ironically the developers have disguised this septic tank by calling it a pumping station! Each month a mobile tanker is required to empty this septic tank because the sump pump is not working.

85

This tanker has turned up at 8am on a Sunday on a number of occasions so far? This is the developers' everlasting going away present, to the current residents' there is no polite way of saying this; they have (shit on us). Seriously how is it possible to accept and leave this septic tank on site it's grossly unfair, the local councillors have turned a blind eye to this serious unacceptable situation, refusing to help in any way?

Septic tank submerged.

Sorry for being so rude, but there is not another word to explain what they have done, which is grossly unacceptable heading into the 21st century. Would the Developers, plus Councillors, and HRH Prince Charles if you recall is the patron of the Guinness Housing Trust, place a septic tank in their own back garden?

The answer is plainly no. So why should we accept it in ours? Then from the housing representative Mr. Day we continually received unnecessary sarcastic remarks such as (due to unforeseen circumstances). The development plus planning must have been planned many years previously, with the developer. Then to rub salt into the open wound once again he states there is. (Currently no demand for the garages locally), and other direct blatant lies is unacceptable and he deserves a severe reprimand.

Both photographs that follow, show the view each neighbour is now facing, their vista blighted by this new structure, of what was a lovely green is now replaced, and compromised considerably by 40ft horrendous buildings which have extremely large windows, overlooking their properties and rear gardens, which is surely unacceptable.

Seriously, where is the privacy, once enjoyed over countless years, with the enforced intrusion of this development now to contend with for the rest of our lives, 'who is responsible for this unacceptable intrusion?' Councillors and all those local officials responsible for this carnage. **Then the monstrosity shown must be removed.**

Neighbours view now compromised with 40ft Monstrosity.

For the above contemptuous situation, this would never have been approved in the more affluent parts of the town, and smartly kicked into touch once mention at any meeting, again showing double standards are prevalent and has always been.

87

Next door neighbours huge twin Monstrosity alongside.

Down at the lower end of the development where all the garages were demolished, now replaced with six so-called beautiful quality houses so our local councillors are convinced, and keep quoting! Another example of excellent planning and professional standards of what is classified as quality housing for the future, looking remarkable like a prison, or very large warehouse placed in our residential housing estate, and regarded as acceptable.

Certainly not in keeping with the houses in the area, additionally another important reason for the devaluing, of all the houses in the neighbourhood. Feel free to comment on what you see as quality housing for the future, in this next photograph offered. These six wonderful houses camouflaged to keep out the nose of the traffic only two yards away.

Unbelievably Six 'quality' new houses replacing all the garages, looking like what?

Extraordinary, this outstanding ugly building should now be demolished, and those responsible should justifiably be sacked for this astonishing expensive mistake.

The open meeting, which was refused on a number of occasions, when the development was initially proposed, was crucial and the most important consideration in a democratic manner, with an opportunity to have our say.

Society demands that before this intrusion into the local neighbourhood, a transparent open meeting is essential to discuss local serious issues, including personal emotions concerning the proposed new development.

A picture can replace a thousand words; there are only four words to explain this building. **Rubbish, inappropriate, unacceptable, Monstrosity.** I'll give you an opportunity to add other words yourself?

HRH Prince Charles, as patron for Guinness Trust. I believe is confident, and experienced in what a monstrosity looks like over the years, would he please add his true personal comments on what this building looks like?

He should be significantly ashamed, with the affect, this new development, has on the local residents concerns, or personal emotions with the above scenario.

Of initially taking the children's play area away, and replaced with the above, new cheap rubbish, prefabricated, unacceptable monstrous 'carbuncle.'

Along with the previous photographs, which have compromised the resident's outlook and views, instead of a wonderful vista of open green?

Now without a choice, are presented with these horrendous ugly looking buildings through to perpetuity.

Alternatively, like a great deal of former residents, who have been forced to leave without a choice, after many enjoyable years living in this close neighbourhood?

Eighteen families which I mentioned earlier, have decided that it is an unacceptable situation to live near these monstrosities, plus having to live nearby a (cesspit), and left since the start of the development, with others including myself to follow shortly why?

Seriously, someone must be totally responsible and justifiably sacked, with causing this exodus of families forced without a choice in leaving the area, because of the foreseeable confrontational hideous new development.

Which the local planners should be utterly ashamed to have accepted as quality, that we have now to live with. Because of this madness, one can only recommend their future as planners would be numbered.

CHAPTER TWENTY

*

Petition to Reclaim Our Play Area

Authorities throughout Great Britain are guilty of snatching extremely important small areas of grass which hold together the local community. When the first attempts to takeover this recreational area by the local authorities, their intention and aim was to make as much money as possible then move onto the next green.

You must be aware of what may happen in your area, in your town, for the future. As explained in an earlier objection, a ploy by the council in allowing the grass to grow, and not maintaining an area over an extended period, preventing the local children who are now unable to play certain ball games on the recreational space in your neighbourhood.

This is sound advice, be attentive and guard against council visitors who are after your precious green with only one intention, to make as much money from each (Section 106 agreements). If the grass is too long, and soaking wet the parents would quite naturally keep the children off the long wet grass in question. Obviously with very long, possibly wet grass, also the rubbish left lying around for weeks, the local residents could not use the field freely, residents walking their dogs as an example several times daily, with many other enjoyable activities called off.

Subsequently with the very same reasons mentioned above, you have to watch out, if the council intend in the future to build on your open space, you have to be alert and scrutinize the council officials visiting your area. You cannot miss their visit, each wearing extremely brightly coloured new florescent safety jackets and normally safety helmets, huddled together busy writing down there shopping list, claiming quite cunningly, over a period, that on a number of visits by the council officials, in establishing that 'the field in question was not been used.'

All councils will go to great lengths in attempting the above scenario. The deals with the developer would have been carried out secretly, over many months previously, or even years and (rubber-stamped) meaning the deal had been completed behind your back, which cannot be proved or disproved either way. Did these so called visits by the council ever occur? As above with long wet grass and a timely 'visit' either when raining or just after, would prove extremely underhanded which would not surprise me, how they achieved these lie's, and it is impossible to prove otherwise.

This consequently is what happens when unlawfully, maintenance is withdrawn for a while which we pay for with our council tax, and is not carried out for a period of time with attempts at securing your recreational area, with a surprised announcement that nobody is using the facility, knowing that with the history of the way local councils think, and apply devious tactics.

'If you are not using it, you lose it.' This is their surprising and outstanding magnificent motto. Which was amazingly, taken successfully from us for the second time in history, without any form of protest from the majority of local resident, is amazing when you firstly consider all the losses and absolutely no gains for the local residents.

Nevertheless, if one, questions the seriousness of umpteen expensive technical issues encountered, with this new proposed development? Even the very small minority of residents had thrown in the towel, after the disappointing result thrown up at the committee meeting held weeks earlier, where only one resident representing the whole neighbourhood is restricted to only 'three minutes' to present all of their objections is highly questionable tactics? Knowing how falsely, the council had treated, also cheated the local residents appallingly at the committee meeting, subsequently with devious underhanded tricks played on us all, allowing only three minutes speaking on behalf of all the community with duck tape used.

Without acknowledgement that the council, had already sold off the land to the developers, weeks before the committee meeting, is setting a precedent for the future dealing, being proved untrustworthy towards the local residents, losing all credibility towards the planning authorities.

Also suffering constantly, with countless confrontational lies, to gain possession of this open space, then with everyone unaware of the fact that the land had been sold off, firstly to the developers Slope partnerships, weeks before the committee meeting, then sold on to (The Guinness trust) some time later for additional huge expected profit.

Without anyone knowing of this sale, of 'our open space' announcing on each occasion that the council still had ownership of the land in question. Further lies, the land was sold in June 2009 shown on (section 106) agreement when requested through the freedom of information act later as proof. 'For thirty pieces of silver no doubt' or more; which is extremely difficult to understand. Certainly, history will show that no respect will ever be shown towards this council ever again, by losing all trust/credibility towards the majority of residents. Because of this untrustworthiness, also unlawful act, by selling the land before the committee approval was granted a disgraceful and unacceptable way to carry out business!

Now disrespect, shown by the authorities, would apparently be returned by showing no respect from the residents, (it goes both ways). You have seen earlier that the ownership of this land was interestingly settled long before the committee meeting, in fact weeks before in (early June 2009).

Further proof if needed, was shown when the expensive hoarding, plus four huge double steel security gates fitted. Consequently this wooden hugely expensive hoarding plus steel gate's surrounding the whole site in early June, erected, at what cost? That was a fundamental fact, which proved they were being 'deceitful' months previously. Stating that the land was still council land, before the committee meeting in late September 2009, was certainly untrue. Those involved and responsible for this deceit should be sacked immediately because they are clearly untrustworthy towards the local citizens, like with the MPs over the years with their expenses, carrying out the above as if it is normal to continually thieving money from the public.

One can only believe that the planning office had their reasons, with questionable motives, and narrow-mindedness. Diplomatically not informing the local residents at an earlier date, that Guinness Trust Partnership had intention to purchase the land discreetly from the developers.

Before returning to further visits to houses in the neighbourhood, this above extremely important outcome has just surfaced, with the housing trust some 11 months into the development. Which completely surprised everyone involved, or interested with the saving of our recreational area? Let me explain, and introduce Guinness Partnership Trust participation, half way through May 2010, quite suddenly a very large notice board was showing at the lower end of the site facing and adjacent towards the main road and passing traffic. Positioned where the local residents would not easily 'notice,' unless you were prepared to walk all the way around the guarded site, some 800 metres in distance.

Without any reason, to walk this distance round to the other side of the site, from the local resident's houses is somewhat questionable? One of our local neighbours while walking their dog had noticed this extremely large notice board that Guinness (Trust) Partnerships were involved. This is a rather well established housing organisation, backed with Government money from Homes & Communities Agency (HCA) offering an impressively large sum of £863,124. To The Guinness Housing Trust However, as mentioned earlier with being proud with having (HRH) Prince Charles, as their Patron.

What reason has the council/developer, of keeping this (top-secret) information; the Guinness Trust contribution from the local citizens? Nearly a year after the development had started in realising this important significant connection so late into the construction is highly questionable and extraordinary.

Ironically, years ago, HRH Prince Charles showed to all, that he was passionate towards maintaining a healthy environment, has he changed at the age of 64 years, in the autumn of his life with his views regarding environmental issues? Plus accepting the horrendous unsightly building in the garage area, looking amazingly like a prison or warehouse, certainly not in keeping with all the properties in the area, extremely poor planning.

Would he be willing to overlook these actions of the developer, by removing perfectly healthy mature trees without any justification? Seriously with abusing our local environment is considered immoral when overlooked towards making money from the sale of this land. Currently used and set aside for the local children to play on, also the residents to enjoy freely. Impossible to believe, that he would condone these actions or concerns with a developer who 'accidentally' cuts down mature trees, which were to be retained?

Surprisingly did not receive an immense fine for each tree cut down intentionally or 'accidentally,' which was clearly shown on the working plans to be afforded protection.

Followed soon after amazingly, by the same construction (Destruction Company) with three other trees, seriously damaged at the bases. With removing the soil, and cutting the roots, to these mature trees with a digger, not affording them the protection, which the planners had requested, with the planning approval. All of these trees were also shown on the working plans, to be retained.

With other serious evidence, of not affording the necessary protection to many other trees, on the same site. (Shown in the photographs as evidence in both chapters 16/37). I cannot believe for one moment. (HRH) Prince Charles, being the Patron of Guinness Trust would knowingly close his eyes to this type of serious mistreatment.

93

To 'our' or any local environment, which has now, been destroyed with the removal of so many mature trees in such a small area in question? Needs answers as to why.

Someone has to be responsible for this massacre, of our once perfectly healthy environment, with video evidence taken before the development commenced, and immediately after.

There is (nowhere to hide) because all the trees have disappeared, cut down with no justification what's so ever. I would not hesitate, to show Prince Charles or any other interested parties, this evidence, of all the trees cut down unnecessary to achieve what?

A handful of prefabricated cheap houses for rentable affordable homes, which could have been built elsewhere, in fact a perfect location just three miles away for a fraction of the price, without cutting all of these wonderful mature trees down.

Choose another area needing regeneration, not on our recreational play area which was designated for very young kids, what choice were the children offered.

Which Prince William could have chalked up as one play area saved, for the year 2012 Jubilee project, a missed opportunity for his Grandmothers' 60years Diamond Jubilee?

CHAPTER TWENTY-ONE

*

Residents, Followed Like Sheep

Now let us return to my visits once again to each house, surrounding the green in our close neighbourhood, some of these neighbours certainly did not have anything added to their water, including my own supply. A great deal as stated previously were not confident with success, once the council had proposed the new development, accepting therefore nothing or nobody would win over the proposed plans, according to the majority of the residents.

'Astonishingly this has proved correct, Importantly you will learn and witness why, after the (Broken promise) by the council to hand back our open space and return as promised years ago back to recreational use. Significantly the council have deviously calculated the announcement of the proposed new development while everyone was busy away enjoying his or her summer break.

Proving extremely deceitful, by this premeditated timing and as mentioned earlier, also withholding important information, such as the involvement of Guinness Trust organization, which should have been revelled at a much earlier stage, was also found to be extremely deceitful.

There are a number of fundamental tools that the local authorities use against everybody locally; some have just been highlighted above. The underlying, reason for writing this book, hopefully will help and guide others placed in the same predicament, with some helpful advice.

You do not have any choice said the majority of the local residents. (Nevertheless, you had to agree inwardly when you are aware of more of the facts later). (With a smile) worryingly add another 'tick' to the side of each signature when hearing this above statement repeated once again.

Most of the residents had followed like sheep, which had grouped together, without realizing or knowing these facts, and continued drinking this contaminated water collectively. Only after revealing my extraordinary findings, at one of our local residential meetings later, they were all amazed that so many had the same negative views, then quite suddenly as if by magic changed their minds and was immediately interested but far too late in fighting for a lost cause, significantly with only 21 days restriction, in submitting all the objections into planning office is grossly unfair.

Being witness on my visits to a flow, of extremely unbelievably silly unexpected comments to follow as an example:

(1) Campaigning against the council it is fruitless act. 'Why is it fruitless?'
(2) The play area is just for dogs to do their business on, (could be correct as long as the owner picks this up, or trains the dog to pick it up)!
(3) We did not have a play area when we were young? (So what does this remark mean)?

(4) Therefore, I do not see why the very small children should be more important than houses. (Extremely silly comments unbelievably stated by a number of naive residents).

(5) Let them go to the nearest park. (Which just happens to be over one/half miles away, across a busy main road)? (Thoughtless stupid mindless suggestion).

(6) The green would have the older kids hanging around on. (It was always policed successfully locally, by the local residents in the past).

(7) Including sharing drugs on the green. (Also at the local parks, and on the streets).

There were lots more bizarre strange comments, which were just as daft.

Has the (Spunk) and inspiration, been taken out of society nowadays, perhaps it may be true something is possibly in the drinking water, to have tamed the spirit, which all true Englishmen used to have in their blood, to protect what is rightfully theirs, like the open recreational space in question for example. When taking on any dictatorships in the past in any subterfuge, you do not throw in the towel immediately.

Below you will find a fine example of a masquerade, which needs some explaining! (Before leaving, the above house calls), and cover the example which follows. Stop and think for one moment of what extraordinary conclusion my visits have achieved. As luck would have it, on two separate occasions, while speaking to the people in the area.

A couple of ex-councillors both gave the very same sound advice, which held me for a while, thinking these two have taught me a very important and significant fact, I had not encountered before which I am pleased to share with you, I will attempt trying my level best not to confuse you. Like all council officials do quite naturally, as previously stated on number of occasions with (end of term exams). You are reminded of interesting facts; you must keep in mind and never forget:

If you submit just one objection, do not make the mistake of including more than one objection collectively, (and it is worth repeating to achieve a sound impact). While attaching two objections or more on the same opening campaign sheet, for people to sign, then all the objections naturally turn into one Objection.

Consequently, you miss out on the impact you where again hoping to achieve. So the simple answer is to separate all objections, and instead of wasting your time overall, with submitting objections into the planning office only. Go straight to where you will attract very much more attention, and possibly a more positive greater success, with your local councillors, you will not regret this positive direct move.

Incidentally I do mean more than one councillor, who most likely be attending the committee meeting to decide on this proposed development? (It is essential to remember this important statement).

Councillors, who finally sanction the proposed development with a section (106 agreement), and decide at this committee meeting, are showing their hand, giving the developers the go ahead to start the proposed development, only after the agreed payment is made. **I cannot stress the importance of the above; you will find it on the exam paper most likely to be the very first question!** (How to handle your objections correctly).

Let us now return to the proposed new development by the council, what does this indicate by the avoidance and refusal of an open transparent meeting, has obvious serious implications, that democracy has been cast aside.

Another extremely important consideration not realised by any council officials, or taken into account, each ageing house bought from the council years ago, has now to be maintained by the current owner. This same owner is now responsible to find the necessary capital to maintain the property, needing this tremendous amount of capital and huge commitment in upgrading these older buildings, which was never considered by the authorities as a serious commitment, in their arrogance when snatching this open space from our area.

When taking over the ownership of the house, you commit yourself to agree and pay a mortgage over an agreed period, possibly 25/30years or more. Additionally running alongside this mortgage, with most building societies in those early days, you had to agree to take out an endowment mortgage (indemnity).

Which in our case was found the same amount of money each month, safeguarding against being unable to pay the mortgage or the possibility of losing your job, or more seriously being terminally ill, placing considerable strain on finances in general?

What I am infuriated and justifiably angry about, along with many other residents, we choose to live in this very quiet cul-de-sac over 44years ago, near to an open small field, realising it had an important (policy background) safeguarding against any building placed on our green, with this significant assurance, that residential housing could not be placed on the open space.

I have kept this important document from 1983 as proof of this official notice, astonishingly my objections which were again completely ignored by the planning office without response, what were they hiding from?

Furthermore, while we were all sleeping dictatorship has taken over, now seriously do you think you should all wake up soon, and sort this unacceptable situation out for the next generation? (I am far too old at 70 years of age, in taking on this task on my own).

Like with the MPs Parliamentary expenses scandal, was sorted out successfully also speedily, through the efforts of the **Daily Telegraph Newspaper**, who were very brave and successful in taking on the power of the whole government well done.

Congratulations on an excellent job, now I earnestly need your help in waking up the British people to this extremely serious scandal, with the way local government are treating the local citizen, in the most contemptible way which is well out of control throughout the whole of Great Britain.

The next generation would not thank us, for leaving this situation for them to sort out. 'We' have over countless years allowed local authorities, far too much power and they are using this same powerful situation rather like Hitler, and other many dictators around the world. Acting as if they are in another world, nevertheless paid by us with extremely large fat salaries, besides with discrete backhanders which are extremely difficult to detect?

97

We all know is going on, but proving it is extremely difficult, you hear this same quote when discussing council disagreements in each town, where the citizens stating once again there is a fiddle going on?

Such as proving the MPs fiddling with their expenses claims, was also thought impossible to prove, but sorted out quite professionally by **The Daily Telegraph newspaper group.**

Going to the (moon) was also extremely difficult, but achievable. Attempting a visit to mars now that is a different matter altogether, understandable impossible at the moment?

Surely the councillors and planners would not leave themselves open to investigation, but have found a 'plan' far too difficult to detect! Years ago the fiddle we all used to call it a (brown envelope job) with absolutely no paper work involved to fill out. With the deal carried out and (rubber stamped) on the phone previously, discretely arranged and undetectable only the touch on the side of the nose.

'Nudge, Nudge (no what I mean, no questions ask) would indicate a deal may have occurred because of something special, (rubber-stamped) over a period of time with the local authorities plus developers, at a secret meeting with the public excluded.'

In our town alone, many councillors have stood for countless years, some for well over 20years or more. The council leader in our town had the audacity to threaten me personally with court action when I asked her a direct question whether the council agreed to nepotism.

After agreeing to well over twelve developments by the same developer in the same town, amazingly the Planning Officer, and the main Developing Officer, both with the same surname 'Bent.'

It may be suggested at this point that all councillors should only stand for one period of let's say four years, which may stop this deep-seated natural open corruption inherited into local authorities throughout Great Britain. Which I feel must surely be implemented now!

Each time the local elections are announced on the ballet papers, the very same names are submitted, making certain that the power in the council chambers does not change significantly.

What amazes me is the type of person, some being Film/Stars, Actors, T/V Presenters, Authors, and many more diverse characters' who put themselves up for election in each ward throughout Great Britain as (Councillors).

Surprisingly a great deal of these councillors who are evidently 'power crazy,' need seriously to seek out a different interest in life.

CHAPTER TWENTY-TWO

*

Car Registration It's all in a Name.

Do you recall, that wonderful funny man years ago, (Max Bygraves) he would always quote, 'wanna to tell you a story'. This story is completely true, only the names have been changed; you would find it extremely difficult, or impossible in making this story up. Please take these next few lines very seriously and pay attention. (I sound like a teacher). 'This most likely will be in the exam later.'

Significantly this was Monday evening 14th September 2009 approximate five O'clock, the day before the committee meeting, concerning a decision whether this small playing field of ours was to be lost forever. When jointly, the councillors have to all agree, **'tomorrow evening,'** only then should the site be handed over to the developers, if successful for the second time in the history, of this same recreational area. Additionally, with the most astonishing confrontational issues' with the council officials using bullyboy tactics, plus open deceit and corruption.

The site in question, has been sealed off with very expensive hoarding surrounding the whole area. This wooden hoarding would have cost thousands of pounds, was paid for by the developers 'Slope partnerships,' including supplying four huge double steel gates also constructed, and locked to keep everybody off site.

These four brand new pristine twin gates, must have been ordered some months beforehand, also have cost a fortune to cement into the ground in four different locations on site. (Proving conclusively the sale must have been agreed at this early stage or weeks before); (Any fool could work this out).

Not forgetting importantly, this is before the committee meeting is held tomorrow, approval has not been granted yet! (Please wait for the punch line).

Only (IF) and I mean a big **'if'** the council won (tomorrow). 'Not today.' Now someone please tell me if I am the slowest snail in town, what is this committee meeting for?

It is blatantly obvious, just like at the **(Routledge institute of Bleeding obvious)** the council have sold the land and had decided on the development at least six weeks ago, when the expensive wooden hoarding was first placed on the ground. It is not until tomorrow at eight O'clock in the evening. Not forgetting this expensive hoarding has been erected as stated some weeks ago, and the gates ordered months before that!

Together, an insult with the planning office asking for objections to be handed in at this late stage; knowing that the land had been sold to the developer, what reason is there for the head of development, Mr 'Bent' doing on site carrying out repairs to the wooden hoarding, plus replacing a broken padlock and already the owner of the 'Keys,' he has in his possession?

So we are now left with 'three' Major problems to solve. (Sherlock Holmes your services are needed bring along Watson if you must). The registration plate on the car Mr. Bent was driving that evening read (BENT).

Curiously as he was alighting from his car, I ask him his name and his reply was proudly (Mr Bent) this confirmed his name. Now please call me (Mr Slow once again) or not, if the head of planning is called Mr Bent. Furthermore, the head of development is also named Mr Bent. Does this sound a bit **'Bandy?'** to you?

Interestingly enough, at a council meeting which I attended at council chambers in town a short time after. A senior councillor who was (chairing the meeting), on hearing the above remark, with both gentlemen called Mr Bent? Stated his interest, with knowledge of both men, and would find it difficult in remaining in the council chambers, with the above statement mentioned and in the interest of his position in the council, would wish to leave this meeting at this vital stage.

Which left me open mouthed in amazement, along with the remaining councillors attending this meeting, having now at short notice to change who was to 'chair' this meeting? This proves categorically that corruption plus a colossal open fiddle is prevalent?

That I had possibly opened a hornets' nest, with the above statement, especially when you consider he was (chairing) the council meeting that evening? Does this also sound rather **'Bandy'** to you, it most certainly looks questionable and confrontational when the chairman has to leave chambers at that particular moment why?

Both gentlemen with the same surnames, my inevitable question to the head of planning, soon after when attending the committee meeting, asking if he knows what 'Nepotism' meant. His reply was instant and to the point. **"If you are suggesting seriously that favours are going on, let me assure you, that we in the council do not take lightly remarks such as yours, so think wisely, you have been warned, of our next action if this is suggested once more."**

Importantly, all he had to say was that the development officer has no family connection; I would have no choice, but accept his answer. Not to make these idle threats with taking court action, referring to what action?

My only question was, and the question still stands, and was never meant to be over challengingly difficult. If he knows what the word, 'Nepotism' meant. Would you please draw your own conclusion as to this set up (Yes or no), 'is there a fiddle going on?' Astonishingly, this is the second time that I have been threatened with court action by these so called councillors, it gets so tiresome after a while with these so called threats.

Just before, we leave the name-calling. Mr. Bent (head of planning) stated he had no knowledge of what the head of developments name was!!! Not knowing the name of the contact, from 'Slope Partnerships Ltd' the developer, after all those weeks or months or even years of contact. Moreover '(Mr No name)' turning up at each meetings without giving his name, regarding this proposed development and a host of other developments by the same developer, in the same town astonishes me and I find it seriously quite unbelievable to accept.

While, you are pondering over my last question. Why the head of planning did not know the name of the development manager.

Consider another important fact; most developments in this town have favoured only one developer, who has already clearly carried out a number of smaller and larger developments in town already over a number of years, with other developments, across town currently half way through development, by the very same developer. Already ear marked for further regeneration, after this current development. I will now leave you with something to consider.

What's the name of this chosen developer over other developers with future developments in this town? Of which several other sites were mention at a meeting I attended last year. I will leave you with a very small but significant clue; it has something to do with a **'hill!'**

Could someone once again, please enlighten me as to the reason, what is this committee meeting that I am attending at eight O'clock tomorrow evening is arranged for? It has already been decided upon with untrustworthy, evidence presented. (So Sherlock Holmes what is your conclusion). Knowing the facts presented to you. The head of development Mr Bent has already the (keys) to the site and is operating, not forgetting the decision is 'fait accompli,' and was settled some weeks ago! In finding everything signed, also sealed before the committee meeting is held, not forgetting of course the expensive wooden hoarding over eight foot tall surrounding the whole site, and was placed their some weeks before the committee meeting by the developer, this is rather unique situation Sherlock Holmes; What please is going on, this is a straightforward question anyone in the planning office should already know the answer.

Even the great Sherlock Holmes, along with his sidekick Doctor Watson should have the answer; there is a (almighty fiddle) going on for all to see. With absolutely no attempt, in hiding from the truth. This is the evidence I present to you once again, Sherlock. How can this arrangement be acceptable as the norm?

Surprisingly I was witness, along with three other independent witnesses, who were present to the whole event, when Mr. Bent from the development company visited the site that Monday evening.

A day before the committee meeting, to carry out essential repairs to the hoarding, plus if you can recall in replacing a broken padlock on one of the four double steel gates.

You can see quite clearly above, that if this dishonesty happens in our town, then could it also replicate itself elsewhere, in all other towns throughout Great Britain, maybe in your town? This very same direct open deceit and corruption is now exposed, and needs urgently sorting out. Was I either very clever, to have noticed the (number plate) connection 'BENT' or by chance extremely lucky, being in the right place at the correct time. To witness the above proceeding, what a coincidence with Mr Bent visiting the site that evening, the day before attending the committee meeting.

Please accept all of the above comments as completely truthful; again, you could not possible make this up! Incidentally, Mr. Bent from the development company was never ever seen again, disappeared as if by magic. Please explain Sherlock Holmes or Dr. Watson as to Mr. Bent's whereabouts it is a mystery? I wonder if the head of planning Mr Bent knows where Mr Bent has gone. **New revelation, as I am about to complete this book. Paradoxically, you would not think I was being at all sarcastic, if I mentioned that the 'Mr Bent' from head of planning has now departed from the planning office. Is this just a wonderful coincidence or what, I ask you Sherlock Holmes once again, is there a gigantic fiddle going on?**

CHAPTER TWENTY-THREE

*

Committee Meeting

You have to be astonished, with the implications and structure of Society nowadays, with having to promote democracy. Is somewhat appalling and disgraceful benchmark for future dealing locally, by council officials? Firstly, refusing to grant a meeting to discuss serious concerns with regards to the new proposed development without debate or consultation, disregarding guidelines' set down by central government.

After seriously slipping up on this occasion, prejudging, the decision of the committee, by allowing the developer to place the expensive hoarding surrounding the whole site weeks before approval, indicating that an almighty fiddle has been carried out by the council officials, and they were caught out on this occasion?

Ironically, as stated previously Mr, Bent from the development company has vanished, and not returned or been seen since that Monday evening encounter, which makes you wonder what is going on. 'Has he been advised, by someone from the (planning office with the same name)' to stay away from this site why?

The committee meeting was held, as always on a Tuesday at eight O'clock, our case was second on the list that evening. I was now ushered to the front to present our case. Astonishingly just before the meeting had started, I was advised that only **'three minutes'** were allowed in presenting our objections, and attempts to save our open space.

Apparently this is normal at all committee meetings, this extremely unacceptable serious announcement the council accept as normal, after speedily reading through the leaflet concerning the contents which was handed to all who attend a committee meeting, and was impossible to ignore. Discovering immediately that it was highly unlikely, or even impossible, to cover our presentation and offering our objections with constraints of only **'three minutes'** to save our green.

While the committee meeting 'leaflet' also advisees one, on how to address the meeting stating three very important ridiculous simple rules. (Please remember reference to all three, for the exam later).

Firstly, (you are not allowed to ask any questions).
Secondly, (you are not permitted to be asked any questions).
Thirdly, (you must not ask any questions to the candidates).

These above simple ridiculous rules must be adhered too. It is extremely difficult also impossible for me to attend a meeting, if you are not permitted to speak! **This left me speechless.** '(Please excuse the pun).'

From yesterdays charade, with meeting Mr Bent on the site, and armed with the knowledge that 'Nepotism' could be involved, my opening line to the chair of the meeting was extremely important and to the point.

"Has this council and local officials taken to encouraging nepotism with its dealings? The difficulty and concern I have, is with the name of the developer, having the same surname 'Mr Bend,' as does strangely 'Mr. Bent,' head of planning sitting to your left madam chair. "Could I please ask a leading question to Mr. Bent head of planning, realising of cause, that I am not permitted to ask any questions at this extraordinary friendly committee meeting."

"Is there a family connection?" A few seconds delay, standing in state of being calm stable and composed; you could say 'equanimity' especially not under any stress. The chair lady replied "that one minute had past and only two minutes remain to plea for the open space in question."

"My second question, which I am also not, permitted to ask at this unusual astonishing meeting. Why madam chair, has the developers erected an expensive hoarding surrounding our field, also fixed four huge expensive double steel gates to stop entry onto the site. At great cost before this committee has given its approval, is understandably confrontational, plus questionable?"

"Alas, I have a third question, which is just as important as the previous other questions madam chair." (Paused looking in the direction of Mr Bent for any reaction to my question). "Has the council sold the open space to the developers before this committee meeting?" Without hesitation, she stated, "would you please stop wasting the committee's time, on silly pointless questions."

I remarked quite loudly without pausing. "Pointless questions, would you please show me some respect madam-chair, the questions are not pointless, they are to the point." Therefore, my remaining time of one minute was spent asking whether the leaflet should be re-written more in favour of campaigners.

"Who, has ever heard of attending a meeting with an agenda, stating that we are restricted and unable to speak, with regards to the unhelpful simple rules stated in the committee meeting leaflet. On this same leaflet handed to us, stating constraints of only three minutes, allotted to present my case was understandably unacceptable in a free democratic society." Pause.

"Also if I arranged a meeting, stating on a leaflet sent out to interested parties, wishing to attend this meeting, mentioning in that leaflet, you are restricted to only three minutes to speak, not many citizens in Great Britain would accept these unbelievable constraints. Therefore are you joking, the leaflet advises the visitors attending this meeting of three simple instructions you need to follow." Those wishing to attend the committee meeting.

(1) Are not permitted, to ask any questions.
(2) Or to be asked any questions.
(3) Nor speak to anyone at the committee meeting.
"Do I understand this to be correct madam chair."

"Then who in their right mind would turn up to this arrangement, and be comfortable knowing that freedom of speech, has been snatched from you"

(Could this possibly be the same arrangement, if you attend a committee meeting in your town, do you have these same crazy instructions to follow, while attending your friendly unapproachable committee meetings)?

My three minutes was well and truly up. Nevertheless, what puzzles me, and I cannot get my head round. Who pays the salaries to these council officials, behaving in a dictatorial way in having to follow these outrageous silly instructions?

Who are dictating to us, informing us taxpayer's/ratepayer's on these extremely silly serious constraints of only 'three minutes to speak,' when attending a committee meetings.

This compliance, of only one representative who will speak on behalf of all the local residents, allowing only three minutes presenting all our objections is ridiculous and beyond belief.

Possibly other local neighbours may have many excellent reasons to speak on other serious positive issues, and personal objections?

Also the audacity of not being able to ask questions must change immediately for future meeting. This is what meetings are for, to discuss issues and debate, also consult with others. How is it possible, not knowing what a meeting is for?

Ironically an open meeting was refused by the planning office who were anticipating and avoiding awkward direct questions?

Obviously, the council had attended the 'Routledge institute of Bleeding obvious,' having already decided on the development, months before the committee meeting was held, which was bleeding obvious!!

This type of straightforward dictatorship and corruption is found everywhere nowadays following on from central government activities'.

Councillors have a history of extreme control and devious corruption, which takes place on a daily encounter, with most local residents throughout Great Britain.

With highly questionable reasons and motives, but everybody just shrugged their shoulders and followed with the same general predictable comment.

"We know there is a fiddle going on, but what can you do about it?"

CHAPTER TWENTY-FOUR

*

Who Owns the Land?

Having already asked Max Bygraves to say that wonderful quote. 'Now I wanna tell you another story.' While I have your attention, please acknowledge seriously the deceit, on how cunning our local planning officials are. Your job is to work out whether I am telling the truth, or are the local authorities representing our council telling (porkpies') 'on who owns the land in question.'

Firstly I will clarifier and make things much clearer; the Committee meeting to decide on the aforementioned open space is to be held as previously stated on Tuesday the 15th September 2009. The importance will interest you after I explain this small but significant unbelievable experience on approximately 11th June 2009 with regard to ownership of the open space. Remembering you could not possibly make this up, it's absolutely true.

On visiting Shortmeadow Green one morning, it had come to my notice apparently, four of the prefabricated bungalows out of 10 temporary units were now vacant, and not being occupied.

The phone call to the housing department apparently was a shock, so it seems to Mr Day who happens to be the housing manager. My direct question to Mr Day was. "In the last few days, it has been noticed that four out of the ten Prefabricated Bungalows, on our former recreational play area are now empty, could I assume by this observation that the rest may soon be vacant. In addition, that the field will be returned to the local residents for recreational use as 'promised by the council' over 20years ago, for all the young children to use." His reply was not very clear; he acted in apprehension and total surprise even embarrassed, and could not answer a very simple question, to ask him his name may have been a less challenging question.

"Are the rest of the temporary units going to be vacated in the near future," I repeated in case he had not understood the question. You could tell by the pregnant pause, that a (lie) was just seconds away.

Furthermore, he was surprised with our unexpected intrusion and interest, with the goings on and the housing department was attempting the impossible, to quietly and successfully empty all the units, without attracting any attention to the local residents'.

This is what we have been waiting patiently for 20years, for the return of our play area as promised once the prefabricated bungalows became redundant, and no further use for whatever explanation. For very sound reasons, which will become apparent, very soon, now the cat was out of the bag! Because he was caught out with the last question my second question was very much easier and more to the point. "Has the council sold the land, does it still belong to the council." His answer was swift without pause on this occasion. "The land still belongs to the council with no intention of a sale in the near future." (A further porkpie).

Another call, minutes after to the planning office, caused as much revelation and also embarrassment and concern, as the previous call to housing department.

The planning office were 'totally surprised' and speechless. "We will phone you shortly, let us find out what is going on," said the planning officer Mr Bent.

Approximately five hours later, still no return call from the planning officer. Therefore, after phoning the planning office once again this was their reply, "sorry we phoned and could not get hold of you" was their reply. "For me to believe your difficulty in attempting to contact me I find extremely beyond belief, having left you my landline plus my mobile number in which to contact me on either I cannot accept as true.

"Incidentally, what is the news with the return shortly of our recreational play area?" Further delay in answering tells you straight away something was cooking. After a short ever lastly spell he admitted the amazing astonishing truth: **"The new development will shortly be announced concerning your open space."**

"What development" it was my turn now to pause, and he acknowledged the fact that I should not have to know any more of the details. "You will soon be informed" with that, put the phone down without another word. What happened next is extremely interesting and significant with regards to who owns the land in question?

Two weeks had passed since my last call to the planning office in establishing, what their intentions were for our open space. It was now noticed each day that the occupiers of the bungalows were leaving at a steady rate, and more of the units became vacate, a further three weeks before all the prefabricated bungalows were now completely empty. The units were now all empty of any furniture. Some men were sorting things like all electrics, and cookers, and rubbish left by former occupiers, from inside the units.

Interestingly I have never been inside the prefabricated bungalows before, I took this opportunity to enter the first unit, while nobody was around or inside and it allowed me time, for a good look inside. Firstly the pungent smell of mould, was detected immediately on entry, this awful stench hit you as you ventured further inside. It was a rather appalling overpowering smell, likened very much to the over pungent smell as you may encounter when entering a fish &chip shop, without good ventilation, but much, very much worse and not very pleasant. This mould could only have formed by not offering enough ventilation into the buildings. They had forgotten the old saying when I used to work on building maintenance years previously, this saying was always repeated from time to time, (heat plus cold without fresh air cause mould).

Trying to imagine only a matter of days ago, very young families over 20 year period, had occupied these units; this was not acceptable leading into the 21st century, by any council standards to have allowed these families to live for over twenty years in these atrocious unbearable conditions. 'Would they have lived in these unhealthy conditions themselves?' 'The truthful answer is no.'

Health and safety was partly to blame, allowing all the small children and their parents, living with this telltale staining of black mould, could be found on all of the walls inside. Now you can realize seriously, why the prefabricated bungalows were now redundant and well past their sell by date. With very small children, having to live in close proximity to this growing mould. What a Health risk, especially if you suffer with Asthma, or have ongoing respiratory problems such as (COPD) Chronic obstructive Pulmonary Disease.

106

While inside the next unit, gatherings more reasons why the bungalows, should not have been made redundant sooner. A rather large person who had entered the unit, which reminded me straight away of Mr Fat Smelly Henderson from school some years ago, suddenly interrupted me. BECAUSE he was fat, he also should be granted a name appropriate to his size, and shape of a person with perspiration problems, and sounded just as nasty. "What the F!!! Are you doing in here he announced in rather a loud surprising manner" before I could answer. His next remark was "get the F!!! Out of here." When I was eventually able to reply amongst,' a string of more unsavoury remarks, which were equally as unpleasant as himself.

Dismissing his ignorance, I asked, "Had the land been sold off to the developers," his reply was swift **"piss off this is private land and has been sold, and presently does not belong to the council, it now belongs to the developers, Slope partnerships Ltd."**

Not forgetting the significance, of other council officials including the 'housing manager,' also the 'planning office,' was unaware that the land had already been sold off!

This large fat smelly worker was holding a secret close to his hairy smelly chest, the only one knowing of the transaction beggars' belief.

I agreed with him that I should leave, but asked, "in future could you take some free advice, and consider respect, on your next encounter with meeting a stranger.

"Perhaps, I could have been anybody with complete rights in entering the units, Such as a taxpayer for instance, or possibly a ratepayer," with that I was again asked to "piss off." With a string of other swear words. 'He needed sorting out' at my age I would not even consider it, but years ago, considering my background, he would have been sorry for those earlier and latter remarks he made:

If this is true, that the land does not belong to the council, why has the planning office, wasted council taxpayers money sending out instructions that residents should send in your objections into the planning office? When all along, the council, along with this evidence, is proof of underhanded dealings against the residents, to claim earlier that the council still owned the field in question is a direct lie, this question still stands who does own the land? (Have you made up your own mind yet)? Another porky Yes or No. Who is lying?

Below you will read my objection that was submitted to the planning office at the time. Concerning the above incident which occurred after my call to the planning office weeks before, also the housing office if you recall earlier. My objection to the planning office follows. **(Who now owns the land, on our playing field)?**

While writing these objections a most important outcome has become known. The borough council, have sold the land nearby which has been used as a playing field for well over 60years. What price you might ask "thirty pieces of silver" or possibly a great deal more. The worker stated this to me in an unfriendly encounter and said that the "site was sold" and he indicated inappropriately for me to "F!!! Off" the site in rather unsavoury manner which I did immediately. I was somewhat shocked to hear the way a council worker was speaking. Later to find, it was not a council worker but a contractor from 'Slope Partnerships Ltd' the new developers. Who had advised me to remove myself off site in a very unfriendly manner why?

None of the residents here in our neighbourhood has heard of this sale. This open space was never reported in the local paper, as been sold. "On the contrary", this open space was promised by the council to be returned to the community, plus secured with the background policy that no residential housing would be permitted on the recreational area.

Once the temporary prefabricated bungalows were removed, we had naturally expected that the buildings once removed, the play area would be returned because of this promise and with good reason. The policy background stated that it was found to be unsuitable for residential housing and should not be considered due to technical difficulties. My objection to this is that no mention of the sale has been stated before 24th June 2009. I was speaking with Mr Day from Housing only Yesterday, no mention of the sale. "What date this year did the above sale transpire?"

This is how underhanded the council are. They have a reputation, also a history of not being transparent in the past, and holding their cards close to their hairy chest so to speak. I also asked the very same question to planning office. "Who owns the playing field" as Mr. Day from the housing department states, that the land is still owned by the council is this truth? The question, needs your urgent attention before any objections, can even be considered. The planning officer stated on the phone in that same week, "that he was not certain of ownership." (Another porkpie).

Even at this late stage, stating the council are still in ownership as far as he was concerned. In addition, not a mention to the local residents is showing total disrespect once again, the authorities losing all possible credibility with the people who have elected them to carry out responsible fair decisions.

Also when contacting our local MP and other senior councillors, who could not help with the truth of ownership of this land used by the residents over countless years in the past. A complete mystery even Sherlock Holmes would have great difficulties in solving this problem, have you guessed correctly?

Only one person as I have mentioned previously was holding the important key in solving this puzzle, he was fat, he was also very smelly, and swears like a trooper?

Had the council sold off the land, are they now stating no knowledge of the open ground sale? This has yet to be clarified.

You will find out, the sale was agreed all along acknowledged with yet another straightforward lie! When in the next local, and nation elections in the near future, we have already made up our minds which Party we will not be voting for, along with the rest of my local neighbourhood.

The one who gets my vote will be listening and communicate fairly. Admission, that over time since my first vote some 50years ago, I was a staunch labour supporter, and would never even consider any other party, not any more.

The power is now in our hands and for us to control, in the next election. Embarrassingly, our local councillor, who quite possibly may lose more than just our respect, or credibility, after losing her council seat in the next local elections surprisingly after just serving one year as mayor of this town?

CHAPTER TWENTY-FIVE

Can You Speak at Committee Meeting?

Incidentally, before attending a committee meeting for the first time you must prepare yourself for an almighty shock, our council have the audacity of introducing a leaflet which without any doubt had been edited by a comedian, this is the evidence to prove the above. Looking through the early part of the leaflet, it remarks that you can speak quite freely to the committee, plus councillors, and then within a few lines of information it states completely the opposite.

What follows below, is the leaflet handed to me when attending a committee meeting, for the very first time, showing conclusively unfair treatment towards the ratepayers who pay their huge salaries.

Remembering, that the committee meeting is to decide on whether the developer can start, after approval granted on the proposed development. Taking on board, the fact, at very short notice of 21 days, to offer all objections against the development, is vastly unbalanced, in the authorities favour. With reference to our essential open recreational space, without any official or personal response, shown towards our objections into the planning office is outrageous. The council officials, planners, construction engineers, building designers, architect, draughtsperson, developers. All of these and many others involved for months, or possibly years ahead.

After secret meetings held, concerning the new development is nothing less than unfair undemocratic, and showing no possible respect towards the local residents. Who importantly have to live with these changes and repercussions, we are fully entitled with an unrestricted time, to discuss our concerns. (Contents of Leaflet offered, with an opening questionable statement).

'All borough councils are committed to encouraging public involvement in the planning process as part of the borough community strategy.'

There are extensive neighbour notification procedures for all planning applications, together with site and newspaper notices for larger proposals. This enables you to make written or electronic comments on development proposals.

Additionally, you can speak directly to councillors at planning and development committee meetings, which determine major and some other planning applications.

(This last remark is their first lie with regard to this leaflet, this is untrue you are not permitted to speak).

This leaflet aims to answer some of the questions you may have on how to go about this and what to expect at the committee meeting its self. It is based on some simple remarkable rules, which the council has adopted to make the system as **'fair'** and easy to operate as possible. **'Fair'** is far from the truth as we are from here to mars. (Please note half way through the above Paragraph).

Who can speak at a committee meeting?

You can request to speak if you object to an application. Which the planning and development committee are considering? Only one objector is authorized to speak against a proposal. Should more than one objector, wish to speak against the same proposed development; a representative should be nominated to express both your combined views. (Proof that the authorities have complete control). Which affectively means only one person to speak for three minutes?

Only in exceptional circumstances, and at the discretion of the chairperson of the committee, where several people have opposed the proposal for different reasons and/or affected by the application.

In different ways, more than one speaker may be permitted to speak. (What the very clever councillors have forgotten, is not reading the leaflet themselves which contradicts it's self all the way through with regard to who can 'speak and who cannot)

In addition, the word 'fair' was mentioned, how this, can possibly be classed as fair). Maybe they need a spell in Mr. Fat Smelly Henderson's class to learn what the word 'SPEAK' actually means.

"TO COMMUNICATE". Which means speaking?
What can I speak about?
Regardless of whether you are speaking on behalf of yourself, or representing on behalf of a number of objectors, the points you raise when speaking to the committee. Should have been referred to in written comments that have been previously submitted.

If you consider that the officer's report to the committee contains factual errors or that the drawings are inaccurate, these points must be raised in writing with us before the meeting. Objections must relate to affect the proposal development and confined to material planning considerations.

(Notice each act, plus instructions are under their strict total control).

You will not be able to speak to the committee on these points, although it was stated in the leaflet that you can speak freely, unless you give us prior notice. (See For yourself. You cannot speak everything is formulated prior to the start of the meeting).

The issues you may not speak about.

- Private property rights.
- Can a developer start a development before approval?
- This leaflet and its contents.
- The applicant's morals and motives.
- Loss of view over land owned by other people.
- Effect on property values.
- Whether the council promotes favouritism.
- Why a septic tank is agreed, surely this is unacceptable.

The committee will not take account of any comments on non-material planning considerations.

How long will I be able to speak for?

Objectors are allowed a maximum of three minutes, but not to speak to the committee. (No Speaking or questions are permitted)

Supporters of the application or applicants are also allowed to speak for three minutes.

Will I be able to speak?

Applications will each be dealt with in turn in the following way: The head of planning and regeneration or planning officer will introduce the proposal. (Notice they are permitted to speak). Those who registered to speak will be invited to speak.

The head of planning and regeneration will present an appraisal of the proposal and, where appropriate, make reference to points raised by those addressing the committee.

Will I be asked Any Questions?

(NO). The council has agreed that the committee members will not ask you any questions.

Can I ask the councillors any questions?

(NO). You may not ask questions to the councillors

Alternatively, take part in any discussion by the committee.

Can I ask planning officer any questions?

(NO). You may not be permitted to ask any questions.

These three very simple questions above you are not permitted to ask is a liberty against all the understanding what democracy and foundations of democracy in any country calling themselves a free society. I am almost ready to say something sarcastic.

(The council are not mindful of the leaflet contents possibly never even bothered to read the leaflet. Most likely, offered someone from another country elsewhere to edit the leaflet, or commissioned a comedian);

Which is contradictory, misleading, and untruthful? Contrary throughout, the way it states a fact, then in the very same line. It means the opposite.

This is a leaflet handed to all those visiting a committee meeting as a guidance on what is permitted at the meeting. First signs of utter madness, surprisingly attending a meeting without being able to speak. Who has ever heard of anything as prepossess and ridiculous as the contents of this leaflet, written by someone without a brain.

This is so remarkable, preposterous, ridiculous, and outrageous. I could not believe the contents on the way this leaflet was edited. All you have read above is absolutely undeniably true, as printed on the leaflet.

You know what I am about to say right now.

'It left me temporarily unable to speak, matter of fact completely speechless.'

111

CHAPTER TWENTY-SIX
*
Three Questions Were Asked

Learning from the past, and always lead to believe, the idea of a typical planning officer with being gifted with creativity in abundance. With academic skills, plus lead to believe to be highly intelligent, also very wise and respected professionals. Now with justification and acceptance in this town, my opinion has completely altered as to the above statement, with the loss of all respect, or any possible credibility, towards the planning office department, their behaviour towards the local residents concerns proved untrustworthy throughout, rather similar to the arrogance (MPs), show with regards to their parliamentary expenses.

Therefore, could they draw attention to the editor responsible for producing this leaflet when one has to attend a meaningless committee meeting, to contemplate whether to modify the tedious script, and make some sense for future meetings? Please firstly consider our intelligence, plus aptitude and show some fairness, and common sense, when presenting this complete nonsense for us to follow, like with our objections submitted, they have not read their leaflet either.

The details along with the contents are comprehensively a complete joke without intention of making us laugh. Which I found quite amusing but disturbing, showing attention to detail is not their area of expertise. Finding it highly embarrassing on how they seem serious with their presentation with this leaflet, saying it is fair to whom, surely not the visitors attending the meeting.

Knowing that all those who attend the meeting will comply, with their simple unquestionable rules, with the contentious remarks of not being able to speak, or able to ask any questions, how is it possible to communicate with the public without speaking! This has to be considered, seriously as a foundation of amusement for the council officials. The quotes, taken from the leaflet handed to me on my way into the committee meeting. (As mentioned previously you could not possible dream this up).

This you can see above is total control (using duck tape) simply so that no questions are asked, or answered. Which I find extremely clever and unbelievable, (Please excuse the pun) 'which left me absolutely speechless' once more. When called upon, to speak on behalf of the residents to save the recreational play area, surprising constrains of only three minutes is highly unlikely or possible with being restricted to only three minutes.

What planet have they arrived from? The planning plus other considerations must have been years in the making, and constrains of only three minutes is outrageous, in presenting our argument against this new development issues, and must be regarded as a complete joke, but who is laughing not the local residents?

(Returning now to the committee meeting, from an earlier chapter, to cover more action. On the leaflet handed out). Walking very slowly up to the table area indicated by the usher at the committee meeting, and paused for as long as I dare.

Looking straight ahead, holding out acting quite nervously until invited to speak by the woman who was chairing the meeting. "Is there a problem Sir," she stated. After a short but lasting deliberate delay in answering.

"My question to madam chair. Which of course I am not permitted to ask. "Madam Chair has anybody on the committee ever read carefully this leaflet handed to the visitors which states quite clearly.

"You are not permitted, to ask any question; also, you are not permitted to speak, to any members of the committee. I find this quite outrageous by exceeding the bounds of what is reasonable or expected in society, or regards with democracy. In total control by the people, who we employ on the council telling us what we can or cannot do, with impossible constraints of only three minutes to speck for example at this meeting:"

"Have the members of the committee taken time out to read this leaflet? If not, why not." (The chairperson told me immediately, you could tell by the way she was hurrying things up). 'Problem was a more pressing engagement such as going out, on to dinner date after the committee meeting, with absolutely no interest with the affairs in hand.'

Announcing "you are using up your three minutes time allowed to speak asking questions you're not permitted to ask."
All was quiet for a few seconds or so then without an answer to my first question. I was asked to return to my seat in the public area of the committee room.

Likewise asked not to interrupt the very quiet committee meeting otherwise I would be asked to leave if any further interruptions occurred. Without delay continued immediately with another question, which had the element of possible favouritism?

"With the head of planning Mr, Bent, also Mr, Bent the head of development Slope partnerships Ltd, seems to me to be showing favouritism, also possible potential fraud, this seamed rather 'Bandy' was my opinion with the evidence set out in front of me that both gentlemen having the same surname 'Bent.' If they had kept this fact of both having the same surname quietly to themselves, instead of allowing the public this information, then how would I possibly have found out this blatantly obvious unquestionable situation. Was this potentially scandalous situation meant to be concealed, or have they on this occasion let the cat out of the bag?"

After mentioning, the above all went extremely quiet in the committee room. The chair asked me once again to return to the public area. Just before returning, I found time to mention a second interesting fact concerning the proposed development.

"Why madam chair, were the developers on site weeks before a decision has been granted to start the development. Having constructed a large wooden Hoarding fixed to the ground, surrounding the complete site. Also four huge double steel gates, in several locations in place around the site. Before 15th September 2009 the day of this committee meeting." Short pause. "Matter of fact for several weeks before this committee meeting; if this is not fraud then what is it, Fait accompli comes to mind." Deliberate pause for a few seconds. "This is an extremely important question, and I expect this committee would know the answer today."

113

The room was very quiet for a short while after this question was asked. Which offered me time to repeat? "I'll repeat the question for the benefit of those who could not comprehend, or have missed the point of the question. As questions at this committee meeting are extremely rare."

"As mention previously, why has the developer's weeks ago, placed an expensive hoarding surrounding the whole site plus erected four expensive large double steel gates?

Importantly with the committee meeting being held today. Then please tell me seriously, why this meeting is being held today when the developers have already been given the OK for the development to commence, before this committee meeting has granted approval. I assume this is why questions are avoided." Again a short intentional pause while looking around the room.

"Remaining highly questionable plus controversial, and seems the whole project is a fait accompli as I have mention earlier. Without proper consideration, and in violation of the very strict planning rules, that a development cannot commence until approval has been granted."

As before, the committee room was extremely quiet for several seconds, and then the chair who was losing patience with me gave a last warning for me to return to the public area. I had this one opportunity, after waiting some weeks to draw attention to this questionable situation that a deal had already been carried out, In fact rubber-stamped some time ago.

"Throughout, the course of this new development it has raised far too many serious questions. For instance the planning office asking for objections to be handed, in weeks after the wooded hoarding had been placed, surrounding and sealing the whole site?

Also the situation with only 4 garages retained out of 51 just to change the site into a free fall site. Taking full advantage so that the background policy affectively does not exist anymore. Consequently the new residential houses can now be built on the green, which is extremely underhanded, now you see why no respect is shown towards the planning office."Looking over towards where the planning officer was sitting without any reaction.

Requested once again, by the chair of the meeting to return to the public area, which I did after my three extended minutes! However, with hindsight, would have preferred to be asked to leave forcefully. Then it would have attracted attention with our local newspaper, to this extremely serious controversial situation. (The main reason this book was written).

Ironically I feel this committee is laughing their socks off, that the development had already started, and there is nothing anybody can do about it. 'Before approval has been granted' in a few moments time by the committee members is deplorable plus unacceptable. Nevertheless, was pleased that I stayed because the housing manager Mr. Day was to speak next, concerning the garages and serious (off street parking) issues.

He stated quite openly without blinking an eye, with tongue in cheek. "That the garages are not in demand, and are due soon to be demolished." (Another huge porkpie, they were in demand by 15 or more residents).

To draw attention I interrupted with a rather loud 'cough' "stating that is a direct lie, there is a huge demand for the garages locally." Astonishingly without any reaction from the chair!

114

His blatant lies which increasingly worries me, knowing the fact that there, is a noticeable demand locally, for the rentable garages by at least fifteen local infuriated residents, of which I am representing, now having to park our cars unsafely in the street.

This can be regarded as outrageous, and untrue, plus unlawful, with showing disregard to the present resident's demands, with the loss of all credibility.

Firstly with the confrontational numerous lies, and secondly by unlawfully demolishing the garages without 'debate or consultation' with future needs of possible off street parking issues, and vehicle security, with regards to the local residents vehicles left in the open, instead of locked away safely in designated garages.

With him being, accustomed to these lies, just to secure the land, to build seven houses, which changed later to six on the final drawings, because of other highly embarrassing problems with this same housing manager Mr Day, (which will be discussed later).

It is astonishing why he feels he has to lie, truly amazes' me. When the development is finished, this will highlight whether his lies will kick him up the backside. On his way to securing future employment elsewhere. Now who is responsible for absolutely no chance of local 'off street' parking needs in the local area?

The planning office or the housing department?

'Neither.'

The full responsibility is with the local councillors, who voted like lambs, when requested to turn up at the committee meeting by the planners and labour party leader, to change amazingly the local policy, importantly from.

'Off-street parking.'
To
'On-street parking.'

Maybe other councils throughout Great Britain will soon follow this fine example?

CHAPTER TWENTY-SEVEN
*
Development Proposal Notification

Legislation altered from the past. You are now entering into an important part of this book, discovering how the local councils plan years ahead, being extremely clever with deceitful account of their actions in securing inappropriately land, by taking liberties when proposing new developments.

Cunningly placing small notification, hoping that the residents do not notice in time, possibly in the local newspaper, in extremely significantly small print, written notification inconspicuous along with many other proposed developments together on the same page, making it extremely difficult to notice. Maybe attached to a lamppost or wall, nearby the site of the new proposed development, an extremely small notice. Possibly the same in your town, to gain a certain advantage with restraints of only 21 days to submit all your objections into the planning office.

What season, or part of the year to your advantage would you announce a development proposal, especially if the development is over ten units in size, which is regarded by a council as a larger size development. Needing necessary publicizing as stated above, in the local newspaper and requires notice placed nearby the development site. Less than ten buildings, the council are not obliged to show any notification what so ever, it is not mandatory. Please pay particular attention to this next important section.

A distinct advantage is gained immediately if the councils notification is placed by the end of June, or better still July, because a greater amount of people are arranging holidays away from the area in question, at this important time of the year: Unbelievably they are extremely shrewd in their timing of the crafty hidden announcements of developments, knowing controversially that the 21 days notice while everybody is away on their holidays enjoying themselves, gives the council a distinct and considerable premeditated advantage.

The council officials have more than a head start and the residents do not know what has hit them yet. Please remember, this is most important and carried out possibly in the same way, throughout the whole country, all councils are singing from the same song sheet. This is where the saying, 'you will never ever beat the council' comes from! 'The timing.' They had months of planning or maybe years, all they allow us residents, is up to 21 days notice not a day longer, you have been warned this is extremely important.

(Additionally, please expect a question on this subject in the exam at the finish of this book). This must have been felt, by thousands in the past without understanding from experience, and too late to challenge, with an organised strong campaign.

The very shrewd and remorseless untrustworthy councils will breach etiquette, inappropriately to gain an early time advantage. Now with only 21 days to muster a successful campaign, knowing positively how the time selection has worked strongly in the past in the councils favour.

116

The manipulative council officials who are laughing their socks off at the residents who cannot understand, how they have been manipulated into losing once again; Against these devious very clever officials (or magicians), who have got away, with yet another trick which was up their sleeve all the time. Another is the new word, (affordable housing). Not council housing anymore.

Which will explain to the public, that you sometimes have great difficulties in finding the proposed development, or scheme, in the local paper or libraries in your area? Not forgetting at least ten units are mandatory, anything less than ten no notice is required. If let's say the local council place notification close by, attached to a near lamp post or wall stating a very brief description of their intentions, your local play area for example maybe chosen, because the local authorities would like to make some money out of it?

They will shortly build on the land in question, only for monetary reasons and inform you that you have only 21 days, to offer any 'objections' into the planning office which will not be read by anyone. Which is their main reason, and advantages once the buildings are built, generating a permanent income for years to come for the council, as council tax!

Your play area for instance cost the council to upkeep as play faculties, also maintenance, just cutting the grass or clearing away rubbish as an example of cost. (No income for the council). Now place 50 houses plus flats on this same area of ground and potentially you have an income of council tax each year, for over 80/100years possibly longer. Now, this is the greed I refer too. Inherent and added with each (Section 106) agreement the council demand payment from the developer. Importantly the developers cannot start the development before this payment has been paid.

Then with the authorization and go-ahead from the committee meeting, the conclusion is that all the local councillors divide and use this money on projects locally in their area, from the (Section 106) agreements a win-win situation. Amazingly each time the council cunningly also unlawfully takes land from the locals, it is noticeably just for a dishonest purpose, to generate more income, then predictably on to the next development to generate even more source of income; your play area is history.

And so on to the next development, money is gained on this next opportunity, the existing current residents are never ever compensated or gain anything from these exchanges, believe me this is mostly true in each town throughout Great Britain.

Serious changes are necessary say most residents, to bring about alterations for the future. And reaching for a fairer system locally, and introduce new legislation which councils will not be in favour of any dramatic changes to their plans? Even policy background is not safe in the hands of all councils, and without warning altered without notice.

By removing the shackles, so that the 'football match' we held some time ago, would be replayed in future with different more transparent rules, and a fairer open match, played with both teams, able to move more freely around the pitch, with more time given over to the local residents, to have their say. Then like magic, astonishingly the situation has changed, see how many goals we score! The result no taxpayers/ratepayers disappointed with this change.

117

An interesting fine example, which follows of extremely bad planning, along with unfortunate colossal waste of taxpayers'/ratepayers money.

A training centre in town closed, over two years ago with the loss of our essential swimming pool, with contentious findings of thousands spent on refurbishments and repairs on the swimming facilities. Paid out of local taxpayers/ratepayers purse, completely wasted without any explanation, as to who was responsible for this colossal waste of £178,000. Then unbelievably the building was demolished weeks after completion of the new refurbishments and repairs.

What plans were they following with this waste of ratepayer's money? Our swimming club had more than a hundred children as members, and as many adults, who were successfully taught to swim, and training life saving skills, each week for both children/adults. Even the town's local senior swimming club and many other clubs used the same swimming faculties continuously each week throughout the years. With full schedules, astonishingly with very short notice within two weeks after the expensive renovations plus refurbishments completed, the centre was closed for good.

We had no choice, many clubs, had to fold indefinitely, and now the town has lost a major extension for teaching swimming/lifesaving, and keep fit, relying solely with only one swimming pool to serve nearly 100,000 people, which makes absolutely no sense with panning for the future, when a breakdown occurs at the main pool, you are snookered, like driving a vehicle without wheels. If another pool exists in town then problem solved.

I called upon our local labour MP plus party leader to look into why the developers who made a fortune after building a multitude of private apartments replacing the old training centre with houses and flats on the extremely cheap old school grounds. Why did they not include swimming faculties as compensation for our loss.

Shamefully not many units out of (174) houses/flats were for rentable housing, all sold on the open market for no less then £200,000/£350,000 not for locals but open for the whole country to purchase. First plans showing (80) units, which soon changed to (120) units, finally ending up with (174) in total, what a huge profit, note the plans changed three times). This was carried out by the very same developer 'Slope partnership' as our current new developer, here on Shortmeadow Green.

By the loss of the swimming facilities, what with the huge profit, they should have offered to compensate and given something back to the town, for our loss of as many as 14 clubs does the council care, not in the slightest. Using the swimming pool facilities each week extensively, and seriously missed by all users. (Unforgivably the clubs do not exist anymore all gone after many years of enjoyment and skills taught). Here in this town as mentioned earlier, having only one swimming centre, with countless people demanding a swim, reaching breaking point at times.

No forethought about future needs for the town concerning swimming, which has proved essential in keeping people fit over the years, young and old. Each council meeting you attend, the councillors are embarrassed and unable to explain who was responsible, for this waste, of such a huge £178,000. Which is a significant amount wasted of our money on one building alone, which was refurbished then after three months closed, and then amazingly demolished a short period after.

118

Which makes absolutely no sense what so ever? Someone must be accountable for such a huge amount of our money wasted, the so called councillors who are remarkably quiet at owning up. Seriously, what is not realised by the very silly councillors, all the clubs had full membership, and amazingly it takes years to establish any essential club in town.

Only minutes by a group of insensitive councillors at a committee meeting to dissolve all these clubs at a stroke, which needs explaining?

'Actions of a few (councillors) are felt by all' the reason for the title as you can see? You see the important statement above with absolutely no plans for the future, all they are focused on is making more and more money (NOW), with no thought or expectations for the future needs. The amazing thing, which I cannot get my head round, with the unexpected closure of the Swimming pool, was that just after refurbishment completed we all looked to the future.

After the local council taxpayer's/ratepayer's spending a fortune on the important necessary renovations, which was again shamefully swept under that very same large magic carpet! After fitting brand new filtering system, new boiler, and many other expensive modifications, repainted both changing room walls fitting new showers. Then leaving everyone, open mouthed, speechless weeks after reopening the facilities, then without warning or justification, closed for good with no explanation what's so ever.

Still to this day shamefully without conclusive reason, for their actions not forgetting the taxpayer's/ratepayer's paid for the very expensive refurbishments, we are fully entitled to an explanation and reason for this closure.

As stated earlier, any club in your town could take years to establish with full membership, can you try to imagine what it was like for all 14 clubs, after all the work and dedication put into running each club by the organisers over the years, is utterly shameful.

Then surprisingly, a handful of uncaring councillors without concern with people's emotions, within a few minutes at a council committee meeting decide, to demolish the building without taking into account.

That all these clubs that used the swimming pool facilities each week, have now folded with huge implications, as to the future treatment of other clubs still variable, and running successfully in this town, for how much longer?

Astonishingly to my amazement after each councillor has shook hands with the developer, after receiving money from an agreed (Section 106 agreement) immediately looks around for their next opportunity to fill the back pocket from the following (106 agreement). One has to congratulate the council officials for their shire determination in carrying out openly this deceit, such as the MPs used to in the past, openly thieving from each taxpayer throughout the country.

Then you hear from everyone while shrugging their shoulders once more, that well-defined statement.

'What can you do about it?'

CHAPTER TWENTY-EIGHT
*
My Old Neighbour

Please consider without smiling, this next event as an example, which has important bearing with 'planning,' but on this occasion nothing to do with the council planning office whatsoever. However, I refer to my past old neighbour at the end of my rear garden. Now you promise not to smile this is personal!

Which I found completely fascinating, only two years later, with the fast growth, of a Silver Birch tree located just inside his garden. If it were not so serious, it would be amusing. Some years ago, my neighbour called Morris planted a wonderful ten-foot Silver Birch within inches of my back fence. Without the knowledge of how a Silver Birch grows, placing the tree extremely close to our dividing fence. With recognising it being a Silver Birch, I mentioned that the branches potentially expand as far out from the trunk as the eventual height of the tree. He had not considered this with his choice of positioning the tree; my greenhouse is within one yard from the fence on my side?

His answer was equally as silly as the position of how close from the greenhouse the tree was now positioned. "I will move, it if that problem exists in years to come." There must have been a method behind his madness, but I am not able to contemplate his thinking. Move it, what does he mean, 'move it.'

After only two years, two branches were actually over eight feet in length leaning on the glass on my greenhouse. After inviting Morris, round to view the possible damage to the greenhouse, so that he could remove the invading branches from possible damaging my greenhouse. With accepting my invitation, he came round saw the two branches that were leaning on the glass, "what is the problem it has not broken the glass yet."

Morris. "What part of this do you not understand, if this was my tree branches, on my neighbours greenhouse glass, and you brought this to my attention.

With the likelihood and expectation of broken glass, and possible injury to any member of your family, while in the greenhouse, the branches would have been removed urgently by me safely without question.

In addition, who pays the cost of the glass, which has to be replaced? "Do you really have a problem not understanding this?" Immediately, came out with the following remark. His next comment takes some beating.

"It's my tree, also my branches, but now your problem". Like at the committee meeting earlier, I was left speechless for a few seconds, and then I stated.

"That he would be hearing from my solicitor, now would you please leave, before I say something rather rude," at that he left still uttering on his way out, "it's not my problem it's yours." My eldest son could see how upset I was, and with a friend, while I was out, removed the invading branches, cut back to the trunk, then placed the branches over the fence into the neighbour's garden, without my knowledge until the weekend. When Morris came round, shouting the odds to me, "that I had interfered with his tree". Therefore, without hesitation my quote made him speechless, on this occasion.

"The tree is yours yes."

"The branches are also yours."

"And it is now your problem:"

Pausing between each remark;

Both my sons, plus my daughter had just arrived and were standing behind him, came round as usual for their Sunday lunch, my eldest son said to Morris, "is there a problem Sir;" with that, he made a rather prompt exit.

We still have serious problems with this same wonderful 'Silver Birch Tree.' With Morris the owner now past away with sudden cancer some years ago. He must be laughing in his grave. Now with two further owners of this house since he passed away. The tree is now huge after twenty years; many other thick branches are now well over sixteen feet into our garden above our greenhouse, the new owner hopefully will consider cutting back safely, the overhanging thick mature branches this year!

After a chat, he seems very much friendlier and amenable; otherwise, the saw will again come into use most likely late in autumn, the new neighbours are still settling in. I will not mind betting, that Morris is saying from where he gone!

"That tree was 'mine' also the branches were 'mine' but the problem is still YOURS."
Now, now, stop laughing this is really serious!

This is the importance of good sensible planning, against the mess over the years, caused by negative thinking, by my old neighbour who neglected good advice.

If the plan by Morris years ago was decided with planting this wonderful Silver Birch tree, in further onto his land, let us say twenty feet or so, the difference would have been a beautiful mature Silver Birch tree by now. To enjoy especially on a windy day, with the huge extremely long branches swaying in all directions as they do.

Besides, great fun watching the squirrels chase each other along the length of the long branches, now that would have been, excellent planning for both us, including the wildlife, which I am extremely excited to share nearby. With not enough people, thinking the same and planning sensibly, this world would be a greater place to share, and enjoy our short stay while on this earth.

A footnote concerning the above subject, which may put a smile on your face, as long as your name is not Morris. My other neighbour at the other end of my garden is a very keen gardener, keeping it looking pristine. She has surprised us by placing a tree within inches of my other fence 10 ft tall, and I am only going to give you one guess as to which type, you promised not to laugh.

Do you really need a clue; starting with (S), second word starts with (H). Inviting her over to view the mature Silver Birch in my other neighbour's garden, left her thinking, also speechless as to its sizes and overall canopy?

121

Mature Silver Birch tree in Morris garden.

My other neighbour's small new Silver Birch tree.

Here is the proof, what would you say faced with the same scenario now be perfectly honest? This young Silver Birch tree is now some 30ft tall and still growing at some speed.

Now will she or will she not allow her tree to grow as tall, it is only inches from the fence as you can see from the photograph. I give up, or is this Morris reappearing in another disguise?

Extremely good news concerning my wonderful next-door neighbour, just before this book was published. Well done Gwen, on a Sunday halfway into January 2011 curiously with noise coming from my neighbour's garden, 'surprise' the small Silver Birch has now been removed. It would have caused a problem if allowed to mature. Gwen was concerned with the speed of growth and was extremely sensible in removing the tree.

That is what I call an excellent neighbour. Congratulations I am exceedingly pleased.

CHAPTER TWENTY-NINE

*

Consideration for the Environment

Always living near to a healthy environment was normal for us to appreciate and enjoyed over countless years, most people's ideal and dream, but everybody's nightmare with having to accept these totally different intrusive circumstances forced upon us. Now we have to endure this latter situation, with the actions of these current cowboy developers, which is totally unacceptable to even contemplate.

Most of the local residents are conscious of the environmental problems posed by inconsiderate council officials, with current redevelopment responsibilities, blinded by accepting money from each (section 106 agreements) without regards to the local environment or resident's personal emotions with losing this essential local green. These impending actions, would be enjoyed by recommending, also implementing these same officials placed into shackles, mainly to restrict their actions.

As in the famous 'football match' in reverse with seriously good reason, when you consider the result of a staggering 40 plus mature healthy trees, were cut down on site unnecessary, without any thought for our local environment. On this development site, far too many trees have been excessively cut down, and many more surrounding the site are surplus to requirements, as far as the Guinness Housing Trust is concerned.

Without any balance or justification for this action, of sheer bloody-mindedness. Please allow me to explain. On the first plans issued, for this controversial new development.

Eight trees were initially scheduled in facing the chainsaw, if that wasn't bad enough, a short while later two more trees discretely added to the next replacement plans the following week. Followed by another unexpected set of replacement working plans, which were altered without announcement, which the local residents were not aware of. With further alterations now changed to a staggering 15 mature trees were now selected to be removed from site, to build rentable affordable prefabricated cheap houses and flats.

Controversially two mature Cherry trees outside the site were now earmarked to be removed, that amounts to 17 trees in total; I was confused, along with the remainder of the local residents, now disproportionately out of control. We were unable to keep up with the alterations to the plans, what are they playing at, the public are not aware of these constant changes, those of us interested in maintaining a local healthy environment, were infused with anger, but the council are not at the least concerned with our feelings or emotions they couldn't give a damn.

HOW HAS THIS BEEN ALLOWED? What rulebook is the developers and councillors following, are they taking instruction from this housing trust (Guinness Partnerships) who will very soon purchase this land from the developers? Always getting away with these momentous alterations to the working plans. Approaching the planning office to enquire about the amount of trees being cut down was a complete waste of time. Stating that the developers had decided with all these necessary changes, ironically the trees are cut down by the council arboriculture group. The plans changed once again at short notice, or changed very quietly without notification not once, not twice, but significantly five major changes to the working plans so far which has been noticed! Instead of being developers, they are into (demolishing and destruction business), with a continued reputation while on this site.

At this early stage of this proposed development amazingly five families had unexpectedly decided to sell up and leave why? Already recorded two cars damaged unnecessary, also huge Lorries attempting to knock down two residents' walls and countless car side mirrors either broken or damaged. Hate to think what rubbish these prefabricated building are going to look like, when you consider that the buildings are 95% made of wood with copious amount of insulation, covering the wooden frame.

Followed with an extremely narrow layer of bricks or thin cladding to cover the insulation. As we witnessed each day over 14 months, with streams of huge Lorries each day having great difficulties in entering on and off site. Attempting delivery of equipment, with vehicles' over 21 metres in length, into a very narrow entrance ending at the lower end of our close, a sharp bend to negotiate, endeavouring to venture onto site with great difficulty avoiding all parked vehicles.

Now that all the garages have been demolished, all cars are left in the road, 'you know what I am about to say next.' They have created and implemented a new astonishing policy called. **'On street parking policy.'**

Inconveniently all parked cars, were made to move each time up the road some 300 metres away, to allow the huge vehicles to proceed onto the development site, as stated from time to time wing mirrors were predictably damaged with the evidence lying on the ground near the car in question as mentioned earlier, two cars were seriously damaged and two resident's brick walls showing scrapes while leaving paint from the Lorrie's along the wall surfaces. Each day for months the local residents were woken early to the sound of very large vehicles parked outside their properties waiting to enter the site before 7 o'clock in the morning which was unacceptable for any neighbourhood to endure over 14 months. Where was the planning?

The so-called working plans have been altered too frequently, since the proposed plans were first submitted some months ago, into the planning Office. Then changed again after the committee meeting, which is normally the very last opportunity for the public to view the working plans? With the last development 'Slope partnership Ltd' were involved with, yet another very much larger development in a training centre, on the old School grounds, this was covered in a previous chapter.

The training centre was being used for all types of training to teach working skills to youngsters plus adults, was now closed, and 174 residential houses/flats now exists; The example I wish to offer, was that the first plans submitted to the planning office initially were a mixture if you recall for (80) flats and houses.

Which soon, altered within weeks to (120) units, mixed with houses and flats? Which the public never had the opportunity with difficulties viewing the working plans at this late stage; The final total, if you recall, believe it or not was (174) a huge increase in numbers of mixed apartments.

But only a very small % of flats were for the opportunity, with affordable renting accommodation. When asking our local councillors, why only a very small number of the houses for affordable rentable housing, nobody knew the answer it was far too difficult a question to answer?

Noticing that the remainder were for the open market, not one unit for the local demand, shamefully with just a handful for affordable rentable flats as mentioned above. Now let me put into words, and make you aware of the sound reason why the council officials along with the developers, agree, with the results of so many more apartments added to the plans.

Collectively with the extra revenue from 'council tax,' their ultimate aim for years to come. Councils are always content with the extra revenue, also the developers, making a huge profit from each arrangement; money in the 'back pocket' is all they are interested in, so to speak. Open fiddling?

It would not totally surprise me, if some building numbers change on this current development, and I will be interested, with some of the surprised changes after this development is finished. The amount of mature trees left standing, would be of interest to me? Why do plans have to be submitted in the first place, if they are not adhere to; How is this just a guide line, the difference of 80units then changed to 120 units followed finally with 174 apartments in total which is quite a significant difference added! They never got round to learning maths, at school; or did they 'when checking the final amount.'

This is the same example, with the removal of so many more trees, on the working plans with this current development, the more trees removed from the site, makes room for lots more buildings. Although I cannot see where any more buildings could possibly fit into this very small area, unless they are the size of a 'matchbox.'

With absolutely, no consideration for the once healthy local environment we all enjoyed and appreciated. Remarkably, Slope partnerships ltd, are the very same developers involved with three other developments currently in this same town. It's not their custom to follow the plans laid down, so more opportunity to increase profits.

'If we offered plans, into the planning office and astonishingly, changed them by manipulating to our advantage.' Just once, we would have to show serious justification with these changes, and would clearly be refused with these alterations involved, this shows double standards are widespread with clearly turning a blind eye.

With all developers activities, (but with private planning applications we are unable to get away with any alterations to the original plans submitted). So many more trees cut down over the planed amount; with the result of seriously harming our environment is not a plan, its mass destruction.

With a perfect example of accidentally cutting down of three trees, and serious damage to three others as a result, these three trees being damaged were also cut down and removed for safety reasons. (See photographs in Chapter 37).

Additionally, on each change with the new plans, concerning the amount of trees, which were also changed on each replacement working plans, would never have been approved or agreed initially with a private planning application.

Noticing, that an increase with construction, adding these changes, some small, others were significant to warrant reapplication, which was adding to the confusion, which I think was the councils aim. With so many changes to the plans, some were very deviously accomplished, through the back door so to speak, unchallenged by the planning office, and will continue, until stopped with legislation.

I cannot wait to see, what is accomplished when this development is completed. Also what is never taken into consideration is the damage to the road surface plus most of the kerb stones and pavement up and down the street had also been damaged on countless occasions, by the extremely heavy Lorries constantly mounting the pavement, the cost to repair this road must have been colossal, each week the road was repaired. As with the last development on the old school, grounds explained previously, how many more addictions and surprising inclusion to this current development will be of interest.

Only the other day, the developers on completion, have constructed a surprising continuous wooden fence across our right-of-way, running adjacent to the lane so that we are unable to walk through the new development area on completion.

On the working plans, it states quite clearly our right-of-way must remain when the development was complete. I drew attention to this with the council planning officer; he was surprisingly in agreement, and having to urgently investigate why the developers have changed these plans, once more cunningly and deliberately constructing this continuous wooden fence importantly blocking our right-of-way with no possible access across the site after completion. Apparently what plans are they following, to assume our loss of access, snatched from us which we have had for countless years the right's, to enter and cross this land, before the development replaced our important open recreational play area?

After two meetings, with the senior management of the development, our right-of-way has now been restored, it would seem at great cost to the developer, having to lay a necessary paved pathway across the development site, plus opening up the continuous fence so that our Right-of-Way is returned. This shows evidently their obvious greed, they were not entitled with this action, in altering this significant important arrangement, with their attempt at shutting off our right-of-way, which we had for countless years in the past, proving categorically this recreational area is unmistakably common land, not private and should never have been sold to the developers?

Importantly I haven't the money to contest in the high court, with proving categorically that this land they had snatch from the local residents, is common land and has always been over time and use.

Given the opportunity I am convinced that I would win by a country mile, with the true compelling evidence presented to the high court. One of the greatest strengths of our local council is the profound thinking and intellectual rigour that goes into the development and creation of its policies, then when it suits them to disregard with the policy created, such as the policy background that our recreational play area, was covered with a policy background that under no circumstances would residential housing be considered on this land, which is covered by legislation and very strict guidelines set down by central government.

127

CHAPTER THIRTY

*

Removal of Two Cherry Trees

Removing inappropriately something beautiful, such as two mature Cherry trees, without debate or consultation, with the local residents in our small close was not appreciated. Fundamentally worth while campaigning against their removal, principally because most bees, butterfly, and many more varieties' of insects, which used to visit each year, now shamefully these trees will not to be replaced.

Returning once more to the development, started on our open play area, astonishingly later it was to get very much worse. The following week I asked the planning office to supply me with up to date working plans for the new development.

Astonishingly hearing that as many as 15 trees on site, plus two mature cherry trees off site, were to be removed. With all of the above trees mention for the chop knowing, any further changes would mean that a reduced numbers of trees, with visits from all the birds and wildlife next year would not happen, gone forever, proof if needed starting with all the bats that have completely vanished from both areas on site.

Including both of our beautiful cherry trees mentioned above, with fantastic pink/white blossom in the spring, one produced the most wonderful white blossom with the Fragrance you could sense from some distance away. The other mature cherry tree outside the site had the most beautiful light pink blossom.

Both trees can be seen in the photograph in (Chapter Two), a pleasurable experience, walking past both these gorgeous trees in early spring on my way down to the garage area, it looked a picture which placed a smile on my face each time in passing. Residents in the past have taken hundreds of photographs of family members against this background. Past memories now history, both have been cut down shamefully by a bunch of fools, to gain a wider entrance to the site without any protest from the local residents.

Who quoted once again, **'what can you do about it.'** How they were able to get approval to remove these two magnificent mature trees puzzles me, one can only assume a 'back hander' was involved seriously, and how much money did both those cherry trees cost us? (Nudge-nudge you know what I mean).

With both humans, plus wildlife missing the aforementioned wild cherry trees such as the birds, butterflies, and most importantly the Bees, have no choice and would have to go elsewhere for necessary goodies, which the blossom trees used to provide. Apparently there are no other blossom trees in our street now it is bizarre, knowing this is a manmade worsening situation, we had absolutely no say in the removal of both these wonderful mature Cherry trees why, only a mad person would ever consider the above, with the removal of these two beautiful trees?

Taken without debate or consultation as mention, in fact there has been no contact with the residents concerning any of these major changes. They talk of democracy which has being lost, this is not a free country anymore or has it ever been?

128

It's run without wisdom, or protection for the future wellbeing of its citizens, or concerns for the environment, noticeably affecting the whole close community which disappeared over 20 years ago by the councillor's greed, and corruption.

Some weeks later, the tree cutters had returned the following day I noticed to my horror and ultimate surprise, you couldn't help noticing from a distance; a great deal more than 15 trees had been removed already, also both Cherry trees outside the site had also been cut down as mentioned earlier. Leaving all the local residents extremely annoyed and flabbergasted, once the trees had disappeared they are impossible to be replaced.

When I approached ever closer, to where the tree cutters were still carrying out their butchery, noticing immediately how many more trees had astonishingly and shamefully been cut down. I was outraged asking the supervisor in charge of the work, "how many have been removed so far." Astonishingly I was horrified; one could see at a glance that a staggering amount, more than 30 had already been removed throughout the whole site.

These bunch at school did not cover maths at all, as a subject (30 trees is not 15) back in the bad old days in the orphanage, you would not make this incorrect calculation, and sit for very long afterwards. Especially when you hear, the final unacceptable total amount of trees cut down unnecessarily in our area.

When supplying new homes in any area, surely the local authorities' main aim and responsibility is awareness and serious control, with potentially harmful affects regarding the environment, and common sense should be your first consideration.

This is why we have strict rules plus policy guidelines to follow; even the council officials have a duty and should be made to follow these same strict planning regulations.

Like us having to follow plans, submitted into the planning office, you can unmistakably understand that double standards have being applied here, when evidently they were constantly stepping over this imagery line, with changing the rules to suite themselves. To my utter surprise, the supervisor stated truthfully, 42 trees had been removed in total at the last count.

The disposing of this many mature trees, when on the preceding working plans for the entire site, were just 15 trees registered for the chop, now this outstanding amount is out of order not sticking to any plans, now the gloves are off. Asking the men who were still attempting, and intending to cut down even more trees, to halt their activates while checks were carried out. (The men stopped and had a break from the competition they were completing in, on how many trees can be cut down in a single day)?

In the meantime I phoned, the council office to make inquires. Speaking with the chief planning officer concerning the above serious situation, of why so many trees were removed than scheduled, his statement nearly sent me to the moon. "Unbelievable they have found out with a (guess), and stated (before actually cutting down these trees), that all of the selected trees, were found to be, in extremely poor condition." (Huge porky pie).

With a quick check on each of the tree stumps, on all but one, were in excellent condition; the supervisor was following instructions from his manager, and compiled with his managers instructions; we did a quick check, on his days work this confirmed that far too many healthy mature trees had unnecessarily, been removed, now this is no joke.

Who can you possibly turn to for help on these matters? Nobody is the answer. However, someone's head should be placed on a good stump, for carrying out this total wipe out, I was furious and like with most men who are hopping mad with anger, it is advisable to keep your distance. What I had not realised, this competition must have been arranged for that day to go for a world record on how many trees could be cut down in an hour? Hurriedly without the local residents knowing what had occurred: Then afterwards say **(what can you do about it)? Which is exactly what they did say afterwards.**

Going by their achievements, that day I would back them against any other team, of tree cutters around in the Country, possibly in the world! This was once a small play area for the local neighbourhood to enjoy, with a very healthy interesting positive lively environment. For the local children to take full advantage of, and continually learn from, this prefect environmental area now in just a short space of time, the area is now representing malicious deliberate wonton vandalism and total devastation.

With my earlier video taken of the area, when the healthy environment was prevalent, and now this video as convincing evidence of this destruction, demonstrating this entire shameful act by those responsible, viewed on pages in (Chapter Sixteen) also in (Chapter Thirty-Seven). Incidentally, what I had to say on the matter was not for young children to hear? It is difficult, to imagine in the 21st Century, how developers, are able to carry out this destruction, when they are supposed to construct, not destroy.

Nevertheless, this proves a serious need, of an official referee or someone to oversee locally, also nationally in controlling the way councils are just ignoring the way developers continually harm the local environment throughout Great Britain, with most new developments. Without being accountable for their actions, the planning office turning a blind eye then continue onto the next development to carry out further destruction elsewhere, to earn a great deal more money with each (Section 106 agreements).

We were witness to this shameful destruction, knowing it is impossible to repair this damage, with so many beautiful mature trees cut down. Which have survived for between 60-80years or more, cut down without any serious consideration or concerns with maintaining a healthy environment.

Before being cut down the Bats used these same trees in both areas on site, and by the law of the land should be protected and also not disturbed in any way, we have all understood this to be true, over countless years in the past, it's the law of the land!!

They should have total protection at all, times? Not forgetting only eight trees were initially scheduled on the original plans offered into the planning office, to be cut down. It leaves me speechless, and nowhere to turn for help in putting a halt to this devastation and madness. Now who will acknowledge the truth, and own up for this outstanding behaviour? The Council will hide away and ignore all the complaints. Until someone with lots of money is involved, then as if by magic 'hay presto' changes carried out immediately. 'Money always talks.'

The workers soon left, after I said a few more words and the words as mentioned previously, were not, for young children to learn. After a meeting with planning officer, no more trees cut down! **'That day'** I must be more watchful, furthermore scrutinizes any more (unhealthy) trees cut down;

You see there is no one you can turn to as mentioned previously, if you are passionate in saving a viable environment, for help and trust in this town or possibly in your town, with these worthwhile serious outrageous situations.

Our town cannot be the only one where this activity is going on, because on the TV, & Radio, also in the local and national newspapers, you constantly hear of this type of destruction to the local environment with planning office approval.

Seriously, the planning office do not check on what the developers are up to, because they have secured the money beforehand with the (section 106 agreement) and could not give a damn, or care less with people's emotions. When regeneration is mentioned in any town, all council officials follow the same pattern, make as much money now, and worry about the consequences to environment, later when someone as I have spoken of, with buckets of money steps in, who is important enough to put a halt to this madness?

The suggestion and intention by this council for the future is that all small open grassed areas will be snatched from the local residents, without listening or considering any complaints or objections from the locals, who keep uttering that well know phrase once again. **'What can you do about it?'**

Consequently the greens cost money to maintain (i.e.) cutting the grass and clearing the rubbish away. After building houses on these same greens, no further maintenance to be carried out in that area, just collect the council tax each year, from each house/flat now standing. You cannot beat this (great plan) by the local authorities and officials, then immediately onto the next area to hand over to the same developers, so that they have a guaranteed income from the next (Section 106 agreement)!

All MPs, councillors and other local council officials, always ignore property devaluation in the less affluent areas, plus residents' emotions, and a whole list of other objections on each redevelopment occasion.

Extraordinary in the more affluent areas in each town, regeneration in their area is regarded as an intrusion, affecting seriously the devaluation of each of their house and would not be tolerated.

Amazingly when you venture into the wealthy areas, you find the council have spent colossal amounts of ratepayer's money on permanent double yellow lines preventing anyone parking in the roads adjacent to their houses.

Venture into the less affluent areas and you would be hard pressed in finding a space to park your vehicle in the road.

Unbelievably the council have sold off the garage areas to the developers on a number of sites in this town. It always astonishes me on each occasion, the disrespect the council officials show, and we ironically continue paying their huge salaries' to carry out these unacceptable actions, WHY?

CHAPTER THIRTY-ONE

*

Our Local Councillor Lost Her Seat

Traditionally most local councillors show a great deal of respect, and are encouraged to carry out the wishes of the local citizens who have voted for them at election time. The consequence of ignoring the emotions of the local residents in your ward, when support is essentially needed happens to be losing your seat on the council.

This subject, you will fully understand and appreciate the time and research in writing this book, to make others aware that when a serious problem such as losing our local small play area designated for the very young children. With totally ignoring the background policy that no residential housing would be considered on the open space in question, then sold off to the developers.

Who can you approach and personally consult with your serious concerns. The children need our support for the future? Positively not the planning office. Certainly not the local police, or the council officials, without a doubt, astonishingly not even our local Mp, who has her own problems, busily concentrating on her own dishonest, 'parliamentary expenses claims and allowances.'

Even our local Councillor, she was strongly in favour, along with the remainder of all other local councillors plus her party labour leader, stating categorically that all the small greens in this town, will suffer the same consequences as our Shortmeadow Green with no if's or buts. With this attitude I can without a doubt bet my pension with her unquestionably losing her seat in the next election.

What each of the above have forgotten, they work for us, not the other way round! Since leaving school throughout my apprentice and working experience continued until my retirement, the labour party have secured my vote, and support over countless years.

Now all that trust along with any credibility and further support has been lost forever, because the councillors sold this common play area to the developers for a pittance, without realising the green belongs to the local residents, they cannot understand it's true value, and potential to the local children, and residents' feelings and concerns.

Many local residents, who feel they have all been ignored and treated disrespectfully, will not forget in a hurry the council's actions with regard to this essential open space, being snatched away from this neighbourhood dishonestly.

It is our opportunity now to ignore her request for support she is seeking, knowing we have the power and a positive plan with the next local elections coming up very soon; perhaps she will listen next time if of cause there is a next time for her!

The question which I have mentioned earlier, where can you turn to for help? When the council abuse the situation they hold and would complain to us with very serious implication if we were to replicate their actions and follow suit.

Our local councillor has proved in the past also presently to be absolutely useless and demonstrated this by acting very foolishly; ignoring the local resident's emotions in her ward she is totally responsible for.

Over many years having never visited this area, and spoke with any local residents about their concerns, which she is totally accountable for. Without the decency in supporting us in saving this important essential green from the hands of the developer. She will perhaps regret not listening, untrustworthy with refusing to lend any support in saving our important essential green.

Even on the previous occasion, over 20 years ago, this same green was deviously taken from us apparently for a temporary period, shamefully what assistance did she offer then: (Absolutely none). Without lifting a finger in supporting us in the slightest, in retaining this open space for the locals, which was promised unquestionably to be returned when the unsightly ugly prefabricated bungalows became redundant, which were clearly not in keeping with the other properties in the neighbourhood.

We waited patiently over this period of time, when approached as previously stated by her, and all the other local councillors that all followed like sheep, who I repeat are in favour strongly, that all other small grassed play areas in this town will also be targeted soon, to 'grow' houses on without consultation or debate also all objections will be ignored with regards to the local residents, they will have to change their minds soon!

If they do not change their ridiculous way of thinking soon, the town councillors will probably start a fight with the local residents in each area, with absolutely no chance of the councillors winning overall, importantly we hold the power now at election time?

The repercussions for their preposterous way of thinking will soon change, when losing their seats on the council soon, all because the very small children were denied an essential very important small play area close by. The local council official's narrow minded attitude and interest, is that these open spaces are for building houses on, changing the background policy in each area which I find extremely worrying, so that the council can fully concentrate on earning as much revenue from each Section 106 agreement. Also continuously collecting if you recall 'council tax' each year from each new redevelopment.

Is it possible to work out a rather simple sum before finishing with this topic, I will try my level best not to bore you with these interesting rough findings. If you average out what the council earns from council tax each year to the nearest £million. Let us invent this imaginary hypothetical town with 80,000 houses/apartments, each year the local council collect from each building, remembering this is only an average sum.

Each house on an average (D or C) scale could be from £1,400 X 1,000 houses =£1, 400,000 for 1,000 houses. Add the amount of houses in the town, let's say 80.000 buildings/apartments, not forgetting this is only an average amount could be something like 80X £1,400,000=approximately £112m in total!

You can see immediately, the county council will take the greater share because they are responsible in providing for education, the police, lighting /road maintenance, provide school building and maintenance, also many other appropriate things like, libraries and many other materials together. Which contribute to providing a service to the whole community in each town in their district? This is just the tip of their responsibility. Now what do local councils provide. When you now look towards what your local council are responsible for locally.

133

It is very little, you would be hard pressed to mention more than, collecting the rubbish each week/fortnightly, additionally, maintaining the council houses, and cleaning the streets, possibly other necessary local responsible requests.

Which happens to be a huge joke, when you count how many times our street 'is cleaned' each year? Only when you phone those responsible, after countless requests, visiting rarely each year with an untimely visit, when most cars are parked in the road unable of course to revisit sensibly, when the road is clear of vehicles. In over 44 years the road where I live, the vehicle cleaner has only visited maybe four times per year as a wild guess. In all that time our road looks rather poor, with leaves each year compounded into the blocked drains. The council are responsible for other maintenance tasks and responsibilities, which contribute towards offering a service for the town; they also collect from central government a portion of taxpayers' money necessary to provide sufficient funds for their expenses for local resources.

If spent wisely and not wasted, as witnessed over the years, they should manage without cutting service responsibilities, especially after you consider the huge salaries the top council officials are receiving.

Well into £300,000 pa plus, for doing what? Now you can see why we are so annoyed, and still in complete shock, predominantly with what has happened to our green, which we were assured that these areas would be retained and maintained for the locals. 'You could say that this comprehensively, is the true reason this book has been published.' To demonstrate initially, and draw attention to this crazy attitude, with officials working on the council, is rather like attempting to swim against the very strong tide which is ridiculous to contemplate, so why do they continually attempt it? Astonishingly, when looking through our local neighbourhood magazine for spring and summer 2010. Now promise you will not laugh, this is extremely serious.

It states amazingly, in our chronicle page six, this is mind-bogglingly and absolutely true; believe me this is not an April fool joke.

Stating that the children may now play in the road, as long as you use a 'soft ball' preventing damage to your neighbour's cars or fences! So when you consider this open statement. (The car, also the fence, is more important than the safety of the children). I wonder is that before they take the play area from the local neighbourhood? Or after all the cars are taken off the street, making it safer for the children to play in the road; 'Please no smiling it's unprofessional.' Is this as daft as it sounds. Or has the world gone completely mad, stating it is, OK to play in the road as long as the children use a 'soft ball'? The damage to each of the cars, would the council pay this damage?

Returning now with the removal of so many trees, to warn against this unacceptable behaviour by these council officials. surely, with these irresponsible actions, with disposing of so many trees, and selling all the essential open spaces, that are so important in holding the communities together without expecting a worsening, affect and considerations for our, healthy local environment.

Aware now that bats and many other birds, plus wildlife which over the coming years, will never return to this area. I am absolutely appalled by the above; it upset not only myself, but also the whole neighbourhood.

Throughout this book, are found examples of serious and mostly expensive mistakes, by the council, which are paid for by the taxpayer's/ratepayers. This should be a wakeup call to anyone experiencing this very same unacceptable treatment in your town, especially if this is replicated throughout the whole of Great Britain.

Action should be carried out affectively not soon, but now, to halt any further harming of the environment as quoted many times before. **It is very much easier to spoil a healthy environment, than to maintain it.**

Councils throughout, seam always to take this easy option, just to acquire a 'very silly' award. Plus fiddle with each and every new development opportunity!

CHAPTER THIRTY-TWO

*

Take a Wonderful New Journey

N ow realisations of different types of wonderful environmental situations, which are now on offer, an interesting free lesson on recognising and experiencing different kinds of environmental circumstances for you to experience. Which should be enjoyed not destroyed.

Now find yourselves an extremely large field, somewhat larger than six football pitches or better still, an expanse area such as a cornfield with no trees nearby will do perfectly. What I would like you to experience firstly is quietness, absolute quietness. Now the first part of this experience should be felt, by taking in this new wonderful experience and concentrate. Stand quite still, with eyes closed if you wish not to be distracted and listen, please stay with that for as long as it takes and relax, a very short while will not achieve the same outcome.

Sit if you find standing is difficult or uncomfortable, extra bonus if you find this experience pleasing. After a while, we will now select a location with a small amount of trees, say approximately between 10-50 trees, remembering how it was when silent:

Experience this change from the last, to show proof of controlled and different environments, the kind of experience now has changed somewhat with the interruption of occasional bird song and rustling of wildlife, in the undergrowth, please stay for a while remembering this magnificent experience, and enjoy this fascinating change.

If you firstly keep your eyes closed intently, (liken to that of a sightless person such as the blind), who see with their ears, breath slowly and wait. On countless occasions if you experience the above correctly and seriously, you will understand with pleasing results.

Consequently it will take some time to appreciate and familiarise yourself with most widespread common birdcalls. Now after you purchase a book, showing all types of common birds also wildlife, that will surely give you the start needed.

You see it now, then hear that sound, then lookup what was that sound, was it loud or quiet, was it a large bird or small that made that last sound. If you have for the first time enjoyed, this new fantastic experience this is the start of a wonderful journey, stick with it now for life, it gets extremely interesting from here on, and worth maintaining.

For the next sighting, remembering the bird or wildlife, which made that interesting sound? You may take that as a casual statement until you realise you are not deaf. If you were unfortunate, to be in that position of having the sight, and not that most important sense of hearing, you would be at a loss.

This is only the start of your tour into another world, with pleasing and pleasant experiences to follow now stay for the best bit, it may last for the rest of your life!

Arm yourself with a reasonable pair of binoculars there not too expensive, but worth every penny. Now please try not to rush, as the planners and other officials would, you are not restricted to 21 days or three minutes (like attending a committee meeting). There is no hurry to collect brown envelopes with lots of money inside.

It will now cost nothing; everything is free from here on, if the developers and council officials are kept out and not tempted into the area. This may hurt some people at first especially a developer or planner with great difficulty in finding a thick wooded area at least a mile square, which has not had all its trees cut down! That is if the planners can firstly understand what a mature trees looks like.

The planners may not have seen a mature tree before, 'or have they.' Planners must know or at the very least remember what they are, if you are into planning, their made of wood, have branches with leaves on, best cut down with no justification and need of protecting! (Right jokes over).

As you make your way into this intriguing environment your sight, plus hearing will also pick up interesting things while wondering what you've missed all your life, and never took the time to appreciate or bothered with before. Because now as mentioned earlier it is free for the rest of your life, to start learning now what made that sound?

Firstly, was it a loud noise? Curiously what made that noise! Can I recognise it again, was it a bird or other wildlife, stop and think for a moment, have I heard it before?

Now with question, after question, you will need answers to maintain your interest, refer to the book purchased, the answers are much clearer now and, getting more and more interesting; with the knowledge picked up on the way in no time at all the binoculars are out searching up into the next 'tree.' (Not the ones that were cut down earlier)

But the ones still standing that is why the trees are there in the first place, for the Birds, Bats, and Wildlife to roost or hide away from dangers down on the ground. (Called planners, developers, plus councillors). 'Most importantly the trees produce Oxygen for us all of us to breathe which has been completely forgotten' by the planners/developers who couldn't give a damn.

Try to imagine each tree holds its own biodiversity of insects attracted and attached to that type of tree, uniquely each tree attracts different insects and wildlife; the birds visit each tree knowing all these facts on how to survive, collecting all that the tree offers.

You are starting now to see what I see, not buildings, but an environment and biodiversity that has to be maintained which is not easy to achieve, with more difficulties than disposing of the trees. Hopefully we have arrived at the most intriguing example of all, which is rather important and fascinating.

Your next visit is placing yourself as far into a thick wooded area as possible, this time be seated on a fallen tree trunk, you're not restricted to time as mention previously, be still and listen there will not be a moment of quietness once the wildlife can understand your no threat to them, you will be surprised and also amazed.

Now surprisingly anything can and will happen, at times birds have landed on my knee and stayed for a while cleaning its beak then flew off in time. On several occasions, they have returned, even on one or more surprising moments which I will never forget, and pleased to share with you, hopefully you will experience this on occasions.

A robin landed on my arm then hopped onto my hand which I lifted towards my face, after a few seconds while smiling I spoke softly to the robin for what seemed like ages. Time was not important he decided when to leave, what a moment and on countless other encounters on other enjoyable visits not only in that wood.

137

But also in many other locations these moments are precious to me and will never be forgotten. Many occasions squirrels and sometimes a rabbit or other wildlife would venture closely, it's amazing how inquisitive the wildlife are toward us human beings, if of course they have your trust.

This is the tops, when wildlife has time to visit us; the pleasure in being connected with nature cannot be beaten. Surely, this is what the environment is like at its very best thus worth fighting for and maintained for the future. (Please remember the exam later).

The ultimate aim for any local authority is to achieve and accept these very healthy dynamic environmental conditions, for the future generations to appreciate.

Unquestionably, with potentially harmful actions of disposing of most trees in our area, would generate awareness when supplying new homes with a responsible approach with future planning.

By attention to detail, also a willing expectation with a response from the planners to start listening and take notice of our significant objections submitted, with local serious important issues plus concerns using some common sense for once, without always showing this pompous self centred attitude of importance.

Proving conclusively with this development, that they have seriously harmed the environment in this area, by removing a huge number of wonderful mature trees unnecessarily without any concerns for our feelings locally!

After removing all of these trees you instantly remove the environment to a different area, wildlife only stay in an acceptable environment. Conservation of the natural environment was affected seriously forever on our open space, when the planners and developers moved in.

It's very much easier to harm the environment than to maintain it, also not to destroy but to enjoy.

These following objections sent into the planning office. Which are equally as important as any other objections offered, but totally ignored without any response from the planning office whatsoever?

CHAPTER THIRTY-THREE
*
Two of My Objections

Evidently our natural, environment was seriously affected quite noticeably, and witnessed by the whole neighbourhood when the temporary homes were first placed here some 20years ago. Safeguarded with a policy background against any residential housing on the green. The planners did not consider the effect, on the enjoyment of neighbouring property values, at the time. We left our trust with these so-called planners and local authorities' last time, they seriously let us down both towards the environment, and guilty of breaking a promise in returning the green for recreational use.

By saying, that our objections were not serious enough objections, to stop the unsightly prefabricated bungalows being placed on our very small essential green, depriving all the small children of a natural designated play area locally. To completely ignore, each objection offered, in support of the open space, potentially brings awareness also concern, that supplying homes disposing of all but a few trees is of extremely serious concern for future plans in any area.

Successfully achieving without awareness, dividing the whole community. Seriously I believe this was intentional, and premeditated against all fundamental rules of society, by our former planning officer.

Without evaluating and applying some common sense towards local resident's emotions, I find it overwhelming; also irresponsible, it would be considerably worse to compound they're mistakes of 20years ago, in squeezing these 21units of flats and houses into such a small area for what sensible reason. With heavy rainfall it would flow downhill causing flooding, with no natural soak away, grass is a natural soak away but has been replaced, with Concrete and Tarmac.

What has the Central Government being shouting about, saying over the last ten years or more, and continues to mention with each opportunity. Do not cover the ground with hard surfaces, so what do the developers do the complete opposite! So where are the Councillors and developers getting their advice from (Mars one can imagine)? Have the planners and decision makers all gone completely mad, having no respect, or consideration for the severe environment impact 20years ago.

This has caused considerable shock to the local residents in and around this neighbourhood; **eighteen families** have already sold their houses and moved on, experiencing   considerably devaluing of their properties, caused by this recent announcement of this controversial development.

Most are looking now at horrendous large buildings only yards from their properties, where their beautiful vista and enjoyment of the trees plus our green has been compromised. Astonishingly showing absolutely no respect, we selected this area to live because the environment locally was healthy and the open space was nearby to enjoy, plus most have taken on a huge financial commitment paying their mortgages over 20/30years,

Which was never considered? Three photographs can be seen in (Chapter 19), which will support the above). Planners when considering planning applications must not ignore these strict rules, which apply to applications submitted, how many serious objections are needed in putting a halt to this madness? The above natural environment is an extremely serious objection on its own, to halt the proposed development, and on this occasion not ignored like on the previous occasion. "When is a green 'not' a green, as mentioned previously, when it's covered with concrete?"

Moreover, this is after the Government has mentioned on countless speeches over the years, reminding everyone only last year not to cover the ground with concrete, and still the developers ignore this important fact today. Do the Officials have problems with hearing or understanding? Please, look at a couple more of my Objections offered into the planning office. For their consideration concerning the local environmental issues, not forgetting this is the second time we have campaigned over this same open designated space ironically with a policy background stating no residential housing would ever be considered on our green?

'Natural educational environmental issues.'

My three children would spend a great deal of time, as all children do quite naturally while growing up, meeting with all their friends locally on the playing field, as all communities have done for many years in the past, until a hand full of inconsiderate councillors have decided otherwise.

Enjoying what comes naturally finding all types of flowers, insects, birds, and a great number of snakes, on occasions over the years. Furthermore, countless injured birds and pets which were taken along to Frank, the local man in our street nearby, who looks after the injured wildlife and pets when needing attention. Frank would advise my children and all the other kids in the area, to return items to where they were found, he would give lots of helpful advice on all subjects and aspects with regard to the environment. And continue attending to the injured birds, and animals found on the green, and in the surrounding area.

With no delay, if their own pet needed a check over, Frank would look to see what could be done for the pet, before going off to the vets. I miss the fun, there was always a predicament and pandemonium, when all the kids were busy enjoying life, and you cannot put a price on this environmental teaching opportunity.

This natural bonding with the community spirit has been lost forever, starting some 20years ago, since some mindless council individuals first placed the prefabricated bungalows, irresponsibly on the play area. So in their wisdom the council officials without applying intelligence and intellectual good judgment, by snatching important small play areas why? This very same objection offered and completely ignored, knowing their awareness of the environment is nil, effectively because their concern for the feelings and emotions of the local residents, or appreciation of the value of the green.

We were all looking forward to the return of the field, but the council officials proved too greedy and deceitful. With breaking a promise in returning the green to its former glory, and beautiful retreat, considered once again for recreational use for the local children/residents to enjoy once more. Soon to be 70 years of age, I am extremely passionate with our local environment issues, which are 'possible to control.'

Moreover should last for the next generation to enjoy, all you need to do simply, is keep the planners plus developers at bay, and all will be fine. Only if we act with common sense now, and consider seriously towards the next generation. I would feel concerned and very guilty if we forget this important point with our decisions today.

With concerns regarding the above objection, this planning application should not go ahead, and be refused on this thoroughly important objection alone, it is disgraceful. If I were wealthy, I would take this council to court, to account for this chaotic state, and unjust intrusion on our local neighbourhood, predominantly for monetary purpose only, with greed their sole aim, snatching this land illegally.

Orchid flower looking just like a bee.

An important find on the green by me, (seen in the photograph) was a very rare orchid, a flower that looked just like a bee? Having never seen it before, or since.

Surprisingly found a short time before the temporary homes were placed on the green in 1991, in early spring. I did not broadcast this find at the time to anyone, but took photos of this flower, amazed that others had not seen this wonderful rare flower located to the side of the green where many other wild-varieties of flowers were found. Having not seen this flower since, which has disappeared from the area alongside where the prefabricated bungalows were placed, which is a great shame and tremendous loss?

141

Over time, we have witnessed that the local environment has suffered greatly in the hands of impersonal idiots, who have evidently totally devastated and trashed the whole area. As repeated many times before seriously we have no one to turn to locally or nationally for help on these matters. Even the environmental law foundation (Defra) a charity that help people use the law to protect and improve their local environment could not help, surprisingly refusing to even visit after my request.

It would now cost a fortune and quite some time to recover, returning the field back into an interesting learning environmental area for the local children, to experience what it was like 20years ago. **This is the one thing I would give the council 10 out of 10, 'for a complete failure' Trouble is they would feel extremely proud in receiving this outstanding award!**

The council, and officials should be accountable for their actions, and should be truly thoroughly ashamed in calling themselves 'Councillors,' that's if of course they can firstly understand what the word actually means. **Now for my second objection.**

Absolutely no consideration for Ecological Environmental issues.

Back in August 2008 a full report from an Environmental Company from Coventry. It suggests a number of ways that 'Slope Partnerships' could achieve certain credits before the development can proceed.

Wading through, all 62 pages of their total rubbish report. Noticing firstly in this inaccurate insignificant report, which failed to include the bats roosting at both top and bottom ends of the proposed site, witnessed over many years by all the locals.

Nevertheless, the full estimate of their findings could have included or appreciate what we have seen on site long before the prefabricated bungalows were placed on our open space. They should never have been allowed to build on the field in the first instant, with a policy background stating no residential housing would ever be considered, we understood this is common ground over many years was secured for all the residents to use freely?

The reason for the difficulties with inaccurate reporting is that we live near to the field 24/7, 365 days each year for over 44years. Being passionate, I see significantly what comes and goes; therefore I would rely on my own findings, concerning Flora and Fauna with the surrounding area of this open space.

No disrespect intended, without any doctor Ship, or degrees, in ecological assessment. I am extremely passionate and proud also take seriously, real concerns with environmental issues, for the present and for generations to come; this I believe qualifies me without a doubt. This so-called environmental company invited from the other side of the country, is an absolute waste of good money plus a direct insult. Investigates on its findings in only a few days, filling out a long winded 62 page report.

With so many increased wrong findings, please stay in Coventry, and busy yourself reporting on things that concern your own area, not ours. (What a complete waste of council taxpayers/ratepayers money again placed under the very large magic carpet by these pompous individuals in authority who haven't got a clue).

Could you at the earliest refuse this application, on the grounds that the environment was seriously affected?

And possible considerations to improve the environment will take some time to return to its' former glory, where the Flora plus Fauna will in time recover for the next generation to enjoy and appreciate, plus wildlife should soon return with appreciation of our actions today. The whole community would enjoy the times we experienced some 20 years ago, on our essential play and recreational area;

We wait in anticipation and see if the council will use some common sense for once, with their decision today. I very much doubt that this objection will receive any consideration or respect it deserves, or even be read by anybody in the planning office?

Approaching the start of the 21st century would generate and bring awareness, when supplying new homes in a responsible manner. Clearly, without disposing of all these wonderful mature trees in this area is essential for expectations for the future.

CHAPTER THIRTY-FOUR

*

No Considerations for Disabled People

Realising Mr, Day's embarrassment made my day, (not his) after taking a trip into town to meet with the housing manager, who showed absolutely no consideration, or respect towards the disabled couple. Mr & Mrs Steal, living extremely close to our green, also covered in more detail in (chapter 48) 'Our other neighbours in the close.'

This same couple have lived here for well over 45 years; you will be amazed with this ridiculous incompetence, by the housing manager Mr Day, without checking on council records that they were blue badge holders. Mr. Steal along with his wife as stated earlier have lived here for many years and have been informed (notice not asked) to vacate his garage nearby his house. Both he and his wife being 'Blue Badge Holders' as mentioned and registered with the council as disabled.

Astonishing without showing compassion or exploring the implications of these findings, and possibilities in getting it seriously wrong. Before covering the above serious subject, and discussing these interesting characteristics, could I firstly mention, if I have called a 'handicapped or disabled person' as such, please do not be offended in anyway. I am a long serving active member plus helper of our local disabled club in town.

However not registered handicapped myself, nevertheless with severe restricted movement after having three separate operations to the same shoulder, finally having a rare new shoulder joint fitted successfully. Also endured open Heart surgery recently to repair a (leaky heart valve), and currently being left taking lots of medication, because of breathing difficulties after this heart operation.

Nevertheless, I cannot see Great Britain needing me in 2012 Olympics so I will give that a miss on this occasion. So we are not knowingly ashamed if called handicapped or disabled, and of cause you shouldn't either. (It is only a tile, referring to a person who needs help from time to time, so please do not be offended).

Returning to the performance and silly activities of Mr Day the housing manager deliberately ignoring this fact, about this disabled couple; the dozy, shameless rather embarrassed housing department manager has quite extraordinary gone out of his way to upset them both with total ignorance.

Causing astonishment too both, by sending a demanding letter instructing them without a compassionate bone in his body, to vacate their existing garage, and move over 300 yards up the hill to another garage block. Have you ever heard of anything as stupid as that? Without firstly checking on their council data base register, of any known disabled person in the neighbourhood, needing any special consideration or concern with the new imminent proposed controversial development.

His only concern seriously (while wearing blinkers) was the speedy demolishing of all but two garages (off street parking) being replaced with seven houses. As promptly as possible, so that the development can be renamed a 'free fall site.' (I will explain in more detail later about free fall sites).

Which maybe an unfamiliar new term you have never heard of before, many council officials will try baffling and reinventing different sayings, which are not commonly known such as this 'free fall site.'

Which I can assure you has nothing to do with apples; falling from a tree. Also 'Off street parking.' (Rentable Garages) Is another term not generally known.

Once they have demolished the garages, which fifteen local enraged residents require, which are currently in demand, this will prove an unsuccessful foolish decision and very silly move. With this local demand being prevalent in our neighbourhood, there is likely to be one almighty row soon, with the local councillors in a 'checkmate' situation looking around for the wheels, which have come of their truck! This huge mistake to empty and demolish quickly but quietly a great many garages without local consideration for off street parking, will come back and haunt them very soon.

Now astonishing the site renamed a free fall site, which is very clever manoeuvre once the demolishing of all but 'two' garages, now changed at short notice to retain 'four' of the garages when the development is complete. (This change was initiated by Mr Day seriously slipping up with the disabled couples requirements).

Back now with the disabled couple, who have difficulties with proving they are disabled, to the housing manager Mr Day? Who would expect this couple to place a flag outside their house indicating helpful guidance to any council officials, that they need special consideration?

On a good day, maybe a short walk of a few yards on level ground could be possible to achieve, but to expect this same couple both Disabled, who are unable to walk too far with the suggested relocation garage some distance up the hill from their house is asking far too much, and out of the question to expect this to happen.

Like me, he is an old soldier and some respect in the autumn of his life would be the least expected, from this experience, professional, council housing organization. Who have been doing this job of messing people's lives around for quite some years? You would think they have learnt some lessons in the past, on how to treat the elderly, plus handicapped people by now.

The Start of the challenge in attempting to save the green.

Example follows let us detract from the above for a moment, to highlight just the power councillors, planners, and local officials are dishing out, without firstly checking on their register. As I happen to be very old, (that is what my children are saying about me constantly), and a member of the (old gits award). I was asked to represent the local residents, attempting to save this valuable essential play area.

The task I have taken on is OK if you were to estimate roughly two or three persons per house, plus not forgetting all the children in the surrounding area. Approximately 250 houses surround the recreation play area and near neighbourhood, with approximately 700 Adults/children using the green regularly each day.

After you work out how many people the councillors are about to upset and lose significant votes, in the next election. Furthermore, have been angered, and who are extremely upset, by the loss of this open space, and the priceless small essential common bit of land, has been thoughtlessly snatched from the local resident for what purpose;

145

A hand full of houses, which could have been built in an area needing regeneration in this town just three miles away, would be my choice, without any environmental concerns or difficulties with construction consideration, also without any serious planning problems regarding objections from resident's in this area because there was no residents nearby.

Alternatively, without great difficulties with construction vehicles would be alleviated with extremely large Lorries entering and leaving this alternative site with plenty of space.

This play area unfortunately has gone forever contrary to statements that central government have been saying just recently, and over the years, that children should be encouraged to spend more time away from play stations because of the addiction with (DS) games and play station in doors, and has proved for very young children impossible or very difficult put down.

Even to my astonishment my eldest grandchild Kai has found the (DS) games intriguing, and we have to control, and limit the length of time between him using the (DS), and encourage other interesting activates such as playing outside in the road, maybe an excellent proposal now that the play area has been thoughtlessly taken from us without choice, **as long as he plays in the street with a soft ball, seriously the council have advised and encouraged this in the chronicle June 2010, you could not make this up?**

Evidently this has proved, in the past to encourage obesity in children, getting little or no exercise which is not a joke, this is a health issue, and should be taken seriously as a problem of concern for the future?

You don't have to force children to play outside just provide them with a small open space, and like a magnet, all the children in the community would be drawn towards the field to play naturally, and run around with other children in the local neighbourhood bonding the whole community together, it's as simple and straightforward as that.

Outside in the open, playing on open spaces like the one which has regrettable been snatched from us. Additionally, the foolish councillors are unaware with the ridiculous situation, and cannot see past their nose, with the harm caused to the whole local community. On the other hand, past the fat Brown Envelope in the back pocket filled with cash, (no cheques' please) they should be ashamed of themselves, it is shambolic.

Not forgetting this could be happening throughout the whole of Great Britain, replicated in your own town possibly? (Pleased I have got that off my back).

Returning now to the way the disabled couple were treated by the Housing Manager Mr Day. Inexplicably someone responsible must be highly embarrassed that the handicapped person on their register being treated in this bizarre and appalling manner and was not considered as an 'important consideration.'

Long before sending out all those demanding insensitive letters, just imagine no checks were made in this area which shows proof, that planning had not taken place!

The couple were both extremely upset when I visited their house, if you consider after 45 plus years with the same garage, and then told to vacate within very short notice, of a couple of days is outstandingly poor treatment to have carried out against anybody, especially a retried handicapped couple.

Within a few days notice with never missing a monthly rental payment, over all those years. I find this unbelievable also thoughtless, you would not think it possible to be treated in this manner, leading into the 21st century by this local housing department.

Both expected to travel some distance, especially when you visualise the pathway up the hill could be covered with snow/ice, and very slippery in winter period.

Which we are currently experiencing at present. Considering also the council is not providing salt containers for locals to address the slippery conditions, one accident and serious fall. Then a hospital visit next, embarrassingly an inquiry after as to why no salt container nearby, why are the disabled treated in this way would naturally follow with this inquiry, much more fun skidding all the way down the street 'on your backside'. **'Which the inconsiderate housing manager needs a good kick in this area.'**

However, consider walking some distance up and down the hill all year round, in heavy rain, and very strong winds, seems highly unlikely and unacceptable scenario for this disable couple.

The chap in charge of housing and responsible for all this palaver is a Mr. Day. Well-done congratulations you have earn yourself an extremely very silly award for this slip up. I highly recommend you to the top of this year's special award. Which will be presented at the Christmas party, well done and keep up the excellent work, and be very proud of yourself, this should be at the very least promotion, for your outstanding performance.

Many other council officials in the past have received promotion with less outstanding performance, three cheers hip, hip, hooray. "For he is a jolly good fellow."

This is what they will be singing at the Christmas party. Let me read you the main part of the correspondence sent out to the handicapped couple above, and others in the local garage area all received this very same letter.

They were told (not asked) to move at very short notice. Could anyone have thought of a better opening line headed by this next chapter, 'Due To Unforeseen Circumstances' which had absolutely no truth associated with the garages, which were in demand as mentioned earlier by a great number of local residents?

In fact months before this letters was sent out in our area, the Housing Manager Mr Day was busy attempting to kick all other tenants out who had rented these same garages.

A great deal of the blokes in our local pub up the road were complaining for weeks, about being told to vacate their garages, this is before we were sent our letters, nevertheless most of the other lads who rented the same local garages, were living on the adjoining estate nearby across the lane, who shared the garage block over many years.

CHAPTER THIRTY-FIVE

Due to Unforeseen Circumstances

S imply remembering, that the housing manager had the knowledge, way back in early March 2008, for well over 12 months previously, before considering demolishing of all the local garages. What follows is the main part of Mr Day's letter sent to each garage holder in the local vicinity. Stating, 'due to unforeseen circumstances,' you will relocate to your new garage at the top end of the road, some 300 yards into the other Garage block, (given a garage number) by the Friday 19th June 2009, if we do not hear from you by the Monday 22nd June 2009. We will assume you no longer wish to rent your new assigned garage, and your former garage rental contract will cease forthwith, followed by your old garage demolished soon after.

Others including myself in close proximity, to the old garages were Mr. Peter Horn, who was also manipulated and not shown the greatest respect either; was presented, with this same standard demanding letter sent out at very short notice to all concerned.

Received letter on the 19th June to vacate the same garage by the 22nd June, if no reply to the said letter, then it would assume that, the alternative garage on offer was not required. Please wait patiently for the remarkable punch line to follow. See if you can appreciate the significance.

'What if the person was on holiday for a week, or possibly longer, on the other hand unfortunately, in 'hospital' undergoing treatment for a week or more? Alternatively, away for much longer period, they are not obliged by rental contract agreement to remain in the country possibly on six month contract, working away.

THIS IS THE REMARKABLE SCENARIO, TO RETURN AND FIND YOU HAVE LOST YOUR GARAGE, AND FOUND IT BROKEN INTO, AND DEMOLISHED!

How would you feel, returning from holiday or from having been working away, in another part of the Country or even aboard, to find the garage empty, or demolished in your absence? Not forgetting that most garage rental is paid in advance, monthly by 'direct debit' so the shortest possible notice is at the very least four weeks' notice, plus with total respect, an arranged meeting to consult with the residents involved, to debate the serious issue with losing the right to rent your garage.

Astonishingly a few days notice, is without a doubt altering the contract signed, when the rental agreement was initially taken out all those years ago, and signed by both parties, wishing to rent the garage; This shows the breach of the contract by the very same council official showing absolutely no respect or concern and importantly in breach of signed contract which is without doubt illegal? Mr. Day Manager of housing department, (Well-done) looking forward I hope to the Christmas party and with the possibility, almost certainly promotion now! Planners please take into consideration the future needs, for us residents, who seriously do need these garages (off street parking).

Mr. Day stated at the committee meeting, that there is 'no demand' for the garages, which will all very soon disappear.

I do hope he is around when the 'muck hit's the fan,' as this is a serious direct lie, towards the local residents: The demand as stated earlier, of at least fifteen, local residents who have shown interest, which were totally ignored and kicked out of their garages with extremely short unacceptable notice, the only logic and important fact in all this, is that needs come first before demolishing the garages, with this new development pending.

We were all forced to move 300 yards up the hill, to the garage block the disabled couple, were offered earlier, heaven forbid for health reasons, like with the disabled couple. With demolishing these garages, what choice is there now for us local residents?

Having as mentioned previously, respiratory problems after my heart operation, now left with (COPD), and would appreciate a garage nearby. Others in this same area may in the future need a garage close by, for the very same health reasons, was this ever considered by the planning office?

There is no chance now, we always had a choice nearby to rent a local garage; this choice has been taken away unfairly without any consideration, we all feel cheated now that the garages have all been demolished; this is an appalling situation we find ourselves in. Incidentally, the insurance on the car would be considerable increased; now the car is not housed safely inside a locked garage nearby, which was never considered with our objections on this very subject submitted into the planning office without response.

Planners should always consider local current issues initially, plus concerns before any proposed development can be approved, its common sense plus unwise to proceed further if found guilty of over stepping the guidelines' set down by central government.

I have found in the past locally, the council officials always resistant any transparency with their dealings with the public in general, holding their cards very closely to their chest. A change of legislation would surely be necessary, to cover this serious mistreatment dished out, towards the residents making it a fairer result overall.

It is unlawful how they have gone about this handling of the local residents concerns with absolutely no consideration for our emotions, with the evidence shown above towards the handicapped couple, as a fine example! Then the impossible demands shown in the letters received, with impossible restraints on moving out of the old garages into the new allotted garages some distance away from your house.

Without a choice or meeting, to find out any possible health problems or individual local issues. Personally, at my age some mornings I have great difficulty walking up this road. Now having to walk to the next block of garages some distance up the road, do these council officials plus councillors care (of cause not they could not give a damn)? (On this occasion with this new development, consideration was never even on their minds, only the cash and corruption). In addition, open fiddling which has blinded their decision-making, furthermore haven't realised the obvious, the housing manager responsible for what has been carried out, is inconsiderate with regards to the individual needs of the current residents before demolishing of all those garages.

By the publishing of this book, also my honest opinion, with revealing all of the above true facts offered, readers can judge for themselves acting as witness, (possibly faced with the same scenario in their town).

Similar to the fans at the arranged friendly 'football match' we held earlier using bullyboy tactics, commonly used by most councils, the reader will make up their own minds as to who is in the right, and who has been cheated! Housing manager Mr Day has stated that there is no demand locally for the garages. (Was that true)?

Now as promised previously to explain in more detail, now that the site has changed, and now classed as a 'freefall site.' All councils look in their towns for brown field sites consisting of, and 'limited to approximately 10 units' needing demolishing, this information which follows is quoted from a government web site explaining a 'freefall site.' is defined, as a site that unexpectedly comes forward during the plan period.

They are defined as a site with less than ten dwellings; such sites are embedded, within the built fabric of settlements, and cannot easily be prevented from coming forward by policy measures. This next statement having value or significance must be remembered it is extremely important; this is how they managed to change our policy background with our green. While carrying out research for this book I came across these facts, so 'Sherlock Holmes' I was the one who solved this fascinating conundrum.

So seriously, why do we have policy background in the first instance, if all they do is ignore the background policy, and change the policy at will, to suit themselves? While under the council strict control, consideration to do the right thing for the local residents will not enter their minds.

Normally restricted in size to just 'ten units' say for instance a Brownfield site consisting of a garage block disused buildings left for a while and without maintenance in the area, made to look derelict and then classed as a free fall site. The actual wording is as follows, land that has become available and is suitable for redevelopment.

With all but four garages demolished out of 51 garage units in total, it is then renamed a free fall site. (I hope that this is somewhat clearer in understanding why it is now called free fall site). Not forgetting the importance with limitation, of only ten units. They have demolished over 47 garages units, which is well over the top of government essential guidelines' which is obviously illegal on this occasion?

The council's action is illegal; when you consider the current local demand of at least 15 local infuriated residents, requiring local rental of the garages, which have not been considered, in fact completely ignored. Some consideration, seriously for the above statement with exceeding the limit on the number of garages units demolished, to achieve a freefall site. 'It is now said to be a development which has become available and is suitable for redevelopment.'

The garage area accordingly, became available and very cleverly executed, when all the garages were quickly and quietly demolished. When this all goes 'pear shaped' and surely this will happen, only then will they realise this fantastic error, oblivious of the concerns with off-street parking in the area.

When you consider the serious facts, instead of demolishing off street parking it can now be quoted, the council have reversed the policy situation. **'You now have on street parking policy.'**

You will not find me laughing I promise!

Nevertheless, that will be looked into later, just brush it under the enormous magic carpet for now, and let other councillors sort out the serious mess later. Inactive for now but I cannot wait for the outcome as mentioned before, when the muck hit's the fan.

However, Houdini the famous magician is employed by councils throughout, to get all 21 units on what was our very small essential playing area and sort out this serious chaotic situation later; With severe on street parking arrangements they have created. The famous magician would be recalled to solve this problem with **'on street parking policy.'** I apologize if this is starting to confuse you!

This will be his greatest trick ever and I cannot wait to see how Houdini carries it out. To get a (quart into a pint jar) should be another trick to witness! Years ago the problem could have been solved by demolishing a number of garages in front so that the criminals who were able, at will to hide behind the front garages and break into any garage at will due mainly because of the design of this garage complex. By only removing the row of garages in front would have eliminate the problem altogether.

This was suggested years ago to the senior council members by others, and myself, but the council were as (dim as a candle) and could not 'see' or visualize the obvious solution.

The criminals would have absolutely nowhere to hide and would go elsewhere, problem solved, always the simple solutions work mainly because it is cheaper and a positive result, all indications show that 'someone' has spent hundreds of thousands on our play area even before the planning application went into the planning office!

Late in July 2009 in what used to be a very quiet cul-de-sac, the council had already completed the deal with the developers, normally years ago called a (rubber stamp) had been used which indicates a deal had already been signed and agreed. In August 2008, a company in Coventry covering environmental issues carried out extensive ecological assessment, on the open space in question, to determine what ecological credits could be awarded. The full report some 62 pages as mentioned previously, took some reading and seamed impressive to the uninitiated, but what caught my eye was the important serious environmental issues that were not present in their report.

First item on their report should have mentioned the Bats inhabit both ends of the green located in the mature trees, which we had witnessed over countless years, which was missing from their report why? Their first initial assessment was a low 2 credits seen on their report, on the same report advised the developer who are to carry out the development; they could achieve another 7 credits if certain work was carried out. Further proof and evidence that since the prefabricated bungalows were placed on Shortmeadow Green, causing very serious physical damage to our local healthy environment.

The area when visited by this company from Coventry was in a significantly sorry state, compared with 20years previous, it was healthy and a joy to observe. This does not surprise me with the inevitably low finding of only (2 Credits). I would have rated it as low as zero. Because the entire site over 20 years was in a compete mess. Compared with all those years previously, it would have received extremely high rating then.

The wildlife could come and go quite freely unhindered, along with Bees, butterflies, and a whole range other insects, and a multitude of other small animals which were encourage into this area 24/7.

Included slowworm, snakes (an adder was seen on a number of occasions) also interestingly I personally witnessed foxes visiting occasionally, were encouraged and unhindered into the area, the wildlife along with domestic pets continually visited the green each day throughout the whole year.

All of us local residents importantly had a natural claim over time, of the ownership of the green, our green settled amongst and between both housing estates intentionally, where the children would play from each estate every day quite freely, until the council decided otherwise and guilty of splitting the whole community in two quite intentionally, with total ignorance? Ironically, most of the local residents from both estates were seen each day on green, walking their dogs, watching over the children or just taking a stroll, and watch and enjoy the wildlife, as normal with regards to all natural communities.

The interfering council officials thought differently with houses, not residents or children using our green, must mention at this stage, an extremely important finding, while looking at each of the working drawings it was observed, that at no stage was 'Shortmeadow Green' ever mentioned, it is as if the green never existed, or importantly ignored by the Guinness Housing Trust?

Surprisingly the whole of development was called the '(town garages).' Intentionally leaving out the fact that the development took over our recreation play area and shamefully, should not be mentioned because it was a sensitive subject!

On the Guinness Trust Website, (Logic homes) explains the site took over a former old disused garage complex, which is completely unauthentic, why do they need to lie.

The garage area was less than 10% of the whole site, 90% of the development was the former 'Shortmeadow Green' an open space designated for the children, and local residents to use for recreational use by both estates in the neighbourhood, is the actual truth.

Another fantastic lie, to go along with the remainder of all the other multitude of outrageous lies, with regards to this development so far.

This explains how the background policy was changed, so that residential houses could be built on our local 'Shortmeadow Green' recreational play area.

Which incidentally did not exist, not in the eyes of the Guinness Housing Trust?

CHAPTER THIRTY-SIX

*

Some of the Amazing True Costs So Far

Horrendously fantastic expensive cost by the council, cannot possibly appeal to my sense of hummer. We council ratepayers are paying, and not saying a 'dickey bird' about the huge costs wasted of our money by the council officials who turn a blind eye, to the way ratepayer's money is spent. This is so serious, even before the planning application has even been approved, and past at the committee meeting.

Starting with the expensive wooden hoarding surrounding the whole recreational area, some six weeks before the committee meeting. It shows openly and unjustly the corruption going on right in front of our eyes.

Shamefully the majority of the local residents were mainly guilty of allowing the officials, to take this wonderful essential open space without a positive fight, and will very soon regret allowing this to happen. Along with the cost of the extensive ecological assessment over a few weeks would not have been cheap. It would run into thousands of pounds sterling. (Remembering 62 pages of negative absolutely rubbish).

Another survey was conducted which determined the sound from the main road. It was carried out to determine and record the very worst sound conditions.

The six houses uniquely designed and camouflaged, looking strangely similar to a warehouse/prison with extremely insignificant miniscule tiny window facing the main road, located only meters or so from the three-meter wooden fence, which was also erected to act as a sound barrier, against the intolerable unacceptable continuous traffic noise 24/7.

This building can be seen in (Chapter Nineteen), behind this necessary expensive wooden three meter fence? The sound from the near traffic will drive the occupiers of the new building, mad with rage making it impossible to sleep at night, mainly in the summer period, with the building placed a couple of meters from the main (A602 road with constant traffic), unless you design this outrageous monstrosity without windows?

Another outrageous 'preventable' cost in 2008 to carry out unnecessary refurbishments on all ten prefabricated bungalows, plus one laundry unit, only a few months after the refurbishments were carried out. Amazingly these prefabricated bungalows were made redundant, a waste of further council taxpayers money? Who paid for this £107,000 repair?

Workers from Germany spent weeks carrying out these alterations to each temporary bungalow. The purpose for this work to each unit, to eliminate an inherent serious (mould problem) each building had internally; it was first noticed and recorded in 2001/2 by local health and safety who were extremely concerned.

Then again, more in a way of a serious health problem found in 2004, the council were instructed to condemn the buildings by health and safety. Finding this out at a council meeting quite by chance. This delay extended into the latter part of 2007, again the health and safety said to the council that these buildings should now be made redundant urgently, reason being that the buildings' were no longer fit for the purpose, with young families living with this serious health risk.

Astonishingly, the council refused to get all the occupiers out why? They were ill advised and went ahead with this crazy idea with this company from Germany, to fix the above serious mould problem.

The company attempted to refurbish and repair the units, on both these sites; this included another site three miles away, involving further unnecessary costs with eight prefabricated bungalows having the identical serious problem with mould. The cost on the other site was approximately £100,000.

I think you know what I am about to ask, who paid the bill for this remarkable outstanding mistake? With two sites in this same town, with the cheap prefabricate bungalows sharing the same problem, the second site only approximately three miles away remembering the German company carried out the very same unnecessary expensive work.

These buildings were also to be demolished. (Only one guess) who paid for the unnecessary repairs once again, have you guessed yourself. 'Taxpayer/ratepayer. So we are entitled with an explanation and justification, as to why this considerable amount of money was wasted on both sites.

With regards to this site on Shortmeadow Green the total cost was nothing short of £107.000, added together the other site as mentioned earlier, it would have been slightly less approximately £100.000 with eight building to refurbish. This was found out by using freedom of information act.

Also added to the cost of the development site, are obviously the building surveyors would have carried out an assessment on this site over months. How much would this cost, plenty? Then along, with the architects, and all their visits and amazingly continued with changes and alterations to the plans they carried out one after the other, saying the changes were necessary, at what final cost?

Five major lots of working plans that I have knowledge of, maybe others. The cost to clear each prefabricated bungalow and make safe is a further necessary cost. Then the costs mention earlier to erect the nine foot wooden hoarding, surrounding the complete site. To further, seriously spoil this fragile environment.

Consider this important extraordinary fact; that this hoarding was erected some weeks before the committee meeting approval why? It's so bleeding obvious there is an almighty fiddle being perpetrated, I feel the councillors have all attended conferences at the 'Routlegde institute of the bleeding obvious!'

The approval to go ahead with the development, which had not been granted yet! Very clever or extremely silly to allow the developers on site before the approval was granted?

This must show to anyone with half a brain, that open fiddling is going on, a done deal had already been struck with the developers.

Now fit four huge double steel gates to four locations surrounding the site, attached to the wooden hoarding (remember this is well before the committee meeting had approved the development), what a huge cost, certainly not cheap. Unbelievably the developers went ahead it must have cost anything up to £100, 000, without a doubt? Now are you convinced was this a gigantic fiddle?

Demolishing all of these garages (off street parking) which 15 at the very least are in local demand, with only (4) saved out of (51) garages.

154

(To achieve what is now called a 'freefall site' as stated previously). With all these costs, I can only draw one conclusion, that the whole development is a fait accompli!

Therefore, I am not confident that our objections you have received will be given due consideration. **This cost was offered as one of my objections, and totally ignored why? You already know why?**

Besides, no explanation as to the gigantic extraordinary fiddle and corruption going on. If this fraud shown to the public is evidence and accepted as normal, just like the MPs with their parliamentary expenses was also taking the Mickey, and needs seriously sorting out with the example presented above.

The developers have spent £hundreds/thousands which shows proof and evidence before the committee approval was granted on 15th September 2009, likewise if replicated throughout the country, and the councillors are spending our council taxpayers money in this way, we are entitled to put a halt to this.

If as suggested, this is carried out throughout Great Britain, we are talking £millions of taxpayers' money Wasted, not forgetting this above, is mainly one site in one town with the above true findings.

Amazingly, the majority of naive residents when I visited their houses in the neighbourhood, while campaigning in attempting to save the green, just opened both palms towards me and shrugged their shoulders, and commented once more.

(What can you do about it)?

Well I have done something about it by writing this 'book.' Moreover, extremely proud that I did do something about it, somebody had to?

This is not to dissimilar to the actions by another 70year old **'Supergran'** from Northampton who took on those six extremely tall raiders attempting to break into the jewellers, using bags of guts, plus swinging her black shopping bag as a weapon, to bravely sort out these six robbers. (Mentioned and covered if you recall in an earlier) (Chapter 9).

CHAPTER THIRTY-SEVEN

*

Democracy Gone Mad

Incidentally, while taking another look, let us stay with our open space, which was subsequently, snatched from us by the successful scavengers, to give some especially fine evidence and examples of 'Democracy gone mad.' With the local children and residents now after some 60years territorial CLAIM on this play area, now denied an essential common local extremely safe play area to call their own, now without choice having to resort to playing in the streets, years ago in London we had no other choice.

Alternatively the council could have asked before remorselessly taking this open space, in a more democratic fashion with a meeting firstly, would have shown a great deal of respect and fairness, now they have lost all credibility with the local residents for all future dealing. Along with the neighbourhood losing a priceless common area to walk the dog and somewhere to unwind, which was rightfully theirs over time, when we chose to live here all those years ago? Importantly the children were never considered with these plans when this new proposed development was at the planning stage.

Without asking the local residents first, the council plus other officials who have affectively lost touch with reality also forgetting we live in a 'democracy.' They remain in another world of their own, without any concerns in general of the outcome of their actions knowing there are strict guidelines laid down which should have been followed. The council plan these actions privately at meetings in complete secrecy, with no meeting or concerns with local residents who will be seriously be affected by their actions.

Subsequently the residents are unable to challenge the council early enough on the following proposed development. Which involves all the local residents in the neighbourhood, with no consultation which I personally think is unlawful, with no regard to the emotions or personal financial commitment of all the private home owners, surrounding the green. Without organising a special meeting to discuss openly with the local residents, is of some concern for the future, showing **Democracy has gone completely mad.** Furthermore, even more reason seriously in making it necessary to promote democracy 'now' not later.

The main reason for writing this book is to put my opinion that I feel strongly that democracy comes first before any thoughtless decision has been made. This next statement is of some concern? Our local councillor has once again informed me, that all other small-grassed areas are to be targeted with no if's or butt's, backed and approved by the party leader and remainder of local councillors.

Once the new development has been completed, the permanent development will subsequently and inevitably devalue even further as witnessed 20 years ago, all the surrounding properties in the neighbourhood this is guaranteed, as experienced on the previous occasion. Most importantly because of the obvious disappearance, that the open space is no longer nearby, which is the reason we selected to live here all those years ago.

Now with justification, we are seriously considering leaving soon because we are upset and disappointed with the outcome of this new development. Additionally, when the open space was taken from the area unjustly, it proved conclusively on the last occasion remembering the horrors when the so-called temporary inappropriate ugly prefabricated bungalows were first situated on the play area, without a doubt certainly not in keeping with the current properties in the area, but patiently put up with this eye sore over 20 years.

Consequently having to except the loss of our essential open space was found significant then, but the difference on this occasion is a permanent loss not temporarily.

Setting precedence for future building on other greens in town. The horror of further, compounding this with a more permanent building development, and loss now of an immaculate healthy environment, which was once enjoyed by all nearby.

Noticeably the officials have destructively gone too far on this occasion, and with their accustomed enthusiasm cut down most of the mature trees surrounding our green.

With carrying out instructions agreed by the housing association (Guinness Housing Trust), holding a completion, on how many mature trees could be cut down in one day, and of cause would anybody record how many! (Well I most certainly did to their horror)!!

If this action was carried out in a more affluent part of this town, heads would swing from any available tree left standing. The lunacy and utter wonton vandalism, of cutting down over '43' beautiful mature trees and others, on site, and off without true rationalization, when viewing the main final working plans submitted.

Astonishingly only (8 trees) were originally decided upon to be cut down on site, on the initial plans submitted. Is this mad or what? Now currently the unbelievable has occurred it is now towards the end of March 2010, while looking over the wooden hoarding surrounding the development site. I counted the mature trees in this small area to the east of the site, left standing. To my surprise and anger, on the first working plans sent into the planning office some weeks ago, eleven trees, were to be retained in this one location at the lower end of the site.

Amazingly last week there were only four trees, each approximately 50/60ft tall, standing in this same location (Both the following photographs were taken from forty yards away showing serious damage to the base of each tree). While viewing over the fence, throughout the site, it was noticed all the remaining trees had very deep trenches some were at least eight foot deep exposing clearly their roots with serious damage carried out very close to the bases of these mature wonderful old trees.

Which were supposed to be protected by the developer, these very same trees along with others that the 'bats' continued to settle and roost, assuming they were safe in this area of the site? Later in March 2010 and halfway into the groundwork with the roadway cut out of the bank, where three other large mature trees stood in a row behind the current neighbours back gardens seen in the photographs.

The developers, had removed all of the earth away from one side of the trees, and cut open the roots as deep as five foot into the ground as seen. Leaving one mature forty-foot tall tree ready to fall with the next puff of wind, turn your back on the tree in question and 'pass wind,' surely the inevitable would transpire. The tree would be felled 'accidentally.'

157

How unsafe all these trees seem, it is not if it will fall but when! Now is that the actions of a responsible developer, to leave these trees' standing, with the row of houses less than a few yards away. Realising a number of very young children play in each of the neighbouring gardens behind this fence. Showing proof with the actions of the developers leaving these trees for weeks in this extremely anxious situation, with a gust of wind how on 'earth' are these tree's, still standing. Again I am forced to state the obvious that these developers must have also attended this same conference centre at the Routlegde Institute of the Bleeding Obvious. It's 'Bleeding Obvious' these trees would not stand a chance with maintaining a vertical position in high winds, we occasionally experience.

One tree seriously damaged.

With very young children, and families living just the other side of this fence. I was concerned and forced to advise the families of this situation. This photograph was taken some distance away. After drawing attention directly to the planning office, only then were the trees throughout the site afforded the necessary protection. **I was forced to inform the police on this matter, which was dealt with urgently.**

Now do you believe me, Are they cowboy developers?

Other trees damaged by the same digger.

Astonishingly, the planning officer did not punish the developers in any way, these trees were left in this dangerous state for weeks, as you can witness from both photographs offered, with far too many other countless trees damaged also on this same site. Without further delay I contacted the Planning Office to check if they had granted permission for the developer in cutting down this many trees.

The protection surrounding the trees in the photographs' above was placed after the planning officer requested the developer to provide this protection. He stated that he had advised the developer to carry out this request, and would check and phone back shortly, to my surprise the phone rang five minutes later.

The planning officer stating that he would like to visit the site that afternoon, to confirm about the missing trees, and view the damage to the remainder, insisting the developer takes immediate action in protecting all the remaining trees on site. He assured me he would contact soon with a result of his site visit. Truly the planners turn a blind eye, they don't give a damn, nor do the local councillors they have already been paid with the (section 106 agreement) that's truly why they turn a blind eye:

This is a first, the planning officer acting so promptly after a complaint being submitted by a member of the public, this deserves a mention in this book! Surprisingly a letter received next day from the planning office, described my findings and worse. Stating that he has written to the development officer, for an explanation, why the three mature trees were cut down, and no protection provided to any of the retained trees throughout the site.

Asking the developer urgently, that protection to all the remaining trees should now be carried out immediately, after witnessing the aggressive extraordinary damage seen at the base of each of the 'retained trees'.

This aggressive behaviour, with cutting down of this many trees, will only add to the confrontation between the local residents, and demonstrates subsequently the carelessness of this developer overall, with regards to not caring a damn, with maintaining a healthy local environment. How was it recorded as accidental puzzles me?

Pausing for extremely good reason, after receiving the developers answer, as to why the three trees were cut down, was unbelievable, misunderstanding by his work force, with a disagreement also confusion, with his instructions was his reply to the planning officer, which is impossible to believe and highly unlikely to be genuine: Therefore, he explained to the 'planning officer' that he was extremely sorry.

How you could possibly argue with that explanation! Or argue with the fact of not receiving a massive fine for each tree 'accidentally' cut down. Also stating that each of the three trees was accidentally cut down, (all of the three trees 'accidentally') you will read how this is impossible.

Officially before a single tree is cut down, a number of checks must be carried out as a formality, and has always been the case, over the years; even I am aware of this ruling, and I am not in the destruction business? Likewise, the working plans are viewed, by the supervisor of the development, also those responsible with cutting down of any trees on site. These workers responsible for cutting down the trees normally have nothing to do with the development whatsoever. They are council arboriculture members who were following instructions by the supervisor of the development.

If the trees are registered on the plans to be retained, those contracted to cut the trees would have noticed this, and refuse this request from the supervisor, otherwise take on full responsibly and obviously be accountable for the 'accidental' removal of these trees, is solely down to them.

How can anybody believe this possible, and classified as accidental? Now would you please believe me, when I repeat, why do we have to continually put up with these unbelievable blatant lies, which the planning office is offering? Who are fully responsible for the actions of developers, and we have to continually remind the planning office, it is their duty, to see if the developer cuts down trees accidentally?

By these so called, highly over paid educated authorities, both with development, and planning office, getting away with these continuous (porky pies). This is most likely to be happening in your town, with developments in your area possibly. Our site cannot be the only site throughout Great Britain where the developers have turned out to be excellent at demolishing, rather than construction.

Each time they will continuously carry out these cunning tricks to get their own way by making deliberate calculated mistakes, (accidentally of course).

Like leaving trees unsafe, (as you have seen by the previous photographs as evidence) then leaving the council arboriculture team with no choice, with having to remove them, stating that they must be removed because of the safety to the public? If we carried out the same as above, firstly you would receive a hefty fine.

Followed possibly by court action and spell inside, for this many trees cut down, for not following strictly the plans laid down, that stated quite clearly which trees were to be retained. This sends out the wrong message for the future, to all those who submit a planning application! When the planning office see you have not followed the plans to their satisfaction, you can now say officially with confidence it was an 'accident' that you cut down too many trees, or whatever misdemeanour against the planning application submitted. Astonishingly, 'double standards' comes to mind; if the developers can get away with it so should everybody else be able to follow their example, showing unfortunate 'precedence' for the future developments.

You can see the developer's 'plan' from a mile away; the intention is that these trees will also have to be removed from this area on site. Which is extremely cunning but intentional by the developers? You must look out for these cunning moves with your developments in your town.

Now the council have absolutely no choice but to remove all three trees for the safety of the current resident's/children, and their properties. With the evidence of compliance, that this 'Responsible' developer accidently cutting down of the three trees, also a Bunch of extremely silly workers! Using a digger, cutting the ground away from the base of these mature trees on site. Leaving the trees in an unsafe, unstable situation, only an Idiot would leave and walk away from. Drawing only one conclusion, carried out by a Bunch of irresponsible Idiots. The photographs do not lie, here is the evidence. You often hear this wonderful quote a photograph replaces a thousand words, (well how about only two words). 'Bloody Idiots.'

These actions we witnessed over months, will most certainly devalue even more properties in the area, with noticing the very serious further harming to our local environment. That we all once enjoyed, over countless years and thought it natural to have this healthy environment, surrounding our area, but would the wildlife ever return to this area, after the removal of so many mature trees, 'not even remotely possible.'

Add together, all that has been taken already, noticeably only four garages remain out of 51 garages, having all been demolished already, leaving serious off street parking, (garages) unavailable to the local neighbourhood to rent.

Now if you think our loss stopped there, please decide someone with a magic wand, concerning this very serious parking problems has rematerialize, simply because of the garages have all been demolished. (Now, no off street parking is possible).

Let's all be very silly, we have no option but to park our vehicles in the street instead of safely away in the garages, so that it will now cause severe parking problems in the street, plus the thieves will be offered an easier opportunity, in breaking into the cars, that are now left in the street instead of safety placed inside the garages.

Consequently without a doubt, the motor vehicle insurance payment will obviously be greatly increased because of this action by these inconsiderate inexperience naive councillors. Other councils throughout Great Britain will now be guided and follow suit.

Effectively, now with a brand new local magnificent policy by our inventive council officials.

Called 'on street parking policy.'

CHAPTER THIRTY-EIGHT

*

Children Can Now Play in the Road

Please believe the above chapter heading, this is absolutely true statement by our local council. Confirming in our local magazine the chronicle June issue 2010 page six, that the children are now allowed to play in the street as long as their use a soft ball. This maybe is a shock to most readers with yet another element in saying a more serious concern, now with increased traffic down a once very quiet cul-de-sac, selected and enjoyed by our family, and many other families in the past, who chose to live in this perfect location all those years ago.

Choosing this area over others, because it was a quiet area with a firm guarantee, secured in the knowledge that the policy background would protect from any building on our small green. This is the main reason we have legislation in this country to safeguard against losing a sound policy background, so we all understood.

This once peaceful area would be interrupted now, with all the children having to avoid the increased traffic while playing in the street, with no play area nearby snatched by the council to build ugly prefabricated cheap houses and flats. With various limited games like running in between the cars and Lorries, chasing after one another, or after a 'soft football.' This is an interesting notice, which will soon appear.

That playing in the street even with a 'soft ball' would be illegal, and any child found playing in the street, would be brought in front of the friendly council committee, to explain why they were found playing in the street damaging the cars and other vehicles, when it is now forbidden.

Because of this damage to the motor vehicles parked in the street, the council are refusing to pay for this damage, stating they are not responsible for this damage. Then who would be responsible and reimburse the owners for all these damaged vehicles'? For the council to officially suggest such a ridiculous statement, proves the irresponsibility of these officials's state of mind. It is not if an accident will occur, with obvious consequences, but how soon before a child is very seriously injured or killed with this increase traffic 24/7, who would be totally responsible, when the inevitable does happen?

The local MP. (No).

The local councillors. For agreeing to the sale of the open space (No).

The planning office (No).

The housing department (No).

Well someone must be responsible for the children's safety. I have an idea, who would be responsible, the local residents who allowed the play area to be taken away so straightforwardly, without any fight. It was certainly worth fighting to keep this recreational play area for now, and for the future. With being passionate with the above, I was prepared to carry out anything in response at not losing this play area.

However, the mainstream of naive residents in the area, assumed that once the council propose a development that's it, throw in the towel.

Stating on a number of occasions 'you could not change the opinion of the council.' Followed by that well known phrase yet again. **'What can you truly do about it?'**

Likewise with all these Bowling Green's throughout the country disappearing into the hands of the developers for a pittance would be another argument against democracy, in dividing the whole community. When will they realise the very serious nature of their actions with a number of serious mistakes including taking this necessary essential play area away from the very young children, who were never considered and included with the planning of this new development.

What will happen if possibly a child is badly injured, or killed now having to resort to playing in the street, where is the choice the children were offered?

The family will need compensation if the inevitable occurred, what sort of compensation could ever be offered, with the above serious incident. You could not even start to estimate an agreed figure of your child or grandchild being badly injured, who will pay? This is like playing Russian roulette, with the children's lives, 'the children have no choice,' but adults do?

Using this simple example, which is easier to understand? Pick any hill in winter with black ice untreated with salt and grit, it is not 'if' a vehicle will skid it's 'when' a vehicle will skid? With the very same scenario, (not if a child is injured, but when).

After being faced, with the above unacceptable situation, you are hit with a remarkable statement from the head of planning office, with his unexpected provocative remark.

A meeting to discuss this proposed development is (wait for it) **'too time consuming'** for the planning office to arrange or even to consider. Now does the above explain. Democracy gone mad?

What have the residents gained above?

Nothing?

What will be gained in the future?

Nothing?

So why should you accept.

Nothing?

An excellent question to ask your local MP. If of course, she is not too busy claiming parliamentary expenses, or lost the seat on the council.

Some of the outrageous lies, from day one with regard to this new development.

1. The single most important extraordinary lie, the council promised to hand back the green to the community after the temporary use by the homeless. That is why it was classified as temporary housing? (Apparently the council officials do not know or comprehend what the word 'temporary' means, it does not mean permanent).

2. The site manager stated at the start of the development, that all of the retrained trees on the working plans would not be cut down. (Evidently proved totally untruth).

3. The housing Manager responsible for the demolishing of all the garages, stated with a straightforward direct lie at the committee meeting, that there was no demand for the garages locally. Additionally, stating that due to unforeseen circumstances? (Both proved to be direct lies).

164

4. Officially the planning application recommendations stated, that the current residents view would not be compromised or overlooked or over dominance, in any way, impacting the neighbouring properties with the new buildings. (This is a direct lie), by the planning office when stated on the planning recommendation as with all planning applications in the past. (Please look for evidence in Chapter 19), as proof of this outrageous lie and disclosure by the planning office.

5. The planning office lied when mentioning there would be no **'significant increase'** in traffic in our street after the development finished. This has proved to be completely contradictory with countless streams of cars and vehicles 24/7.

6. Stating that there would not be a significant difference with the parking in the cul-de-sac, after the development was complete. This has proved another straightforward lie, with constant difficulty, and inadequate parking spaces for our cars and vehicles 24/7 in our street, which was never experienced before the development.

7. After stating that no more trees were to be cut down, five months after the development was completed, over 42 mature trees were cut down adjacent to the development in the lane. (This evidence of this can be seen in Chapter 16).

Subsequently with five unbelievable reasons for this action, by the Guinness Housing Trust.

1.   Firstly, the mature trees were a danger to the new residential buildings.
2.   Secondly, the trees were blocking the light into the buildings.
3.   And thirdly, the trees were interfering with the TV reception.
4.   Fourth reason their vista was unbelievably compromised by the tall trees close by.
5.   Finally the tall mature trees were blocking the sunlight onto the Solar Panels situated on the roofs.

Which was fantastic planning in the first place, what came first the trees or the buildings?
(Like the chicken or the egg situation, which came first)?
An interesting quote below to all council officials.

'If you cannot tell the truth, don't tell a lie.'

CHAPTER THIRTY-NINE

*

Could Have Been Curtains for Me

Must cover an unpleasant topic now, but absolutely necessary, to be included in this book, you will soon understand why, so please be patient while I lead you away briefly from the above development, just for a short spell.

To explain a further excellent example, with democracy gone mad, but with a horrible more sinister twist, and a serious outcome with me still able to discuss and report on it's unfortunate outcome on this occasion with me as the 'Guinea pig,' so to speak. It involves central government right at the top, down to where it hurts at our level, the taxpayers/ratepayers! I will expand further after the main incident.

Quite some years ago, my wife and I before our marriage, had arranged one evening to go to the' Odeon cinema' in Craven Park, Harlesden North West London in the NW10 area, where we both used to live. On taking our seats at the rear, in front of a five-foot hoarding of this once huge Cinema. We had immediately noticed out of 100% of the audience, we were in the minority, only 5% were of white descent English home bread.

Consequently and unbelievably was allowed and ignored by the government of the day to be out of all proportion in just a few years in our town of Brent. This was amazing, and predominately the most overseas visitors from Jamaica, congregated in a cinema audience that I have ever witnessed, after countless visits in the past to this same cinema, which could easy hold as many as 2,000 people and this night was a fall house:

This was exceptional number of foreign people, the type of film and its preview involving white girl and coloured boyfriend, had most likely encouraged this selected audience that was explained, so colourfully. However, ignoring this fact we settled down to watch the film called. (Guess who's coming to dinner) a 1967 Film we had saved up our money that week, it had raving reviews on this film.

The main stars were Sidney Poitier, Spencer Tracy, Katharine Hepburn, also Katharine Hepburn's (niece) Katharine Houghton playing the (girlfriend) and directed by Stanley Kramer. To explain the film briefly, very rich girl, who fancies black boyfriend and invites the boyfriend back to the very large rich parent's house for dinner by the girlfriend, but the snobbish rich parents were in complete shock, and utter surprise to find the boyfriend who was exceedingly smart and quite pleasant, spoke excellent English, but was black.

With only Minutes into the Movie, I was astounded with this annoying early interruption, this man, leaning over the back of the five foot hoarding, with a noticeable strong Jamaican accent.

Accompanied by at least five others of roughly 30years old or thereabouts, not home bread Jamaicans but overseas permanent visitors, much older, you could tell that because they had only started coming over from Jamaica a few years previously. The visitors now well established a foothold in towns such as Harlesden in North West London. Eventually the whole of the Brent area, where the black Jamaicans congregated in mass, were not born here in the United Kingdom.

Nevertheless, were invited in by the government of the time, not integrated in a sensible way witnessed over time when we were living in the area. It very soon was completely out of control, far too many had settled in such a short period, in the same area.

Quite a percentage came in illegally, but ideally, if the government had some serious control on the numbers at the time, it would not have been so bad. This group were in this cinema just to make trouble, which was blatantly obvious; you certainly did not have to attend the Routledge institute of Bleeding Obvious.

Sometimes one person pays to get into the cinema, and then finds prearrange fire door behind the curtain, with a push bar on the fire escape door with no alarm is made exceedingly easy, so others get in without paying. Uniquely, this group of coloured men must have carried out this same procedure many times before. With confidence and no security, it was made exceptionally simple, very much easier to enter without paying.

Soon after the start of the film we were singled out, they started by prodding me, and stating very rude comments which were not complimentary remarks. "What they would like to do with my girlfriend." After telling the man to go away, otherwise I will call the manager, to remove you lot out of the cinema, you felt uneasy also very uncomfortable staying where we were, but without a choice or spare seats nearby.

It was a packed house, as stated earlier predominately overseas visitors that had settled in England in their thousands, with absolutely no control with their numbers, we decided to remain seated; hopefully they will soon go away! Seconds ticked by before the very same comment, "didn't you hear what I said" the same Jamaican repeated his first remark once again, still prodding but with much more force on this occasion?

I said to Janice my girlfriend "stay their I'll return in a minute," while passing this other white guy two seats away, "I asked if he would look after my girlfriend," he had heard most of the earlier comments by the black man, and said he would keep an eye out.

My intention, in going to the manager's office was halted by this same group of Jamaicans, who had position themselves in the very dim light, behind the rear of the five-foot hoarding, blocking, my way to the manager's office. Without uttering a word more than "excuse me," in attempting to squeeze past while making a gap appear.

Immediately without warning, felt a very sharp unanticipated sudden pain in my back, followed soon after by two more, in very quick succession in the very same area, near the Kidney and just above.

My first defensive spontaneous kick at the assailant stopped any further action from this person. I believe he would have surely suffered a very badly damaged knee joint, from the force applied to that first and only successful kick applied just above the kneecap.

It was extremely difficult, feeling sorry for him as he started rolling on the ground screaming like a baby, while not realising at the time the true nature of my back injuries at this stage. The intention as before, was still finding the manager's office, so forward I continued, but the same black man who started this commotion and confrontation in the very first place, was now attacking me from the front and on this occasion with a knife, which I saw too late to avoid in the poor dim light.

Without being aware it went down the left side my face, with some speed from my left eye, down the face ending at my mouth;

167

At the same moment, instinctively my leg was again employed in defence, accurately taking him down with one kick strategy aimed again at the same area top of the knee, which I heard a sudden crack identifiable with a bone being broken.

Consequently, in my normal regular training down at the boxing club each week, will always prove successful in stopping opponents in the street doing any further damage. Besides, in training, it works a treat first time. Used for real, my instructors were correct, in advising the long limb, to carry out the most damage, plus in keeping the opponent at a distance. While looking around very quickly, to see if there were any further attacks from this group of idiots. I could see the first person, who had carried out the stabbing to my back, was being helped by two others away from the area, still screaming like a baby in pain through one of the fire escape doors.

'I almost felt sorry for him also.' The other bloke, who knifed my face, was also speedily being taken away screaming also like a big baby, by the remainder of their group, hurriedly leaving by the same door. Likewise I honesty really did genuinely feel apologetic for hurting him!! After leaving me now holding my face, which was streaming with blood, to stem the bleeding, I held my handkerchief with both hands pressing firmly as my First Aid training came in handy. This must have taken only two minutes in total from the stabbing in the back to their escape out the fire door nearby.

With lots of commotion, including my girlfriend Jan screaming for help, along came the manager trying to take command of the situation at this very late stage. The police did not take very long in getting a grip of the situation, cautiously checking the cinema for further knifemen, after their checks finding many more than a lorry load of knives and other weapons discarded on the floor of the cinema, starting their body search of everyone in the cinema, which was about to be closed indefinitely.

Seriously, I question what is going on with these black people, always carrying all these knives and other weapons' around. We never ever had reason to want to use a knife on anybody; it is not in our culture. The Government at the time invites them into the country to attack us at will, with the true intention of killing somebody without any former provocation; this is unacceptable, and very nearly succeeded in killing me that evening, luck was most certainly on my side that night!

In the meantime, the number of police had gathered around where Jan and I were waiting for the ambulance to arrive. One of the police officers asked me to show him my face, which was still being held quite firmly, by both hands. As the pressure was released slowly and cautiously, on the handkerchief to show the inquisitive officer the injury, the blood streamed out in all directions. Immediately I resumed pressing with both hands applying as much force as previously.

It was difficult not noticing the inquisitive copper had fainted on, and alongside me. With my back feeling quite wet I asked another officer close by who was lifting the other police officer of me, to investigate why my back felt extremely wet. On lifting the clothing he had turned as white as a sheet and was unable to stay, it must have been worse than it felt, "bloody hell."

Luckily, the ambulance crew had arrived just in time and immediately took control of the situation I think just in time as I was on my second length of breaststroke, with the amount of blood loss on the ground, also with this loss, I was now starting to pass out and felt extremely weak all of a sudden.

What interested me more than anything was the reason with the ambulance crew's delay, stating an interesting fact, with hearing the discussion the ambulance crew had with the policeman, was a complete revelation.

They were explaining to the policeman, that by mistake they had gone on another call to the other cinema called the 'Coliseum.' Nick named, '(the flea-pit)' near the Royal Oak pub, which was just down the road from this cinema, they were directed to the (the fleapit) by mistake. Ironically by coincidence, another serious incident occurred simultaneously.

A similar stabbing had occurred involving a white fellow out with his girlfriend like myself, attacked by three black men. Why do these idiots think that this is acceptable, it's our country not theirs? Still the government just ignores all these stabbing at the time, and still these incidents occur on a daily encounter. Why?

CHAPTER FORTY
*
Rivers of Blood

Parliament in the late 60s invited huge numbers of foreign visitors into the country as mention in the previous chapter, astonishing the government also MPs, were not reacting, allowing it get out of control, without any controls as to those invited into the country. Seriously the MPs also the government officials are not the ones, lying on the floor, swimming in a pool of blood. Enoch Powel who was Tory MP in 1968 quoted the above chapter, heading (Rivers of Blood) with direct positive meaning.

Then was sacked by his party, joining the Ulster unionist as MP. Remembering Ted Heath did not take kindly to phrases such as 'Rivers of blood.'

While I was currently doing a few lengths Breaststroke in a pool of my blood, on the Odeon cinema foyer floor. Waiting for the ambulance crew hopefully to stem the blood flowing from a number of orifices, which the foreign visitors decided to make with their weapons, while attacking me for being English why?

As long as the MPs, plus government officials are not directly involved, nicely hidden in central government, until it gets completely out of control: (Well it was out of control then, and nothing has changed since). This is still prevalent today even after all these years, which is unbelievable with no wisdom or understanding, while entering into the 21st century. The answer is so simple, as always;

Ask the visitor why England is essential for them to settle here. If their initial reason is persecution like I keep hearing them say, then stay in your own country and attempt to sort it out, instead of passing this extremely serious problem on to us. We are now at breaking point with far too many serious incidents accruing each day, it can only get worse if nothing fundamentally, is sorted out soon.

With far too many having now arrived; and we are forced to live in cramped isolation, so that the predominately foreign visitors have taken over our entire major towns and cities, overcrowded completely throughout the whole of Great Britain. Without sensible integration into our very small island, you have to be blind not to notice, but extremely silly to allow it to continue.

Any further delay by the ambulance, crew in getting here by just a few extended minutes, and the outcome would have been curtains for me. What with further blood loss, still proving a serious problem, mainly with the back injuries. The ambulance crews, concentration with the bleeding was their immediately concern, and attended to that first which truly saved my life. The very same ambulance crew carried out an excellent job, at stemming the bleeding to my back, giving them 10/10 for their excellent work.

Now feeling the immediate benefit and relief, as soon as they held the pressure, stopping any further blood loss too my back I started feeling the benefit immediately. The same team asked if I was able to keep the both hands holding the handkerchief in place.

Without a doubt, I was able, because being a experienced teacher in first aid, now they were ready to move me into the ambulance with me jokingly, saying you two look after my back, and leave me to attend the front;

They both smiled on hearing that last remark, at least I was still with them, they were happy to agree to this arrangement knowing importantly the statement I submitted that I was an experience first Aider. While remaining conscious, he will allow this understanding but reinstated his commitment to my wellbeing.

Another ambulance crew stopped by to see if help was needed, and lent a hand. This spare driver was used to drive the first ambulance, while the first crew attended to my needs. The more experienced first crewmember was eager to check on my face by now, which I would not release. With his experience touch and confidence, I conceded.

After this quick peak, he made a sound by rounding his lips, and breathing in fast, only an 'experience plumber' would make that sound. (Just a slight pause, before stating you will need a new boiler sir). This indicated immediately, to me the seriousness of what he had seen by swiftly reaching into a steel cabinet and placed another large swab over my handkerchief and taking over the compression from me. Asking the driver how long before we get there. It was only then that I felt very much more confident of my survival and started to relax. While all this commotion was going on all this time.

Poor Jan who was by my side, not able to help in any way, she was very concerned I could see in her beautiful face every time I caught sight of her assuring her I was OK, with tongue in cheek! We had gone though a lot in let us say 30 minutes or so, it seemed very much longer. All week we had been looking forward to seeing this film.

Along with all the rest who came to see the movie that evening, was spoilt by a handful of black inconsiderate idiots. Resulting, that nobody managed to see the film that evening and we still haven't seen the movie to this day!

I was very nearly killed, and still not a racialist, against any immigrates as long as it is well under control, which has left me with a permanent large facial scare, which is still quite prominent, from my eye down to the corner of my mouth. Which has spoiled my good looks over the years? The three stab wounds to my back, which even after all these years, I still have problems with.

The Odeon cinema was closed, that same evening for an indefinite period, and was never reopened accordingly, with inadequate security in the building, the reason given by the police. Now this was meant to be kept brief and to the point, of expressing my opinion, explaining that. **'Democracy gone mad.'**

Continuing years ago, as mentioned previously the MP called Enoch Powell at the time of me being attacked was concerned seriously, with the amount of overseas immigration pouring into this country, without any control with numbers entering Great Britain.

Immigration was in those early days, completely out of control, and the government of the day was turning a blind eye, making no attempt to control this flow of immigrants entering the country, nothing has changed over the intervening 44 years?

Enoch Powell stated a well-known statement of exactly what happened that evening in both 'Cinemas' locally.

'RIVERS OF Blood.' Was he correct?

171

Of cause he was. With being ridicule at the time, but nobody was listening. Incidentally, as mentioned earlier, this evening with two very serious incidents involving stabbings with white people being the victims.

You need to sit up now think very hard, does this explain quite clearly, look around in each major town or city in this country where you live proving exactly that.

'**Democracy has gone completely mad.**' Moreover, needs sorting out urgently.

CHAPTER FORTY-ONE

*

Who is in Charge?

By now with immigration in free fall, the overseas visitors invited not by the British people, but those voted as members of parliament (MPs) to represent the British society with no planning or checks. No one would disagree, with the plan of inviting overseas visitors into the country, but under some very strict control, with limitations on the amount.

Integration carried out in the proper sensible manner, spread more evenly throughout Great Britain, would be quite acceptable and achievable in those early days. Not allowing the overseas visitors to bundled together congregating and settle into the same areas, like ghettos. An area of any town, or city years ago with the majority of white people has now been replaced with densely populated with people from overseas.

Fulfilling and taking a firm hold in these towns/cities, some way from the mainstream of British people who have been forced out. Then also bringing the rest of the extended family, through the back door illegally on most occasions over to stay permanently, which has occurred over many years, and is continuing today out of control, you had to be blind not to have noticed.

Which has proved an impossible situation of too many foreign visitors coming into the country to stay? If proof was needed, take Harlesden NW10 as a fine example of the overall mess, with allowing far too many overseas visitors in where I use to live; I will attempt to keep this brief and to the point.

Very soon after the first visitors arrived here in this country, within a couple of years a house that would have, let's say normally two adults mother and father, plus maybe one or more children. Now changed completely and replaced with a property owner (landlord), who would provide accommodation with no less than twenty-mixed race people, crammed into the lower part of the same house. Then cram the same amount up in the top of the same house once the white occupiers were all forced out.

This is the absolute truth, of what truly happened over a short two-year period in our street. The government officials and all the MPs plus councillors, completely ignoring what was going on. Was repeated, all the way along Dayton Road NW10 where I used to live, also in all the streets in the surrounding area. As the white English people were being forced out, by the intolerable conditions thrown at them, with provocation and nasty remarks each day in passing. Importantly the English people were suffering this discrimination, not the overseas visitors.

Furthermore, with an unfriendly attitude in passing as you walk passed their house, now occupied with overseas visitors, not in a pleasant friendly neighbourly way. The (MPs) were ignoring what was going on, wearing blinkers, with serious consequences affecting the majority of surrounding residents, with positive 'discrimination against the former occupiers.'

All of these properties now sold to the landlords, who instigated the move in the first place, making it unbearable for the former owners, until the owner caved in and was forced out. Witnessing this exodus until I was forced out eventually for the very same intolerable reasons, with a rude awakening, what the (MPs) had started was acceptable for them, but not acceptable for us, the MPs were distancing themselves from this worsening situation, as long as they were not living next door to the above situation.

Throughout Great Britain, over the years using the town of Harlesden as an example, which is in the Brent area of London as mention earlier, shows proof of serious overcrowding with overseas visitors, in all the towns surrounding the Brent area, the very same exodus of Londoners, unbelievable leaving in their thousands.

We were, eventually forced out of our house for the very same reasons as mentioned above, with humiliating heckling, and jeering by the foreign visitors nearby, stating as we were about to leave the area.

"I told you we would get you out eventually", smiling with further rude comments as we were loading the van ready to exit the area. The MPs knew what was happening at the time, and did absolutely nothing in stopping the mass departure of true Londoners who had enough of this humiliation, and left to settle elsewhere well away from their former homes.

When you consider, I had many exceedingly close mates who were coloured, and were absolutely horrified to see what their own kind had done, to my face and back, being highly ashamed at the time! Nevertheless, this did not affect our friendship in any way, we continued to support Queens Park Rangers (QPR), And of course the (gunners) Arsenal, deciding at the last minute which one to visit each week.

On many occasions I can recall being the only white person among a group of let's say ten black mates visiting the pub first, then on to the match. When I announced, to my mates that I was leaving for the reasons mentioned previously, they were extremely upset but what could you possibly do, my mind was made up, it was time to move on and exit London without a choice, shamefully forced out never to return.

Surprisingly, we were the very last white people in Drayton road at the time, disgracefully force out by overseas visitors why? Seriously Why did I need to leave it's my town where I was born. Although I love London and hated the thought of having to leave, the daily abuse we received got to me eventually, and I will never ever return!

To summarise, in Drayton Road well over 200 houses throughout the length of the road, all white people moved out in just over two years, which is outrageous also unbelievable, the landlords were to ones to blame.

Choose at random any town in the London area, firstly what % of the town has more white/coloured people. This book was never meant to dwell into politics. Nevertheless, the evidence and answer into what % is only showing the seriousness of the increasing problem, with foreign overseas visitors now residing in the United Kingdom. We will have to change the name of this country very soon from Great Britain too (Great what) 'Mess' would be my first suggestion? Because of the overcrowding which has occurred over the years? Seriously, this is not a joke! The problem is now impossible to be solved; it's here to stay, and can only get worst. This has to be **'Democracy gone absolutely mad,'** and could have been controlled years ago if the MPs knew how to used their brains.

174

If having a educated guess on the % of White people occupying Harlesden alone, my best guess would possibly be 20% or less. The remainder would be increasing overseas permanent visitors.

In the Brent area overall possibly 30% white the remainder foreign, would be a wild guess covering the whole of the Brent area. Outside London, let us say Luton 40% white possibly less? What about Croydon, with a significant numbers of foreign overseas visitors, even more serious problem than Harlesden. This is madness, and should have been capped; from the start it is now a serious concern over the whole country, this is now proving such a serious problem, I can foresee the white people will then be the considerable minority throughout the entire United Kingdom. (I have as promised kept this brief and to the point).

Returning now to the recreational area on 'Shortmeadow Green.' Noticeably, when I visited well over 250 houses, to muster up support for the campaign against the play area being snatched from us. Most houses visited, the occupier stated with their opening line, also open palms, hunching both shoulders at the same time.

Stating, 'what can you do about it,' that I was wasting my time campaigning against the proposed development. What they hadn't realised, was the tough unforgiving point, that over time let's say some 60years or more, you have an increasing claim and positive common ownership, more than a common right to stay put, and fight for the green, and win by a country mile.

With this being, the most 'important point of this whole argument.' We had a serious 'claim' on this open space and the council should have 'asked not taken.' Only a very few houses visited, considered seriously that the play area was conclusively worth fighting for. 'And hats off, to all those thoughtful genuine fine British people.

The rest deserve this loss of this essential green, and they will live to regret this loss shortly. Until they sit down, and think very soon of the consequences, that the loss of the green is now history, and the developers are now thinking of their next conquest already before even the very first brick is laid on this new development site. This once again is 'democracy gone mad.'

You have to congratulate the local council officials for their tenacity; those who through in the towel, before the first round had started, made the victory extremely easy for the council officials plus developers. The majority stated that any proposal the council propose is not worth campaigning against, because the council have a history of winning, on all other proposed developments unchallenged so far. "WHY"?

We all know why, this country has changed. To suit the weak, who cannot be bothered to fight for what is rightfully theirs. Then they are the first to complain afterwards when it is far too late to do anything about it. (This is completely true);

We are now witness to the police constantly visiting this new development. On one occasion in early January 2012 with countless police vehicles possibly ten vehicles in total, to arrest a number of new occupiers dealing in drugs, this occupier in one of the flats was immediately kicked out after only a few weeks occupation, by the 'Guinness Housing Trust.' Who had done a marvellous job in vetting this person?

175

Yet another person who has also been vetted closely by the 'Guinness Trust Housing' is refused and bared in any of our shops up the road, because of constant stealing?

With yet another visit by the police on another occasion to stop a fight which got out of hand by two new residents, showing damage to the front door glass broken and boarded up afterwards, this damage to the front door, has still not been repaired.

This person was also given his marching orders, and requested to leave. After only a few weeks opening the development, what on earth is this area going to turn out like for the future?

The Guinness Housing Trust, seam not to give a damn, they surely must have vetted the people carefully, examining somebody's background before determining the suitability of those chosen, how did they seriously get it so wrong?

Plus of cause, placing an unacceptable dangerous smelly permanent 'septic tank' positioned only yards from the current local resident's rear gardens.

CHAPTER FORTY-TWO

*

Too Late to Change Your Mind

After losing the play area, it certainly again surprised, and amazed me. Curiously, the same majority of people mentioned earlier, who stated the green was not worth fighting for, suddenly realised it was worth keeping, but was far too late in saving the important open recreational space from being sold off to the developers.

The dominance and strength the planners had shown, was far too clever for these residents, who did not stand a chance, against all the untrustworthy performances, and constant lie's you have read about throughout this book. In selecting the correct seasonal timing, mentioned previously to propose a new development when most people were on their holidays, and were unable to help with this campaign. This is another extreme classic display of 'Democracy gone absolutely mad' and I feel that this next incident, should be included in this chapter, and should not be excluded from this book.

A group of Muslim extremists, (please excuse the pun) at this time of the year, were walking on extremely thin ice. Some time ago in Luton, the soldiers from the 2nd Battalion Royal Anglia Regiment, who were marching through the town of Luton? Surrounded by crowds of well-wishers, who were extremely proud to see them marching through their town. Were horrified to find the soldiers placed in a situation with this large group of Muslim extremists, all on state benefits and handouts, from the government, holding up placards one stated 'Islam will dominate the world' another 'freedom can go to hell.' What is more insulting in a public place, screaming out towards the Soldiers 'Rapist', 'Murderers'? Which I have no understanding of why?

If I was their company commander, in charge of that very proud group of soldiers: My decision on that particular day without hesitation, would have been to halt the battalion, turn and face this group of foreign people, detain, each and everyone, then place them were they deserve without delay. In an aircraft, and return them back to their own country immediately, no questions asked. In any other country throughout the world, they would be placed in prison and the keys thrown away.

On the 11th January 2010 at Luton magistrates court, where they were found guilty of screaming 'rapist' and 'murderers' at the soldiers mentioned above who were marching through Luton town centre.

Five, were given conditional discharges, for shouting 'baby killers' and 'terrorists' and waving placards at hundreds of soldiers returning from Iraq. Outside the court, they were surrounded by a mob of supporters and boasted, they would do the same again. Furthermore, on state benefits would prove evidence once more. 'That Democracy has gone completely mad' are all the MPs in this country as soft as butter, every indication shows this to be true. When one considerers other factors with 'democracy gone mad.'

Why is the England football team manager not English? What truthfully are we proud of when we say we are British? When presently all our banks are foreign owned?

Also our energy suppliers, Gas, Electric, Water plus coal, providers are all found to be foreign owned, and getting away with charging outrageously high prices. Most, English football premiership teams have foreign managers, followed by a great percentage of the teams in the premiership have an overwhelming amount of overseas football players why?

Give me £6million in wages and I will justify this fee by selecting my team that would beat any other team in the world. Example Arsenal, with most of the team consisting of French players for countless years, with a French manager of all things, which I cannot accept, more of an insult to all their supporters. I will only resume supporting the gunners with an English manager, Tony Adams possibly, would be my first choice because he would inspire the players like when he was their captain over many years.

Additionally, with all Arsenal players being British, by the way, Tony take some good advice when being interviewed as the Arsenal manager, hold your head up and show you are proud. Each time I have seen you speaking on (TV) you are always looking down which shows considerable weakness instantly. (You learn about this when boxing, always hold your head up, you will certainly see were the next punch is coming from).

Excellent news from down under as I am typing this page, we have just pulled off a marvellous win over Australia, furthermore won back the ashes after some 24years. Now that is something to be proud of well-done Andrew Strauss, shown in today's newspaper the headlines showing on the 29th December 2010. 'It's gone barmy down under, as sensational England side have retained the urn' congratulations, this is only the tip of the iceberg. What is underneath? You may wonder where this is leading.

Consequently, we lost against the Germans recently in the world football championships all of the British people would like to know what is going on, with so many foreign players playing in our football premierships teams. Is the fundamental reason our game is not up to scratch, and has no chance of improvement until serious changes are made, you don't have to be a brain surgeon to work that out, but it would help?

Does (United Kingdom) own anything in this Country, what truthfully are we proud of anymore, when we say we are proud to be British? Let us now change this situation and have something to be proud of.

The old boy Ron Harrington, who joins me each week to play snooker down at the CIU club, is also a staunch Arsenal supporter like me, would dearly love the return of all true English players, plus English managers in our teams? It is also expensive to expect pensioners like us to pay these colossal prices just to watch a game of football nowadays, also for the Football Association who is made up of ex players from the past, insisting we have a foreign manager in charge of the England team is preposterous. Would the likes of Germany, France, Italy, Spain, and countless other countries ever consider introducing a foreign manager, managing their own team?

Not likely, seriously what must these other countries think of our football association decision, some years ago; to look aboard for a manager is unthinkable.

And highly embarrassing for the whole of this country to except all those years ago, when the unthinkable actually occurred along with paying these foreign managers £6million in salaries. Without success over the years has proved justification for not choosing a foreign manager.

178

Before leaving football and covering another interesting subject, the very latest fantastic news, our local football team was through into the fourth round of the F/A cup.

After beating, Newcastle united 3/1. This is payback time, after we went out of the cup 13 years ago in 1998 playing against the very same team. To an Alan Shearer disputed 'goal', which did **'not'** cross our goal line, the linesman should have gone to 'speck-savers,' what a berk!

Could I drift away from football to mention an interesting episode while working for British Telecom some years ago, in connection with complete trust and abilities of a fellow worker, Norman Penn while working on underground cable maintenance, repairing telephone cables?

On this particular day while working in the countryside well out in the sticks, a 50-pair cable was faulty with a great deal of customers without service due to this faulty buried cable. The point of mentioning this episode of my (BT) experience you may find most amusing concerning our inspector Harry (G). Who was in charge of us engineers' with a famous quote repeated each morning when inquiring as to the whereabouts of the location of a buried faulty cable?

Allow me explain, Norman the other engineer (a spurs supporter) working alongside me that day, had located the fault and the location of the dig-out with confidence on countless other occasions in the past, with success over many years of experience, and could be trusted unquestionably? After two hours digging, the hole was approximately three feet deep, three foot wide, and six feet in length.

In four hours, we had achieved six foot deep, by four wide, and eight foot in length, it was now time to pack up and make safe for the day, and resume the next day.

Continuing from yesterday to repair this faulty telephone cable, after a further four hours the hole was now down to ten feet deep, by six feet wide, and over eight foot in length. With great difficulty in removing the earth over the top of the massive hole, with bucket loads of earth and steps in the hole to make it easier to accomplish the removal of all this earth, to get down to the buried joint. Any other pair of engineers would have given up by now and thrown in the towel, Norman, along with myself was confident with the location of the buried joint.

Along with a concrete indicator, I had noticed but withheld this information from Norman before the start of the dig. It was lying hidden in the long grass that the engineers place nearby, when the cable is first laid in the ground years ago, most probably knocked over by a lorry or tractor at sometime.

While having a break at lunchtime our inspector 'Harry G' arrived to see how we were getting on with finding the fault, astonished by the size of the hole we had excavated, stating that he would get the digging gang to further excavate if we were sure of our location of the fault.

Within an hour of their arrival, the gang had reached the concrete lid, of the 6ft coffin now twelve feet down from the surface. (The name coffin) with reference to the type of cover placed over the joint to protect the joint.

We were spot on the nail; the joint was as suggestion by Norman right in the middle of this vast excavation.

Now here comes that famous quote first thing in the morning as expected the inspector Harry (G) with his words of wisdom announcing to all those within ear shot. "I knew it would be their boy."

Looking over at Norman after the anticipated quote was mentioned we both smiled, but I was smiling also with the knowledge and disclaimer of the concrete marker, which was kept a secret from Norman, and still remains lying in the extremely long grass a short distance away, sorry Norman!

Lesson learnt from the above example; always trust the bloke you are working with explicitly, 'well most of the time.' (Even if he happens to be a Spurs supporter).

Wishing all those old engineers who may by chance read this book, good luck hope you are all keeping well and in good physical condition, do you recall that same quote of Harry's each day?

"I knew it will be their boy."

CHAPTER FORTY-THREE

*

Change Policy Background

Before continuing, may I apologises for neglect in not mentioning so far, of the nice neighbourhood who share the loss of the play area unjustly taken from us indefinitely. On what was called 'Shortmeadow Green,' in general, just an open common space, which the entire local community used to enjoy.

Was altered and affected significantly, some 20 years ago, when the inconsiderate council officials initially took the green from us, stating that central government needed to use our small field for a while, even with an important policy background. The reason given at the time, for temporary housing now acting as evidence similar to the Berlin wall, which also lasted over 20years, dividing what was once a flourishing lively exciting local community, now gone forever and missed by all.

Acting and currently remains like the Berlin Wall, dividing the whole community in two deliberately by the fault of our extremely greedy council officials. Ironically, only those people over 20 years old would appreciate this fact, which divided significantly both east and west estates, splitting apart our friendly neighbourhood, and local vibrant friendly community. Each of the residents came together as communities do, each day on the green.

The council officials completely discarded the rulebook, plus importantly government guidelines by taking the gloves off and fighting dirty, the background policy with serious local concerns with the planning application, was also torn up and discarded. These councillors I believe will answer to the consequences soon, when the muck hits the fan. Unaware of the local resident's emotions with a broken promise, also secured with this official Policy background, which protected against any residential housing being, placed on our recreational open space.

Noticeable the same policy was held on the council documentation and database some years previously, stating that our Play area had an important policy background history as I have mentioned previously, that the green would not ever be considered under any circumstances for residential housing, which could not be clearer. This council, has now reneged on this promise, and very cunningly and most underhandedly reversed this admission to the background policy, without anyone locally knowing of this change on their records. Now let us try explaining briefly, until we get round to 'Hazel Jones' house, my close Neighbourhood which takes some beating.

You would not believe how well we all have gelled together over many years; a number of neighbours were directly affected, with the extraordinary behaviour of the council taking our very small play area. These families decided at tremendous financial loss to themselves, with selling their houses and reluctantly moved away.

Electing, to move away regrettably, because of the devaluation of their properties, plus the developer has placed a (septic tank) a cesspit placed yards from their properties, which has to be emptied each month by a tanker, you know when it needs emptying by the horrible stench in our neighbourhood which is totally unacceptable.

181

This same arrangement with placing a septic tank was also unacceptable with the temporary bungalows, over 20year period, needing to be emptied often, at the very least each month. Effectively by the loss of this recreational area for the very young children, replaced with these unacceptable atrocious buildings are now compromising their vista.

I would have followed but the loss of £35,000 devaluation on my house, caused by the placement of the ugly temporary bungalows on our green, put a halt to our family leaving at the time. Not forgetting importantly 95% of the houses are privately owned in our neighbourhood, residents were fully committed to repaying mortgage's over 20/30 years.

Which was not taken into account by the planning office, when first deciding on the proposal for this development, which has truly devalued seriously all the properties in the area. Some like in our situation, have paid off their mortgage's over a great number of years, but cannot understand or accept the devaluing of our properties once again, because of this permanent new development has taken our small open space indefinitely?

Asking how the close is when you meet up with any of the eighteen former families occasionally, saying quite truthfully, they left because of the loss of open play area nearby.

Regrettably would love to return, because of past wonderful joyful memories, some have seriously regretted the move. However, never recovered the devaluing of over £35,000 on their properties at the time, and had to purchase accordingly. Nevertheless, on hearing of the council had reneged, on a promise that the green was not being handed back, were pleased with their earlier decision to move when they did. Another extremely silly personal situation concerning the way authorities treat the taxpayer can be summed up with this next wonderful specific example, again without consultation or debate!

Many years ago, the county council decided unwisely that a main road would be placed only yards from our rear garden fences, along with a roundabout set on the junction a few meters from my rear garden, with a high mask lamp situated in the centre of this roundabout, approximately 80 meters in height.

With these lamps switched on each evening, as we entered our rear garden from my house, all our family members had to shield against the brilliant light emitting from the five lamps shining into our garden, which I feel was completely unacceptable intrusion, again without any consultation or debate.

Therefore on a number of occasions, wrote an extended letter to the county council, inviting them to come and view this unexpected infringement, on my family's privacy.

Personally my special interest has always been passionate with looking at the sky on a clear night, especially in the winter months, which was now impossible, because of this high mask lamp with five bright lamps now situated and positioned so close to my rear garden. The following letter was sent to the authorities at the time, showing a negative attitude towards this serious problem. This letter was for the attention of a 'fine spark' called Mr WG Doolittle.

Customer Service Officer.

My Ref: NH/WG/13670.

You may recall sometime ago, with our last correspondence, which I requested also (pleaded) on a number of occasions for either yourself or one of your field engineers or both, to visit our property and view the high mask lamp from my families perspective.

This request was refused directly, without any consideration of my families feelings with the following concerns. For you Mr 'Doolittle,' and your engineer to view the unbearable, unnecessary, unacceptable brilliance, the high mask lamps are currently emitting locally into my rear garden, without the opportunity or a meeting to consult or debate this serious issue.

The main reason I addressed this letter to the (customer service officer), was never meant to be funny, or in any way sarcastic. It was to remind you that you are responsible in offering a service to the ratepayer, who is fully entitled to this service.

Over a period, and on four separate occasions, I have invited senior councillors in town, followed by other local councillors to view the lamps unacceptable brilliance.

The reaction each councillor carried out while visiting our property was also to shield the brilliance the lamps were emitting with their hands held to their forehead, on entering. Each visitor on entering the rear garden recited roughly the same comment.

"Wow" "that is bright, and surely is unacceptable, followed by how long have you put up with this, why have you not brought this to our attention before now." (I did when the high mask was first installed some years ago), without any response, after writing countless letters to the local councillors plus the county council complaining about this sudden intrusion, which was completely ignored on each occasion.

This shows Mr Doolittle not only patience, also tolerance on my behalf, and our family over all those years, you can appreciate my annoyance with your attitude you showed some time previously, stating that the problem was far too difficult, also impossible for you and your team to resolve with an accurate assessment, while super glued to your office chair. You are paid a fantastic huge salary each year to carry out a service to the public which I feel you failed to offer.

Only a short while ago I made contact with your department once again, and was received by an extremely pleasant gentleman call, Mr Steve Pedigrew, who was sensible enough, unlike yourself to consider an essential home visit. Which has resolved successfully, this impossible problem to our satisfaction, cheaply, plus conclusively, without your negative attitude towards solving problems?

Steve brought down an exceedingly tall gentleman called Tim, an experienced street light engineer. I did not catch his surname nevertheless both gentlemen's remarks were the same as the councillors previously. Tim remarked jokingly "we should send you a bill for the light source we are providing freely." He along with Steve needs an addition to their salaries, for offering a supreme service, which you were unable to provide or even contemplate. They both followed my well-used remark and quote; that I have followed over the years, when faced with a difficult or impossible problem to solve. I think it would be to your advantage, and an excellent idea for you to possibly remember also consider for all future impossible problems. When approaching any difficult or impossible problem.

(1) Try firstly to get over it.
(2) If that fails, try going round it.
(3) Failing both of the above attempts, go under it.
(4) Next attempt to go through it.
If all of the above fails to solve the problem, then find another way?

This has always been successful for me in the past, and on this occasion appreciation to both Tinny Tim, also Steve Pedigrew, who was extremely successful in solving this difficult, impossible problem, to a satisfactory conclusion, for me and my family with less brilliance emitted down into our garden.

May I finish on a final note which may surprise you, I am not a councillor, or an (MP), also nobody of any importance with lots of money or influence.

Nevertheless, having just completed this book and considered seriously with including this above situation, and hope you might learn from the manuscript.

Please read this book, it refers a great deal with the way those in authority; treat disrespectfully taxpayers who pay huge salaries to those 'bright sparks' in authority for occasionally doing absolutely nothing.

Just as your name implies, you 'do little' in providing a service of any kind to the public, while your backside is super glued to your office chair!

CHAPTER FORTY-FOUR
*

Our Close Neighbourhood

Again, we return to our neighbourhood, starting with the person who has put up with me since 1968 in that memorable year we got married. (I cannot remember a thing, it is a blur). She has kept her good looks and has weathered over the years like a prefect wine. I could not have survived, without her very bossy control.

With understanding straight away who is boss, and to prove this I carry out all the washing up and other necessary chores around the house daily, only to keep her happy and content. (Bonus points lads).

Just to give me a rest, she used to work locally, but recently gave up this idea that I should have a rest from her, now in the autumn of our lives, has taken to coming shopping with me! Mainly, as I start thinking, the shed needs a good clear out, or contemplate other worthwhile jobs we men find to do.

If she was not so gorgeous, I would have left her years ago. (Now lads, you could not beat that as a chat up line, could you!) Use it wisely or think up a more apt, statement each day, you find it puts them off, and puts a smile on their beautiful face.

What I really cannot get my head round, is this concept that is now accepted as normal, living with a partner rather than choosing someone to get married too. Which seems so insecure but is now out of fashion to get married? It is perhaps simple to understand, that it is vastly too expensive to commit to marriage these days. This shows my age drifting away from the subject; now let us get back before more grey hairs appear.

My next-door neighbour on leaving my house is a perfect neighbour; she is a quiet, well-spoken woman with her two growing up lads. You could not wish for better neighbours, who I would not swap, are exceedingly quiet, never in all the years they have lived next door, neither of us had any complaints and would not change this arrangement, the very best. Unfortunately has decided to leave and sold her house regrettable because of the unacceptable new development.

Years ago as you turn the coin, it was a completely different story in this same house when my children were very young. In this same house 'Jerry' the husband an Irish builder by trade, would go off to the pub after work, and you knew he had returned because the piano (Joanna) would spring into life.

Quite loudly for all to endure, showing absolutely no respect for anybody, for up to two hours or more, 'if of cause I aloud it.'

Each evening, or sometimes-early morning, would be the same, knocking on his door loudly because my children needed some sleep, and of course my Wife and I, needed to be up for work at half past six in the morning. He was half-deaf or because he was playing too aggressively. I would equal the loudness with trying to stop this raging idiot, with his daily (or nightly) entertainment! This is when you appreciate and respect the alternative, and end up with excellent good neighbours.

His wife Joanne in the end locked the front door. 'She' like us, had just about had enough, and could not put up with the early morning entertainment anymore, (I never paid him for this entertainment by the way). And with me joining in the racket did not improve matters with me banging on their front door, which was out of tune to his piano playing.

She was the complete opposite, very kind considerate and understanding person, nice to talk to and we both liked her a lot, in the end, he took the hint and left.

Nevertheless, would return a few times a week after a few drinks up the pub, with forgetting that his wife had closed the door on him, with the familiar serenade; in the early hours trying to attract the attention of his wife, who would refused to allow him in.

It was so unfortunate the way it turned out so quiet in the end, unfortunately he was suffering with cancer and the inevitable happened very soon after, I felt very sorry for his wife and Son Tony who was a work colleague, working at (BT) with me for a few years.

Regrettably he followed his Dad a few years later suffering the same with cancer; he fought well but lost the battle at a very young age. The cancer had returned after some five years, but unfortunately he lost the fight, and passed away without any pain, we are still in contact with his wife Joanne.

Continuing round the close, our next neighbour, is also very friendly whom again I would not change as a neighbour, over the years she has been our friend and continues this friendship? We have over the years taken advantage with her Son, who often visits his mum. He has an unsigned contract over countless years as our local plumber, the very best, and lucky to be able to call upon his services, with a number of emergences over the years. An excellent plumber and the salt of the earth, would not tell him this to his face otherwise he would put up his rates, but if you need to discuss non-urgent work you have to chat his mum to get his attention.

This same house some years previously, housed some of the worst neighbours any neighbourhood could do without. For some years, the council would place neighbours from hell in her house we were very pleased not to repeat this episode. When you have for a while experienced very bad unsociable neighbours, which the council have to move them from one area to the next, you most certainly except with open arms excellent neighbours like Jill. Our concern as with the temporary housing on our very small play area, over 20 years was a revelation.

For us now to anticipate the outcome with this new development, which is on a permanent basis now, we experienced some undesirable neighbours over that extremely long 'temporary' period. Who stayed for a while in the prefabricate bungalows placed on the green over the years? Most were OK but all you need is just a couple of neighbours from hell turning up, and you put up with the cards you have been dealt with, or move.

The council are sometimes in pursuit, and looking for a hiding places where difficult neighbours from hell could be placed, hopefully not choosing here on this new current development. Already with the new development only 6 months from opening the police have regularly visited, one person was dealing in drugs and has been thrown out of his flat.

followed soon after with yet another serious incident where a second person was also asked to leave. It has only recently surfaced, that yet a third occupier has been barred from all the local shops for thieving!! One can only guess how the people were seriously vetted?

186

Progressing onto my next neighbour, who is a hair stylist and for years has cut my wife's and my daughter's hair, plus presently our grandchild Kai. She has been exceedingly happy since a successful birth of a lovely Son; you can see her overwhelming sense of enjoyment in her eyes since the birth. Moreover, she has not found time to land back on earth since, or to get back to work, she is busy enough with her new arrival. We are all overjoyed with her recent bundle of joy. Proceeding further round the close, is a person who is quiet and we have found him to be an excellent and wonderful neighbour, with a big smile and the usual chat in pasting each day.

Next Mr & Mrs Horn whom I nickname 'Mr Blower' after his surname, another sufferer like me interested with golf and plays a good game. Who have both shared the close with us for well over 45 plus years, their two children were great friends, with my three children? Always in our back garden each day, also played together each day over on our open common recreational space getting up to mischief and enjoying themselves.

Mr Horn would on occasions test my home made wine from time to time. I must mention before going round to the next neighbour, concerning a surprised letter from the council official regarding the garage they are renting.

How would you have reacted after receiving a classic invitation by the local council surprisingly to vacate your garage at very short notice of only three days, is highly questionably when you firstly consider this is a monthly agreed contract?

Both Mr & Mrs Horn, who received a very urgent notification, along with others locally, had received this very same correspondence requiring immediate action, this appalling treatment from Mr, Day the housing manager with reference to the renting of the local garages, which the council classify as (off street parking). The contents of this ridiculous letter stated without concern or compassion demanding that you must vacate your garage without hesitation.

'Due to unforeseen circumstances.' Now how can it truly be possible to be unforeseen when the council are attempting to turn a brown field site into a free fall site illegally of cause, by demolishing all but four garages out of 51? Replaced by six horrendous houses which are clearly not in keeping with the other properties locally, looking remarkably like a warehouse/prison. (Seen in Chapter 19).

Knowing these facts a full 12 months previously is amazing to be classed as "unforeseen circumstances."

CHAPTER FORTY-FIVE

*

Mr. Day's Knighthood

Relentless appalling treatment by this same housing manager is understandably unacceptable, with the letter just mentioned, received by a number of our close neighbours, when you consider firstly the letter was received on Friday informing our neighbours to vacate their garages at extremely short notice on Monday. **'Due to unforeseen circumstances.'**

Continuing further with the letter, which Mr Horn received, you must take over another garage approximately 300yards up the hill from your old garage block, if we do not hear from you within the next three days. We will assume you are not interested with the alternative garage on offer, and your old garage will be demolished, and your current rental agreement will terminate forthwith.

Any council, offering a long serving tenancy that has no history of non-payment, or late payment offering this above unacceptable notice, remembering that there are strict rules within the rental agreement, which applies both ways. With regards, to renting the garage over all these years, with a contracted, 'monthly' rental agreement, with only three days notice! Is highly questionable also, it is unbelievable, breaking all the rules laid down when creating a legal or moral obligation and contract.

When sifting through the contract it states quite clearly that a months' notice must be given to the tenant, and likewise the tenant must follow this agreement of one month's notice by letter to the council. This is not the only sufferer of Mr Day's actions; I among with a great number of others without a choice, had to move some distance up the road and had to accept a garage in the other block.

Weeks before, a number of other local garage owners stated while visiting our local pub up the road, they too had received the very same standard letter, to vacate their garages in the same garage block at very short notice, with no if's or butt's had to vacate at extremely short notice, were also treated in the very same appalling manner by this same housing manager. Mr Day will very soon receive his very special award.

Maybe the Queen may even consider seriously an (MBE or OBE or possibly you guessed it a 'Knighthood.' Now that would be more appropriate, for this person to be 'Knighted' and a certain promotion to chief executive in no time, for his outstanding treatment to the local residents.

Again, this is the principal reason this book your reading was published to highlight, and to show the rest of the country the way councils treat their local citizens, certainly I bet in your town you must be treated in the very same disrespectful manner. It would be impossible to make this up, this is really happening in the 21century.

Their sole aim is once all the garages are emptied and vacant. The site reverts into, and is classed as a Brownfield site, then declassified as a free fall site, which means that land has become available and is suitable for redevelopment.

Mr, Day or should we start calling him "Sir Knight" in advance, who stated at the committee meeting quite openly a 'porkpie' that there is no demand locally for these same garages, which is utterly untrue and a direct, lie!

As mention before with as many as fifteen locals, I include myself on that long list that has a need of a garage (off street parking) nearby, this is why he should be Knighted I would be first to highly recommend. "Sir Day." Wait if you can as I continue round the close to Mr&Mrs Steal's house, as the treatment gets extremely serious with regard to both being handicapped Mr. Day's actions or should I say Sir Knight (excuse the pun). So hold your breath and please no smiling promise!

The next house on the start of the close is Tony and his dear wife, and their three grown up daughters, one of his daughters has just handed Tony and his wife a granddaughter in May 2010. Tony used to work at (BT) with me some years ago, where we became very close work mates, and used to attend swimming training with our local swimming club, in the early mornings, and I do mean early mornings. For quite a while just to keep fit and swim in the masters competitions throughout the years, like Tony living next door to me years ago another BT work colleague.

Have you noticed three of us all with the same first name 'Tony.' Years ago when at work, out of approximately 150 workmates in the BT depot, 25 had the same Christian name 'Tony' it was murder when Tony's name was called out. Those of us sharing the same Christian name would all look round to see which one needed to take notice on that occasion. In our close, two more with you guessed it with the same first name Tony!

Just as the start of 2010, Tony had a bit of a scare on his 50th Birthday with sudden serious pains to his chest; he had to go into our local hospital for a few days for checks. Hoping it does not prove too serious, after further tests should be OK.

Returning once again to my house and looking left, a close neighbour over time who we have a great deal of respect, who for some time was also not too well, and unfortunately treated for the Big (C) We all hope she will stay clear after treatment, hoping for a successful outcome for the future, good luck. While in the early days of her treatment to clear up this frightening devastating illness. I used to help with cleaning her car and other helpful tasks praying for fine result very soon, now her son is back living with her and her family have pulled together for the future which is fantastic.

Unwelcome concern in our Close. Before carrying on round the close, let me mention something that had seriously concerned me, about the happenings over a couple of years in the past. My main concern was thought to be extremely serious, serious enough for the health and safety to be involved with.

When you consider Jerry & his son, passed away with cancer, also John at number No11, another gentleman at No 9. And three others all within a very short worrying period, in total eight people in our small close out of twenty houses, all with same on their death certificate 'cancer', is of some concern and worry.

Would you have good reason, to start worrying like I did, faced with the same serious predicament in your near neighbourhood? At the time, and in secret from any of my other neighbours, I contacted a senior person at the department of health and safety, with my deep felt concerns.

189

With immediate attention, tests were carried out and without a known cause, it was thought that the lead Water pipes supplying the area which may have a barring, but without concrete proof! These lead water pipes were immediately changed throughout the close with plastic, noticing that replacement to all the lead pipes supplying utilities later followed throughout the whole town?

Asking the officer in the health department, am I next or is someone going to look closely into this problem, which is causing all these questionable deaths. Worryingly it seems that the problem could have stemmed from the 'lead' water pipes as the strongest contender, which served the area for many years.

After the new plastic run of pipes, replacing the old lead water supply, it was not conclusive but no further noticeable fatalities added to the problem. Checked each day on 'waking' and I am still here thank God, it was extremely worrying at the time; you could not be sure whose turn was next. How many more fatalities' needed in this very small close, before it becomes a very serious problem to act upon?

Now leading on towards the next house, is a young woman, who has three Daughters and one Son, and extremely fantastic news, she is now a nanny with a grandchild to care for in late May 2010. All her children were taught to swim by myself when much younger, unfortunately as I happen to be their Swimming Teacher at the swimming club and also with their school swimming lessons.

It was always good fun, with lasting memories; their children always enjoyed the swimming lessons. I had attempted on a number of occasions to drown them all, but without success, I suppose health and safety would have been concerned, because I don't think its legal is it? In addition, their mum would not offer me enough money at the time!

Margaret and yet another Tony next. It should have been named Margaret & Tony close. (At one time, in the close would you believe it, there were no fewer than six Tony's and six Margaret's then as one would leave yet another would arrive, it was uncanny.

This next house along used to belong to very close friend of ours Ada. Who unfortunately lost her husband John to cancer many years ago? She has down-sized, and moved nearby in a lovely flat, which she finds manageable and very much smaller for her; she keeps it spotless, and fortunately has the most wonderful neighbours who keep an eye out for her;

Unfortunately she has had a number of falls recently, injuring herself seriously and with some concern to her family; she has now safely entered a local nursing home and hopefully she will be looked after, by the staff and safely out of harms way.

190

CHAPTER FORTY-SIX

*

Long Weekend Away with Hazel

Against my better judgement and understanding, the next neighbour, Mr and Mrs Jones. Richard's wife Hazel is the most domineering woman in the world, moved into our neighbourhood when Ada left, since arriving it has been a nightmare for all the local residents worried, if her front door opens as you pass by her house.

Even our postal worker David is hesitant when opening the front gate, which has a noticeable rather loud squeak on opening. Hazel I feel should be reported to the local Police, with the way she treats her poor husband Richard, and poor Harry their dog, even her daughter feels sorry for her dad. Who looks as if a golfing holiday from her would do him the world good?

We should be forced to play at least one game of golf each week, whether we like it or not. As you may have guessed by the last statement, I get on well with the poor old boy, nevertheless try to avoid Hazel if possibly when invited to one of Hazels tirelessly (Soiree) confrontational weekly afternoon tea's.

Stating that the local mayor or local dignity, had phoned to announce an urgent important meeting very soon which she has to attend. Even on one memorable occasion we choose to take both away. For a long weekend, Richard would have to bring Hazel with him, 'why' to one of those 'Warner holiday' breaks. I really shouldn't' tell you what happened because one of the staff at 'Warner's' named 'Tony' is presently serving time in a special hospital, with serious problems in not knowing his own name and other such simple tasks. 'He now needs special care 24/7 for life:' Because of his encounter with 'Hazel' on that very short break away at the weekend.

All right, you forced me, but do show some concerned for poor Tony, in that special hospital. I was selected to drive, with losing the toss with Richard. On a number of occasions on our way down to Hayling Island, in Hampshire with Hazel in the back alongside my poor wife Jan. She would break into involuntary comments like "mind the bus," or "watch out for that cyclist" just like in the (TV) programme.

'Keeping up Appearances.' however, she is somewhat worst, in real life which you will hear about soon and judge for yourself.

Eventually we arrived at our destination on Hayling Island, avoiding all buses and cyclist and other imaginary obstructions in the way, while Hazel was still busily chatting to the Wife. On arrival, you find the reception area, in the vicinity standing close by to the woman at the reception with a welcome smile was the unfortunate 'Tony,' who was a normal looking chap.

With most likely a driving licence, past his lifeguard proficiency 25 metre certificates, also certificates on rifle shooting, along with proficiency with archery, possibly other proud passes on his 'CV' which looks most impressive.

After the receptionist had carried out the welcome details and handed the keys over for our apartment, she smiled and introduced the person standing next to her with that equally welcoming smile, "this is Tony."

"Hello, if you would be interested in any of our sporting activities such as shooting arrows into targets, or rifle shooting or other sports, Tony will assist even if it is your first attempt; do not be afraid to have ago."

Hazel was truly even at this very early stage, mesmerized and fixed on poor young innocence Tony, who was showing the normal interest towards any new customer being very helpful as he spoke to our group of four in general. "Shall we put you all down for the rifle shoot at ten O'clock tomorrow morning, also the archery in the afternoon, at three O'clock, which is your preference?" "Both" said Hazel immediately before he had a chance to say, right then.

Poor fellow he hadn't realise what lay ahead, neither did both my wife and myself but tomorrow is 24 hours away, so let's settle in and make ourselves comfortable for this evening, and have some fun.

After the evening meal which was excellent, and a few drinks later to lubricate the places that needed lubricating, delighted to be resting up after our drive, now settled down, and watching the enjoyable evening's entertainment laid on. This weekend was dedicated to Elvis Presley lookalike, first showing tomorrow evening?

Hazel, was a lifelong nuttier with anything to do with Elvis Presley. After the journey down, it was time for bed so "good night both, see you at breakfast." With my wife stating, "your with me not Hazel" "oh sorry."

In the morning, I knocked on the door to Hazel and Richards apartment; the door flung open, you couldn't help noticing the way she was dressed in sporting gear not forgetting her handbag, "are you ready for the off."

After having a good hearty full English breakfast together, we glanced at the site map and made our way in good time, down to where the rifle shooting was being held. On arrival, there was a gathering of approximately eleven others interested in the sport, and all very enthusiastic and eager to take part.

First question to the group in general was "hands up those of you who have never done any shooting before." A number of individuals including Hazel, indicated being a complete novice, and were extremely keen to be involved in the enjoyable new interesting experience. Tony went slowly and carefully, though the safety procedures and covered all aspects of safety, including most that can go wrong when dealing with first timers, using the weapon that is so unfamiliar to them. He had not encountered on any one like Richards other half before, a new experience to add to his (CV).

Continuing with the safety talk; for instants "if the Rifle malfunctioned or you may have forgotten to take the safety catch off," showing the entire group, present where the safety catch was on the weapon.

"Please remember under no circumstances, do you turn around like this; holding the weapon stating it does not work, while still pressing on the trigger at the same time."

You have only one guess, as to who was suffering from selective memory loss, and was the only person in the group who did not understand fully, the above safety talk.

She was still mesmerised with Tony's good looks. Each person scheduled to shoot was enjoying the new experience. Each had shot five lead pellets into the target in front, some very good surprising shooting, excellent results.

Including my lovely wife Janice, whom I think was extremely lucky, beginner's luck I would say, but was never brave enough to say that to her face. While showing me her outstanding results, from her first target, from 25 yards, and wind assisted, she had a perfect arc with each pellet into the bull's eye, less than the size of a fifty pence piece now that was showing off don't you think, that was lucky or what? These were only her practice shoots to get the feel of the weapon!

Now for the people who have never touched a rifle before, including none other than her 'Highness' Hazel, who choose to be last in their group because she was an extremely '(shy introvert person)' to the firing line, on her own because of the odd number of clients selecting to shoot. Causally Tony placed the five pellets in a small round steel pellet lid, just as he had carried out on a thousand occasions before.

The good lord up above was the only one knowing what was going to happen next, in fairness should have consulted with poor Tony with some sort of warning, any warning would have been helpful. Breaking the rifle in two was too difficult a task because with most women also some men, the spring on the weapon was amazingly strong. Consequently, they needed assistance with the technique with breaking the weapon in too, followed by loading the pellet into the gun with being unfamiliar with the loading procedure of the weapon.

Hazel handed Tony her handbag, which was fair enough Tony delayed his attempts with assistance to break the rifle, to sling Hazels handbag over his shoulder, seeing that Hazel was having difficulties as describe above. The outcome, which was extremely funny on its own, with Hazel's attempts at breaking the rifle in two. While adjusting her handbag that had slipped once again off his shoulder for the third time, already, he seemed so skilful one would reckon he has done it on many other occasions, maybe when out with his friends clubbing in the evening possibly!

Now if you have not been shown closely, or took any notice of the actual loading of the pellet into the weapon earlier on, when Tony was giving an excellent demonstration her mind was on other things, and someone who will remain nameless! Had not taken a blind bit of notice with the perfect demonstration carried out earlier. Sure enough, you need accurate guidance with your very first attempts, which Poor Tony was quite willing to carry out, if the day light was still with us.

His patience towards all the other beginners was first class, but I think he suddenly realized he needed more than the usual customary encouragement with this young woman, who was sent to test his breaking point.

Now (Richard) who is well into his later years, and her long-suffering husband, was standing next to me while all this was going on, with a knowing smile. After three more attempts, with placing the pellet into the correct orifice in the rifle Tony was indicating, saying the round end in the hole "yes" and push the pellet in "yes." Tony was encouraging her attempts in stages.

Slowly Hazel attempted to return the barrel, in line with the butt of the weapon seemingly a comedy on its own, moreover would clearly justify £250.00 on the TV. Show, 'you have been framed' while trying to return the barrel to its firing position, the pellet had fallen out, and landed very near to the open steel lid holding the remainder of four pellets still to be fired.

But was not noticed by Hazel, nevertheless, Tony had picked it up off the firing bench without Hazel noticing and was holding it between his thumb and fingertip ready for her next question, as to why the 'rifle is not working.' Worryingly for Tony, she had looked back into our direction on several occasions, with a smile of satisfaction knowing Tony was there, this turning around to face the audience on occasions, was of some concern to Tony! If of cause she could successfully load the weapon?

Now where should you be looking while firing the rifle at all times, 'To the front,' like poor young Tony was frequently advising, on each occasion she looked round smiling at her husband and us knowing she had poor Tony's attention fully.

I am certain now she fancied young Tony, as I mentioned more than once to her other half, while the master was tutoring her. Now with the rifle not loaded, but was cocked and ready to fire, finally she was taking position still with Tony holding the pellet between his thumb and fingertip, and adjusting his handbag, which had slipped of his shoulder once again, waiting for the obvious from Hazel in a few seconds. After the rifle fired, Hazel turned to Tony with a smile, and said, "Did I hit the target" Tony slowly but reassuringly asked her "what is this pellet doing between my finger and thumb."

She said. "That was a fantastic trick, how did you manage that" Tony had explained to Hazel that the pellet dropped out while she was attempting to close the rifle. Seeing that time was getting on he loaded the weapon himself, and offered the rifle fully loaded with the safety on. Advice was being feed slowly and clearly to Hazel, with the necessary pauses with each instruction, "hold the butt to the shoulder, and look through the sites, when the target comes into view, then slowly press on the trigger."

She was still aiming forward but at 45% degrees to the right of the target. Instructions from poor Tony, who was standing behind her, were obviously being totally ignored, "saying to your left please," repeating "further to your left please." Meanwhile she had attempted pressing the trigger. Suddenly without warning, she turned to show Tony that she had a problem with the rifle; Tony immediately altered her line of fire by grabbing the rifle along the barrel, and pointing it sky wards. What Tony had only just realised of the group of spectators, had all taken to the ground for cover, and some had managed to hide behind some bushes close by.

Hazel was also wondering where everyone had gone, oblivious to the possible danger while still asking Tony why the weapon did not work was her only real concern. While facing towards, where we had all been standing; with sweat now descending from his brow he showed, Hazel by pointing out that the safety catch was still on.

Now it was possible to aim at the target once again, Tony who is an excellent shot held the barrel towards the target on this occasion, and asking her to pull the trigger, low and behold positive hit on the target. As a result, a broad smile of satisfaction on her face as once again she turned to face us all.

We all acted on impulse, once again, diving for cover with the rifle pointing in our direction, so Tony quite professionally pulled back on the rifle to face towards the target area. Immediately all of the audience started to applause as they had returned from their hiding places, behind the bushes, with smiles of relief.

With no more serious breaches concerning safety, the shooting commenced without further incidents. Only one important statement Hazel shared with Tony quietly as she was vacating the firing area.

"Would I have done better if I was wearing my spectacles?"

CHAPTER FORTY-SEVEN

*

Hazel Preparing for the Olympics 2012

Funny, but surprisingly you could see Tony, had been seriously affected by this encounter with Hazel, and was acting most strangely, looking to see where she was at all times and I'm sure he started to twitch. I clearly noticed this twice which was not showing before. Meanwhile Jan my other half won the women's shootout, while I quite fortunately won the gents competition, the man who came second to me was an excellent shot, and was unfortunate in not winning, several of his targets hit but remained upright.

We had to shoot at weighted targets in the final shoot-out, which needed a greater deal of accuracy shooting right at the top in precisely the correct area of the target, before they had any chance of falling, and were awarded higher points.

With more difficult targets positions, with smaller holes to shot through to reach your target area behind, plus being different size targets' obviously the smaller the target awarded you with the higher points.

Some of his shots were excellent, certainly good enough and should have brought down the targets, from what I saw and that is why I was extremely lucky to have won!

Asking my challenger, 'had he been in the Army', which he replied yes? I told him that I had served with Middlesex Regiment at Gordon barracks in 'Hamel' in Germany. What a coincident and utter surprise, he had been there at the same barracks serving with the REME roughly the same year with the REME being attached to our regiment what a small world! We shook hands, and reminisce for a short while on all those years spent in the army, which I loved plus enjoyed every moment.

Just before we all parted the shooting range. Tony reminded all that the archery was at 1500hrs this afternoon looking indirectly at our group, with his eyes fixed towards Hazel. Still adjusting his handbag, with that noticeable twitch which was getting more noticeable somewhat out of control, asking Hazel if she was going to attend this afternoon? Besides, had she ever considered taking up archery possibly start training for the next Olympics in 2012? She smiled and said, "See you at 3 o'clock" in a girly fashion as if she had been flirting, on her first date. After we had left the firing range, and were walking back a short distance towards the main block of buildings, surprisingly we heard someone calling behind us; it was Tony waving his handbag towards our party.

"Hello have you forgotten something?" Spontaneously, we all laughed, while Hazel ran back to collect her handbag from Tony who smiled and said, "Enjoy your lunch, looking forward to the archery this afternoon." After a couple of pints of the best, and our belly full, we slowly headed back in the same direction. Returning to the identical area as the shooting this morning, to find most of the same crowd with a few newcomers had joined our party. Tony and his assistant were heading towards us carrying all the equipment. Hazel had elbowed her other half, stating. "Look Tony's coming; we should have some fun this afternoon."

"Good afternoon, all," with a deliberate pause, looking in the direction of our group, smiling while eyes fixed towards Hazel, still showing signs of the very same obvious occasional twitch, plus involuntary head movement.

Thank you for attending I hope you will enjoy yourselves, we are here this afternoon to show those of you who have never used a bow and arrow before, and to encourage all of you to participate. Please pay particular attention while I run through, some important safety points, and carry out a demonstration.

"It is both for your safety and for our safety and the safety of others in the general area on site, not to attach themselves to any stray arrows while passing by! Who have no desire to be killed with a wayward shot?"

Continuing on with the safely. "The target will be situated on your left or right at right angle of 90 degrees, dependent on whether you hold the bow in your right or left hand." With the remainder of the safety illustrated. He gave a prefect demonstration, with three arrows fired into the target some 25yards away showing slowly each time how best to attach the arrow to the cord. Two of his arrows landed right in the bull one just a fraction outside the bull we all congratulated Tony by clapping saying well done.

"Please can I have those of you who have never used a bow and arrow before on my left, the remainder to my right with James as your instructor?" Only three had not tried archery before, one of the two girls you guessed correctly was Hazel. Who immediately with her finger pointing towards the sky, asking Tony "could I go first please?"

With being extremely shy also very keen to continue her association with her instructor, Tony beckoned her forward to the front, with open arms as if she was a long lost friend. The remainder of us were on the right with James, but able to see what was going on with the other group. Now the pregnant pause was not meant by Tony, looking closely into the eye's of Hazel, standing as if in a trance directly in front of her, you would think they were about to embrace, or Tony was hypnotised by Hazel!

Truthfully, he was still suffering from the affects of this morning's shooting, with the same involuntary occasional twitch; He had obviously developed from this morning's shooting returning rapidly. He did not move his stare for several seconds, she raised her arm that had her handbag attached and asked Tony her instructor to hold it again for her.

Which he very kindly and obligingly carried out, as if it was the normal common reaction for the instructor to try out a prefect stranger's handbag, which was carried out in such a professional manner. You could see, by the way he placed the strap of the handbag over his arm so naturally, just as he had done that morning, with a smile only a comedian could understand. He must have practised this, on many occasions before, as we witnessed this morning, and was quite comfortable in leaving the handbag dangling over his arm.

There was not one person standing there who was not smiling, or laughing or like myself absolutely doubled over with pain, with Hazel and Tony's performance. With a straight face and looking at Hazel thoughtfully, he said "pick up the bow please" which she did with the target at 90 degrees too her left, while holding the bow in her right hand and faced Tony, waiting eagerly for the next line of instruction. Tony spoke slowly, and quietly, reassuringly asking Hazel where the target was positioned!

197

It is a simple, but extremely fundamental question in archery, one needs to know, it helps if the target is on your left, and it would naturally be advantageous in holding the bow in the same hand. As he was saying the above, he reached forward to change the arrangement that Hazel had the bow in the right hand still. His handbag was getting in the way and hitting her legs, while it was dangling from his arm.

With professional ease, the handbag was again repositioned over his shoulder; with the handbag now safely out of harm's way, behind his shoulder. Now with the bow in her 'correct' left hand so he 'thought,' he ask if she would reach for an arrow which she did, without taken her eyes from Tony's face, asking "what do I do now," with a innocent shy smile? Which was a fair question as it was her very first attempt with archery.

You would never have thought so the way she reached for that arrow without taking her eyes off Tony's face, and suffering a great deal with nerves at the time! Not forgetting the occasional glance toward her other half and the rest of us, who were trying to contain ourselves, and thoroughly enjoying the free entertainment carried out before us.

The time was fast approaching the release of Hazel's first arrow, which Tony had great difficulties setting her at 90 degrees to the target, plus his problem with his handbag, which was continually slipping from his shoulder and repeatedly he would return it so skilfully.

Tony's dedication in achieving customer satisfaction was 100%, adjusting his handbag which had slipped once more just at the vital moment. Hazel started pulling back on the cord, still pulling back enough with the bow now starting to shake with tension from side to side. Suddenly and unexpectedly, she released the grip on the cord involuntary before poor Tony could say quite loudly, down a bit.

Too late, the arrow missing a number of seagulls and pigeon pasting overhead, which was very lucky for them, and continued straight over the very tall trees behind the targets, some 200 yards away. The outcome was that after two more attempts at the target by Hazel, with the loss of a further two arrows in the same direction, which were never recovered. Tony had a sudden bad turn, after Hazel's next amazing statement. "I think I should have placed the bow in the other hand because I'm right-handed".

It's a mystery why a perfectly healthy young man in the prime of his life suddenly, needing help and assist away from the shooting area, still holding his handbag firmly, not allowing anyone to remove it from him, you could hear Tony repeatedly reciting the safety rules aloud as he was lead away by other members of staff. The archery was naturally suspended for that afternoon, while other members of staff were summand. We were all very concerned with this regrettable and unexpected situation. Still not knowing or aware, what actually caused this very sudden breakdown, while taking a slow walk back to the main reception area? Noticing, an ambulance outside the main building poor Tony still repeating the safety regulations, while being helped by two gentlemen in white coats into the ambulance, still holding 'his Handbag' close to his chest, which Hazel said he could keep. Warner has sent us a very nice letter, also the contents of Hazel's handbag, in the letter it stated that Tony will be well looked after and the handbag will be returned when Tony decides to let go. 'Sorry to report, showing no improvement yet.'

We all wish him a speedy recovery, all because of his encounter with Hazel on that unbelievable day! "That was an excellent weekend, when are we going again!"

CHAPTER FORTY-EIGHT

*

Our Other Neighbours in the Close

Over now to our next close neighbour, and proceed further round our close, they have two beautiful girls who are extremely friendly, knocking for my grandson Kai occasionally who enjoys their attention. They are relatively new neighbours to the close only arriving approximately one year ago. Both girls get on quite well with Kai; on a fine day with the sun shining they spend time in our garden, or out the front playing and all enjoying themselves with the other children in the close.

Meanwhile their next-door neighbour, who are showing all the signs of wishing to keep their distance, and seems unlikely to change as neighbours with no noticeable smiles, without the daily greeting have just like the last neighbours, only been a short spell in the close. The main reason, as explained earlier with so many relatively new neighbours arriving in the close, was certainly due with losing our open recreational space and play area, which was why they choose to live here all those years ago. If you look towards the title of this book you get a greater understanding what is meant by: 'Actions of a few' (councillors) at a committee meeting, 'are felt by all,'

One thoughtless decision by the councillors at the committee meeting can make a huge difference, and seriously affect the whole community for years after, just for the greed and serious corruption that's going on.

Their next door neighbour who surprisingly is very quiet, over the years, always gives a friendly wave, saying good day which we respect, regrettably has recently lost his wife quite suddenly which was extremely sad. Their immediate neighbours always saying good morning also, and smiling each time with welcome chat while walking up the road, is another neighbour who has been in the close for well over 45years. Surprisingly he agreed all along with the development but regrettable placed their house up for sale recently, I seriously wonder why!!

Suggesting our next neighbour as our oldest friends is an understatement. We have known these two since joining the neighbourhood well over 45years ago.

My wife enjoyed going occasionally over the years to bingo, with Margret infrequently winning but socially looked forward to a pleasant evening down at the Bingo hall in town. Also having a cup of tea and chat, either in our house or in theirs. I think to get away from me for a while! Which I look forward to this arrangement, for a bit of peace and quiet while she is over there with Margret she is not nagging me;

This same couple that Mr Day, (Sorry I forgot he was Knighted earlier), from the housing department had not realised or considered both are disabled, and registered blue badge holders down at the council office. As mentioned previously.

This Mr Day, should be 'Knighted' for the way he treated this couple, deciding without using his brain first, to send an enforced standard letter mentioned earlier, with the same contents as my other neighbours had received locally, demanding that the garage he rents from the council, should be vacated urgently.

Matter of fact within the next few days' due mainly, to 'unforeseen circumstances,' at very short notice of just three days, which is a direct 'lie' in classing it as 'unforeseen circumstances.' If no contact is made with the housing department by Monday in 3 days time, they will assume the alternative garage on offer some 300yards up the road from where they live is not required, and the former garage will soon be empted and demolished at the earliest, due if you recall to 'unforeseen circumstances.'

When George showed me the letter he had received, I could not stop smiling, he has known me for all those years thinking I was wrong to smile the way I did, he did not see or comprehend the ridiculous side with the contents of this letter, or the significance of the housing manager's negative concerns.

After reading it a second and third time, while having great difficulty in trying very hard to stop laughing in front of two mates, whom we have known for years, they were unimpressed with my actions at first, and could not see the serious side of the contents in the letter they had received. Both understandable were in terrible shock and extremely upset with the unforgivable contents found in this letter, from the housing manager.

Anyone would have been upset in receiving this type of correspondence, let alone a disabled person, his wife was in tears I have never ever seen her so upset before, which made me rather annoyed.

Initially I was going to phone 'Sir Knight,' but decided a personal visit to the housing department would be best. Looking forward to seeing his face, when realising his huge mistake, would make my day, not his. On arrival at the housing department, while waiting for Mr, (sorry) Sir Knight to receive me, this delay gave me opportunity to look through some leaflets in the reception area racks. Ironically, the first leaflet I reached for, states that the council are concerned that all handicapped people would be treated fairly, and special consideration for the disabled at all times: (What a joke).

I was just opening the second leaflet, when Sir Day was standing in front of me, smiling from (ear-to-ear); jointly we were both smiling, him not knowing what lay ahead and why I continued to smile as he uttered. "Can I be of any help sir?"

"Firstly, this leaflet I have here I gather you do read these leaflet's, it states that the council will always look after the handicapped, plus disabled with serious concern at all times, you most certainly can help, if you could initially explain the contents of this letter to me, which has upset this disabled couple in our close, can you please explain who is responsible for sending out this letter." I paused to allow him an opportunity to answer, without any response.

"Without consideration for the above situation it has your name down below, signed Mr. Day is that correct, why no checks made before sending out this demanding and inconsiderate letter to this couple do you not have a compassionate bone in your body."

His smile quite suddenly disappeared; in its place was a look of despair, of someone who has just being told, he has lost his job. Still looking at the letter, he turned to walk away I asked for the return of the letter, which was handed straight back to me. Still without a word of explanation also in total shock, while attempting to walk away from me, you could see from his expression he was looking for a rather large hole to disappear into, probably a very large 'black hole.'

"Mr Day, by your silence would I be correct in assuming you had no knowledge of the couple being disabled and established on your register as blue badge holders. How unprofessional and shameful without any checks locally just proves how compassionate your department is towards the disabled plus handicapped, with reference to local planning issues. "Besides, the couple are registered with you as such on your database, this very same standard letter sent out to all those renting garages locally, showing no compassion towards anybody, only total disrespectful attitude."

Mr, Day heard me say this quite clearly still without a word of apologies, while still walking away I said quite loudly. "This is the same person, like the remainder of the authorities in this town with a reputation and history of shameful dealings towards the public, with showing this same arrogant attitude, towards the proposed development." (Others in the reception area were listening intently with utter amazement).

"Regarding our recreational open space with no meeting since day one showing unprofessional blind judgement, with greed plus corruption being your only motive."

"Would you now at your earliest, personally apologise to this couple reassuring them in your next common sense letter, the responsibility of yourselves having made this outstanding mishap. On this occasion, showing some compassion and make it look as if you are concerned with their welfare not your own with your reply."

He assured me that he would sort this out immediately, and urgently investigate this situation. Turned once more without a compassionate bone in his body and swiftly left.

Astonishingly, the main development plans were soon altered two days later, importantly showing a special single garage planed to be built, next to the couple's house.

Which indicated how serious this huge mistake was to the council? They reacted promptly showing how highly embarrassed they were by not realising or checking the disabled person was living in the close, (matter of fact extremely close to the green). The local papers would have been extremely interested in this confrontational story; it certainly was rectified in record time, surely with a 'promotion,' not punishment for Sir Day!

Bad news followed within days, the garage that was promised to be built alongside the disabled couple's house. Cancelled once again, by the architect, instead of seven houses to be built in the garage area, now changed to six houses, leaving four garages to remain instead of two, which were seen on the final working plans. Truly this proved highly embarrassing for the council!!

Now with six houses looking remarkable like a warehouse/prison, replacing all the demolished garages and the disabled couple satisfied with keeping his old garage, and not having to move a considerable distance up the road after all. Just as a footnote, the main working plans were altered twice since, five times in all. Sir Day was finally 'Knighted' so I hear! Continuing round the close yet another recent new neighbour, the former couple in this house left only a year ago, again because of the loss of the open space.

These relatively new neighbours with two young children, who are rather annoyed with the situation of not having a play area on their doorstep. Their estate agent assured them when purchasing their house; they had a green within yards of their property.

'Which was absolutely true could not be closer to the green?'

201

Also promised that renting a garage locally would pose no problem what's so ever, after being told previously by the same estate agent, that there were lots of garages nearby to rent from the council. Only moved in last year, days before the development was due to start, and the wooden hoarding placed around the site soon after.

Now you can see for yourself, the damage a handful of 'councillors' can seriously affect a once happy thriving community. When attending a committee meeting to vote and agree that our recreational open space will shortly be snatched from us, which the locals thought was safeguarded with a policy background against any residential housing being placed on the green.

Even the estate agent had no knowledge of the development proposal, that's how well this planning application was camouflaged?

CHAPTER FORTY-NINE

*

Respect

Let's now as promised earlier, take account of my time spent in the army, which I alone in my intake of 67 national service blokes, uniquely was the only volunteer recruit signing on for no less than nine years. All the remainder, of my intake of lads called upon to serve their two years National service. Without realising this fact at the time, that after our intake of conscripts' serving their time there was, only one other group called up to serve national service after ours in the whole of Great Britain.

Before the end of conscription in November 1960, only realizing or aware of this unique fact, of being one of the very last group to be called upon to do compulsory national service, we were not conscious of this fact, until half way through our 13 weeks training. May I firstly explain if I had not signed up when I did for the Army as a regular soldier? I too like the rest of the lads above, would have had to enlist and serve my two years national Service? It was my decision at the time before the letter arrived on the doormat, and would have informed me.

Her Majesty's Government has chosen you along with all others of your age; would it be very inconvenient in asking you to arrive at Ingus Barracks in Mill Hill, in London? On the 5th July 1960. If of course, this date is not convenient then two big blokes accompanied by a Provo Sergeant, who will kindly show you to your destination and introduce you to the guardroom apartments, where you will be well looked after in your early days of enlistment in the Army!

In addition, her Majesty would like the pleasure of your company for the next two years, you will join the rest of the lads of my age 'willing' to serve National Service for the next two years and counting the days to demob. Why, I was singled out as the only regular in an intake of 67 Nation Service lads is a mystery to all, and can only be explained as a very serious cock up with the recruiting office.

Being totally responsible or irresponsible giving me the incorrect date in joining up. I think to my knowledge history was made on that particular day, with being the only regular soldier joining an intake of disgruntled nation service lads who started arriving three days after my arrival. Moreover, a joy in meeting and welcoming, the only friendly face for quite some time and you will find it compulsory to like him! Who will be your Warrant Officer, or more commonly known as (Sergeant Major) (RSM)?

A drop down from Warrant Officer, is everyone's friend and very best mate, is your 'Company Sergeant.' His one and only roll if (CVs) were around in those days is to be a 'Bastard.' Apologise for swearing but there is not a more apt phase in the dictionary, which best describes his attitude towards the innocent young recruits, when initially he presents himself for the first time.

Very quietly, states "pay attention you horrible lot" meaning every word, while introducing himself to the raw Recruits.

He will always look down the length of his big nose and smile down at you, as if he enjoys being a 'Bastard' and has worked for years to achieve this status, so you have to respect him for that alone. In addition, each sergeant in the army has a unique talent, with eyes in the back of their heads, and do not miss a thing;

May I step back just for the time being to explain my decision in volunteering to join the Army, rather than wait for the inevitable call up papers which would have arrived shortly. My older Brother Paddy who is four years my senior, being much cleverer of the two, with academic skills along with a modicum of brains and being a highly intellectual.

When called up to serve two years national service some years before me, had chosen the Royal Signals Corp, and instead of becoming a real soldier. He had a cushy comfortable time in the signals, playing around as a Radio operator.

He was sent to very interesting postings such as Hong Kong & Singapore, inspiring me in making my inevitable choice in joining not as a national service victim, but choosing to sign up as a regular soldier.

Nevertheless, took the bull by the horns and signed up to become a regular soldier, not for three years, or for six, but for no less than nine years, or if it suited I could have extended my stay later to 22years. Choosing nine years was my choice and decision at the time, a good balance leaving the option to continue later.

Considering my background, as a youngster, in orphanages, and institutions all my early days, I took to the army as a duck to water, fully prepared with inbreeding with the rigors of life already established.

Whether as a voluntary recruit or National Service Soldier, I was destined to end up in the forces in one roll or another eventually. Very nearly settled for the Navy at one time, but my brother persuaded me towards the army. Furthermore, having never ever regretted the foreseeable time committed, loved every moment of this wonderful experience, and would recommend this training to any youngster.

What a pity with the young people of today without any form of training, or way of gaining 'respect' for themselves, or others. They should all have continued, this wonderful worthwhile experience, being tough enough to face the rigors of life ahead with more meaning. The very first thing you learn is 'respect,' not only for yourself, but for everyone you meet. not just a select few, just to gain advantage, and favour for your own needs, similar to the MPs/councillors, feathering their own nest, but a natural inbred respect, for all aspects of life.

Like with the importance, of writing this 'book' drawing attention to the vast amount of disrespect, shown by the so-called intelligent high almighty council officials, and others in authorities, such as members of parliament, (MPs) who have over the years proved not to be so trustworthy, with their open fiddling going on. Sorted out quite successfully by none other than, the **'The Daily Telegraph newspaper group.'** Who started the ball rolling with a successful push, and endeavours, further triumphant and successful conclusion? With intent on exposing, the open fiddling of the MPs parliamentary expenses, which evidential would have continued, without even blinking an eye while openly claiming more and more expenses. We would surely all be securely placed into prison, for carrying out these same actions, of stealing.

Astonishingly and unbelievably the MPs are in an important powerful position, in writing legislation and passing laws of the land, setting a fine example for us all to follow! Showing absolutely no respect, and disregard towards ordinary citizens of this country, who put them all in this position of power. As mentioned previously we would all be serving time in solitary for half of what they get up to. Serving for a period, managing and controlling our lives without due care or any respect. They could have gained this same respect in the forces. **Where respect always follows success:**

While I have your attention, amazingly for countless years the government has operated and run the country in a inherently unpredictable way, made up with three main political parties which for years have made a complete mess at this task:

One senior political party is only interested with making and securing as much money as possible for the wealthy, that's their main aim.

The second senior political party was always seriously interested in helping the working class, but have clearly for many years in the past, also presently lost their way, placing themselves in no man's land.

This next senior political party do not know which direction to take, and will always remain so, until they focus on something to follow, and crucially head in that uncertain direction:

Now I can genuinely without exaggeration offer you the best choice ever, which would achieve something positive without a doubt, just when a new party is essentially required.

The name of this interesting new intriguing political party would be called the **'Fair Party.'**

Honestly, why these other three parties have not chosen this name is a mystery, just the name implies a significant meaning, and positive ring to it.

FOR

ALL

INDIVIDUALS

RIGHT'S

It would be a direct shock and beyond belief to all the other senior political parties that introducing a new party at this moment, is just what is needed seriously with flexible important new ideas, with some positive dependability.

Each Member of Parliament representing this new party would be handpicked with strict positive morals to act in a fairer way at all times.

Evidently over the years a great deal of MPs in the past, have proved untrustworthy and are just there to feather their nests, and make a fortune, while super glued to their parliamentary seats, then collect a fantastic pension at the end of their service as MPs. Hoping to live the rest of their lives in shear comfort, while millions of others in the country are seriously suffering?

205

CHAPTER FIFTY

*

Early Days in the Army

Life in the army, especially in the early days will always be remembered by each recruit. My first day on arrival, with an old brown suitcase in hand, being introduced into army (not forgetting I joined as a volunteer regular recruit) surprisingly was offered my own personal butler, (batman) in the army!

Actually, he turned out to be some nation service bloke, skiving on light duties; He was attached to the previous intake just finishing their 13-week training and was given the task, in showing me around for the next few days. Which I believe was unheard of, making me feel rather important being waited on in the army, 'but that's life some ones got to do it.'

With his help, also his experience plus general knowledge, he got me nicely settled in within the three days showing how to polish my boots, also Blanco my kit and press the uniform ready for inspection, arranging the bedding each morning into a box section, which is a skill on its own.

All hell broke out, when the national service lads joined on that faithful Monday morning. What this fellow did not ask me, over the last few days while he was assisting me in settling in, was understandable a shock to him when eventually he found out, and the penny eventually dropped!

That I was a volunteer regular recruit, well he never asked. No national service bloke would even speak to a regular without good cause. The rest of my new intake had no idea, until payday a week later, this again was a revelation to the others in my barrack room after pay was distributed to each soldier, and it caused a sensation for some time after.

With, obvious ill-feeling amongst my fellow 'inmates' for a short while anyway, or maybe that was inappropriate word 'inmate' to use in these circumstances, which we found ourselves. On our first payday, we were all asked to assemble in no particular order, and wait for your name to be called out. Starting with (Mr, Jones first), 'Pte Jones' "Yes Sir" he would come out from the crowd, and after marching up to the Paymasters table come to a halt and salute, shouting out his name clearly, also the last four digits of his army number, remembering to say, "Sir" before returning to where the remainder of the intake were gathered.

Otherwise the Sergeant standing nearby would remind you directly on how the officer should be addressed. The money that 'Pte Jones received' because he was on national service pay, was a measly £1-1shilling per week (a Guinea in old money), he would then say thank you at the same time Salute and turn, slamming his feet as loud and fast as possible, and march away with thanks for nothing attitude so I noticed! Without the officer or sergeant detecting this same attitude.

Next 'Pte Smith' with a repeat announcement as all others before him had done, with gratitude for serving our Queen and country, after a number of others in the intake having collected their pay.

I could hear my name suddenly announced 'Pte Casey' "Sir" as before repeated last four. Suddenly, as if by magic the room went extremely quiet, you could just about hear the heartbeat of a fly in this very large room, this is how tranquil the room was immediately the paymaster announced £3-15shillings, "thank you Sir." Saluted and turned marched away towards the waiting crowd of lads, some speechless others in complete shock. The very same room as described earlier with being difficult in hearing the heartbeat of a fly was suddenly the complete contrast, with many thinking the paymaster had with oversight and inadvertently mentioned a sum out of the top of his head! The buzz around the room had built up that loud that the next name "Pte Gapp" was impossible to decipher above the nose and had to be repeated several times by the paymaster.

"QUIET" you could here by the 'Sergeant' bellowing out one instruction "QUIET" at the top of his voice once more, which had instant effect resulting with a very much quieter room. The Paymaster called out silently as all officers normally do "Pte Gapp please."

Platoon sitting on the wall, I am standing sixth on the right.

Whose attempt with proceeding forward with a rugby type charge passed me and two other lads, in passing his foot 'accidentally' descended on top of my foot with some force, with him being some 15stone in weight or more, and me wearing soft plimsolls shoes it was no contest. Incidentally, a well (meaning pathetic) "sorry" in passing.

You could sense that rugby or wrestling was his former pastime. When he came to attention in front of the paymaster, the wooden floor felt like a sudden earthquake seemingly any action carried out by Pte Gapp would demand respect, being one of the largest person in our intake.

With me still limping on his return, to where I was trying to stand on one leg, I said quite bravely, "thanks you bastard." Immediately the Sergeant came over to me and placed me on a charge, for swearing in front of the officer. Unsympathetically at double quick time, he marched me out of the building towards the guardroom limping all the way, with what felt like a certain broken bone in my left foot.

On reaching the guardhouse, I was left outside still marching (hopping on one leg) on the spot, he returned outside still shouting "left,-right, Left-right," in double quick time. Because my left foot was starting to throb, still suffering from the weight of that Elephant Pte Gapp, who 'accidentally' on purpose finds my foot supporting his huge blubber for those fateful moments.

He noticed my difficulty in maintaining the marching on the one spot slowing down, and shouted halt, due to the injury to my foot I had already stopped. You could see his contempt and compassion he was 'showing' that he was very sorry with my encounter with that 'elephant Gapp.'

By continuing his shouting, his mouth was an inch from my nose; well this is what you have to contend with, when learning a lesson and not swear in front of an officer in future. Once inside the guardroom, it would be terrible and frightening for most other lads in the very same situation, but more of a curiosity for me apparently with not having the pleasure of visiting the inside of a guardhouse before!

Other blokes would be shaking in their new boots, (or plimsolls) worried as to the next episode anyone without my institutional background and experience would be just as concerned, also worried at the retribution before me; the schools in the past you accept punishment as the norm. Having a short stay in solitary confinement and quietness you treat as a well earned rest.

On our visit to Germany after our 13 weeks training you have to join the regiment, and placed into a Company in the Battalion. Our company was 'C' Company which was like all the rest of the other three companies with approximately 100 troops in each platoon. In the next photograph the men you see are all the drivers, (not skivers) we all worked extremely hard!

Us lads in the MT yard, Blossom on the right then me, followed by Andy.

The three on the right were all boxers, and mix work with training and enjoyed both, but are able to carry out all the normal duties in the battalion. The evidence is in the previous photograph while on the assault course our platoon sitting on the ten foot wall which you have to clamber over on one of the test which the (PTI) physical Training Instructor would encourage all to attempt with full kit on, which was not that easy to achieve with full kit.

CHAPTER FIFTY-ONE

*

Court Appearance

E ntering towards the guardhouse building was an experience on its own. Hearing the sergeant shouting left right, left right, all the way into this large room to where the Provo Sergeant was seated behind his desk, immediately asking me for all items to be taken out of my pockets. Searching for anything, which could harm the guardroom personal, then a quick body search all over checking my pockets, entered all of my contents from my pockets into the register book.

After placing all my personal items into a large envelope for safekeeping, followed by quick march into the cells, and the door slammed after my entry. This treatment would have been intimidating for most lads as mention previously, but for me time to practice yoga and meditation for a while. Which I carry out each morning, was missed that morning because of a sequence of events not allowing me the time needed that morning.

Carried out most days as a daily ritual, with fantastic benefits' overall started many years earlier at a comparatively young age, after reading many books on the very interesting subject of yoga of all types, great deal of enjoyment over the years.

Either through, 'physical exercise' or through, peace of mind, with stretching all muscles throughout the body, achieving a feeling of satisfaction throughout, sets you up for the day. Until inevitably you have achieved a nice relax state, you take full advantage any time during the day. If everyone took time out such as mention above each day, 'there would be no wars just peace.' While starting my count down, into this relaxed state I overheard the guardroom staff calling out, "did you notice that bloke Casey in there, is not in the least bit upset or frightened with being in here."

Evidently, the damage to my foot was not found to be any worst than bruising, when the medical Officer checked the next day, with me still limping around from the elephant's attempts, at swashing a fly just to collect '21 shillings' on payday. Without a doubt, when I see Pte Gapp I will find out why that elephant chose to stamp on my foot, asking whether he did it on purpose, I have a feeling this was no 'accident' after the medical officer had left stating I was on light duties for a week, and to report sick if the pain got worst.

Fancy that light duties without attempting or even trying to skive off duties, which must be a first! Still this was good news, relating to more time to relax but not looking forward to the punishment for swearing.

Without awareness, things were going on that soon involved me. The Provo Sergeant had been instructed, to release me from the cells in the guardhouse because of very interesting events. Pte Gapp had spoken to the Sergeant involved with me being placed in detention and had mentioned to the sergeant the stamping on my foot was deliberately carried out, and was it possible to release me from the guardhouse. It didn't take the sergeant only a few seconds to decide the fairness of the situation, and made a swift phone call to the paymaster who turned out to be a comedian inwardly, stating to the sergeant.

"let's pretend we are going to crucifier him then release him soon after, just to teach him a lesson." That was their plan, to teach me a lesson that swearing with an officer being present, is unacceptable in the army. I reckon the entire guardroom personal were in on this joke, about to run its course and in a short while, the penny will certainly drop.

With all my processions still in the envelope and carried by the Provo Sergeant, also accompanied with two enormous giants acting as escorts, I felt as if I was the murderer being taken to the gallows and about to be hung.

The way they were acting this charade out, instead of marching fast at double quick time across to the other main building, it was carried out in a sedate leisurely slow motion at my pace because of my injury, but never the less the sergeant was not holding back on the 'shouting.'

On entering the room, while still marching very much slower than the last occasion, I was lead first past Pte Gapp, who to my horror was breaking into an uncontrollable smile, while trying to muffle the nose, which straightaway got up my back, even his size would not stop me putting one on him just for smiling at this situation. The culprit standing there smiling like a Cheshire cat while I was about to take the punishment. All went quiet then the officer who was doing an excellent good job at not smiling, asked.

"NAME" "What your name Sir", 'No your name, and Number', (he was trying hard not to burst out laughing). "Name Please" said without hesitation from the very patient Officer. "Pte Casey followed by my last four numbers Sir" while glancing over towards 'Gapp' as if looks could kill, I did an excellent job.

"Pay attention and look to your front" shouted the sergeant from the side. "The charge you are facing is that on such and such a date and time, you did utter a rather disgusting swear word out loudly, which was heard throughout the room and witnessed by all present at the time, including myself." The Paymaster paused before stating. "How do you plead" "Well the bleeding stopped some time later Sir," was my immediate reply. All those in the room suddenly spontaneously burst out with laughter, I was the only one holding a straight face. Inwardly I had great difficulty in not smiling, what with the last remark just submitted, well if you are going down for something, you might as well have a laugh.

"Pte Casey" stated the Officer in a straight face he found extreme difficulty in maintaining. His next remark was not quite as amusing. "Adding now to the charge of being deliberately insubordinate towards an officer, now included on the charge sheet, is that understood."

"Yes Sir." "Can fully justify immediate return to the guardroom, with serving more time inside maybe teaching you that swearing in front of an Officer is unaccepted, and deliberate insubordination will not be tolerated." Pause. "Do you understand" "yes Sir."

"I'll repeat, how do you 'Plead' not Bleed to the charges now." "Guilt Sir". "I did swear Sir; if you had an elephant suddenly standing on your foot I believe you may utter the same towards the animal in question, Sir." "While being molested by this so-called animal Pte Gapp has admitted that, the stamping of his foot onto your foot was his fault, and would like to apologise for his actions, spoken rather slowly by the Paymaster."

With a smile saying "Sir, I will accept his, apologise for his 'accidental' provocation, in charging forward to collect his pay Sir."

211

The Officer made us both shake hands and forget about the incident altogether, 'what a grip.' In reply the Officer stated in my defence. "Due to this extreme provocation, by this so-called 'animal.' We would recommend your immediate release and please resume your training forthwith, once you feel well enough to rejoin the rest of the intake."

"Thank you Sir" turned and marched slowly out of the room with most of the audience presently, laughing their heads off. The Provo sergeant handed me the envelope and smiled in passing, well that is worrying sign seeing a different side of the Provo sergeant.

Andy met me just outside for a formal introduction this time voluntary shaking of hands. Stating "Andy is my name I hope your foot is OK, very pleased to meet, under different terms,"

He was quite well spoken and surprisingly agreeable for an 'Elephant' "my name is Tony and would appreciate in future if you wouldn't mind, not stamping on my bloody foot. Now we have been acquainted and on speaking terms is a brilliant start with both our army carriers." Hopefully, many more other pleasant encounter's which were soon to follow. Andy asked, "Was it that bad staying in the guardhouse all night," my immediate answer was "I could do it standing on my head" (when you consider some of the yoga positions) two of which were carried out last night's session, for five minutes exercise on my head on each occasion:

"Come on Tony lets nip off to the NAFI drinks are on me, if you're paying." I smiled with approval and bought him a couple; we talked for some time followed by a short episode of my past in the boarding schools.

Guessing correctly, saying he was a wrestler also a rugby player before entering into the army, this is what you must do, pick your 'friends' carefully. Andy was most impressed a few days later with my activities in the boxing ring, during (PE) lesson.

212

CHAPTER FIFTY-TWO

*

Settled a Score in the Ring

Treating somebody respectfully, will soon be taught towards this show of contempt and unnecessary animosity, chiefly targeted towards me being a regular soldier, will be altered on Tuesday in the gymnasium in only a few seconds I guess, after entering the boxing ring. To explain further, one of the national service lads a Welsh bloke who had a bee in his bonnet was always giving me grief over time in training, for absolutely no reason other than the fact that I was a regular soldier.

Given the slightest opportunity concerning him being a national service, and me being a regular soldier this individual needed sorting out, indeed this needed sorting out sooner rather than later, and now was his perfect opportunity so he thought, or did he think!

He indicated to the Physical Training Instructor (PTI) that 'we' should contest in the ring with him being roughly the same size and build. This selection suited the (PTI) who agreed with us being next to contest in the ring, using conventional Queensberry rules of boxing, and of course, not forgetting your brain. With 'only three one minute' rounds, with the PTI as referee sounded a fair arrangement to me.

'Well some people judge a book by the cover, most read inside, but this bloke did not entertain either,' perhaps he should have. Moreover, may wonder or wish he had very soon, maybe within a few seconds the way I see it. We had only one minute to wait before I learnt the significance for the rest of my army carer, was about to form in less than one minute, or possibly less.

Perhaps acting should have been my speciality, for the performance shown by myself that morning, before entering into the ring I put on an act of being extremely nervous and frightened, deserving of an Oscar at the very least. The bell had rung at the end of the last bout, with one poor fellow who was very brave but needed the necessary skills against the punishment he received.

Returning to my next carer opportunity with acting, suddenly I produced the twitch and continued this twitch quite noticeably, fearful of what was about to happen. You could see quite plainly my dislike and nervousness, with being in the ring with this pumped up animal with a shirt covered in sweat and on how fit he looked, egger and keen getting carried away with the stationary post in his corner thinking the post was me, his preparations carried out ready to proceed with the battle against the English and the Welsh.

More to the point, a regular against national service, 'who' would show the scars of this confrontation? Describing what looked like facing a tiger already prancing around in his corner, pretending to fight an imaginary boxer in front of himself, even I was feeling a little anxious and panicky! The (PTI) called us both together in the centre of the ring, just to cover the point that he was the referee, stating "we should listen to him and carry out his instructions, is that understood" looking at both of us then touching gloves.

The bell rung and he continued hearing the bell on the way to the floor of the ring.

He made I suppose, the classic mistake a bull in a china shop would be ᴄ. make, towards a waiting unexpected glance to the side of the head, with the glov left ear. Which you cover in training, most serious boxers know of this move to unbaḷ the opposition, I have witnessed this over the years of training.

On his way down to the floor of the ring, I was able to stop his head and face hitting the floor, with a crushing affect, already both eyes were rolling ended up looking towards the top of his head with classic knockout. The site the Doctor would witness when called into the ring, when a boxer is left lying on the deck.

This first fight was so important and remembered for the right reasons. The significance I did not see it coming. (Excuse the pun) excused most duties when fighting for the British army later against other regiments throughout the army, and when officially representing army, against other British forces Army, Navy, additionally Air force.

Andy my most recent acquaintance was most impressed with arms outstretched, greeted me while I was departing the ring, saying, "That was most impressive, the best lesson that Welsh bloke will ever learn in his life, just before your fight I overheard him say that he was going to 'kill you,' when given the opportunity," (metaphorically speaking of course). "Where did you learn how to box like that, when you entered the ring I fully expected a bloodbath not in your favour of course, and with good reason, covered my face with both hands momentarily, nearly missed what actually had happened well done.

Incidentally I see the twitch has suddenly disappeared what was that all about." With a smile it did not need an answer.

It hadn't gone unnoticed by the (PTI) who was refereeing the bout that I could 'fight' even with only two seconds length of this bout, he now put me with another potential victim later in the same morning session of (PE instruction). What the Army will always look after is its boxers, to symbolize the regiment against other regiments; this is a well known fact, in all fields of sport within the armed forces. Later I was through along with Andy, Blossom, and several others for the next stage of boxing the following week.

With boxing, you will find some boxers very much like the Welsh bloke, who risk everything, and open with attacking move, towards the opponent on entering the ring, on occasions this surprise attack does work. This has always proved extremely risky to open like that, without using the brain first.

After countless hours of training and learning different skills, you would never risk an open attack, without finding out whether your opponent will either firstly attack, or use his defence in the opening seconds of the first round. Andy may be spot on, stating this bloke has learnt an important lesson of 'respect' although it does seem a stalemate essentially.

If you wish to stand any chance of winning any fight, using both timing plus your brain, along with importantly experience, followed closely with skills learnt over many hours in training, and an awful lot of luck to follow. Together our intake continued with the army training over the next thirteen weeks.

Like the comedian who stands up and tells one joke after another, in front of a very large audience, with the same 'brave' timing, but different end result with the same 'punch line' (excuse the pun).

...d possibly explain the reason why this coverage has any bearing, with ... the importance and the meaning of the word. **'RESPECT.'**

...oke down to me, mean an awful lot more in general, than just the word ...nce, of the word respect is seen in all occupations and lifestyles whether ...now sincere respect or make-believe. Then when that person is not present ...eone about that same person, with contradictory thoughts and remarks, which ...be regarded as disrespectful, without the person presently aware of this fact.

I would like to follow with an excellent example of respect. This fine example that comes to mind just recently, and a perfect choice for an entry into this book. Showing true 'respect' for others, which I feel merits an award for outstanding aptitude for the welfare, of one of her visiting customers in our local pharmacy up the road.

Mrs. Indira Shah and her husband in charge of our pharmacy in our local shopping area. This wonderful woman exceeded her normal duty, with supplying a service to the public, while continuing her busy schedule with preparing prescriptions; she went out of her way to assist the postal worker, serving their shopping area, which included this same pharmacy. He was unfortunately off sick suffering from the consequences of the 'swine flu,' currently affecting thousands of unfortunate people in this country some seriously, others mildly only a chemist or doctor would be aware of this person's ability to resume work. The very point, of this being entered in this book, showing the ignorance of his employer. Post office Head Quarters, 'apparently sacking an employee while off sick with swine flu is like hitting someone below the belt.' Is uncaring similar to kicking someone while on the floor injured, without an understanding or concern with his medical circumstances, is an appalling outrageous act by his employer the postal service.

Actions of our local chemist, in recognising his dilemma, have now a bearing on this fortunate person's future, through her actions successfully, accomplished, with him being reinstated back to work? Notwithstanding her physical support with contacting three separate individual (Post Office Head Quarters).

Only after a successful petition, and a great deal of luck carried out by the entire local people, headed by the accomplishments of our local chemist. Whom I personally, feel should be nominated, for her outstanding concern for one of her customers, her friendly postal delivery worker.

The outcome for this person's future would have been devastating for himself, also his wife along with two small children. He was reinstated after the post office looked seriously into this highly embarrassing case.

Consequently it would have been a totally diffident story if the local chemist had ignored this local scandal, and serious issue, involving a post office worker. Successful outcome now, for this lovely family was truly remarkable, by the actions of our local chemist. This is truly what I feel respect is all about.

Another very important aspect, with this book referring to the astonishing way councillors, and local authorities, including planners, housing departments, show very little respect or concern plus compassion towards the local resident's emotions, when proposing any new developments.

All you hear from the local residents on countless occasions is **'what can you do about it?'** without firstly considering a meeting which is extremely important, plus respectful. With money their only concern, how much can we fiddle out of the taxpayer on this occasion! You give your vote supporting the local councillor, when they need your support. Then they refuse to support you just when you need their support most. This is clearly unbalanced in their favour, showing no respect what so ever.

Along with other fine examples with regard to Respect being shown above, while in the Army you show respect to the officer and likewise respect will be shown in return. 'Andy most importantly owned up to the Sergeant' about 'accidently' treading on my foot.

Which truly did occur as, explained above. This resulted with my early release out of jail. Proving a marvellous example of the word 'respect' and now long lasting friendship as a result? Incidentally without any report showing on my records, which was extremely important to me:

With a number of fine examples, throughout this book showing where the importance of respect also proved necessary. 'Look throughout, for these examples in each chapter.' renaming the book from **'respect'** to my other choice. **'What can you do about it?'**

Then on to the current title. **"Actions of a few (Councillors) are felt by all"** was extremely difficult for me to decide on, but hopefully proved the correct choice in the end!

Respect starts from within the family, without a doubt, you must show respect towards your parents, then onto the school you attend, most children show a great deal of respect towards their teachers, but a tiny minority in each school showing positive disrespect.

Deliberately taunting the teacher with unruly behaviour, until the teacher eventually loses interest with the teaching profession altogether, with disastrous devastating consequences, the remainder of the class suffering the regards of this small minority which have a knock on affect on all their education with the teacher unable to teach?

Held back by this tiny minority which could escalate at any moment out of control towards anarchy? On leaving school, life completely changes, and respect accounts for every aspect in your occupational choice, from now on, if shown respect, you will quite suddenly realise, others are now showing their respect towards you, which is found pleasing, when you are on the receiving end, and applied for the rest of your life with a great deal of success, proved on each occasion?

Time spent with the other lads for 13 weeks training in the army, teaches respect, which is extremely important. You may have gathered by now throughout this volume, respect is paramount and must never be ignored.

CHAPTER FIFTY-THREE

*

Interesting Discussions

Total loss of respect was shown, if you recall by Mr, Bent from the planning office, stating it is 'too time consuming' to call a meeting, when the local neighbourhood are about to lose their essential open recreational space, enjoyed for well over 60years. Nevertheless, having a serious rightful natural 'claim' on this important open space over time, it belongs 100% to the local residents having gained absolutely nothing with this important intervention.

It could, and should, have been argued in the high court, concerning this serious natural claim over time, however, with absolutely no chance of winning against the council, having and using an abundance of taxpayer's money available, will obviously win any court action by a country mile.

My personal pension, plus life saving would be lost in defending this action, but I did seriously consider the above knowing I had a very strong presentation, and still believe this to be the case, and with the opportunity would win significally if one could trust the fairness in court action? How on earth did they manage to change the policy background? Firstly, by throwing away the rulebook, then fight dirty using unconventional rules, similar to getting into the boxing ring without gloves on.

Importantly with no referee present to oversee what is going on, using bullyboy tactics. Secondly and just as important, not allowing an open meeting with the locals to discuss the serious local issues, before the approval was granted to start the development. Then by magic, the site turned into a brown field site, immediately without anyone locally being aware of this fact. Followed closely by changing the land into a free fall site, which now becomes available and suitable for redevelopment which meant importantly, only the garage area not our recreational play area:

Third and most important serious issue with breaking government guidelines as to the limitation of approximately (ten units) demolished. Learning from my research on (free fall sites), this is illegal what the planners and developers have carried out above.

With 47 garage units demolished is far in excess, of the amount or quantity beyond what is socially or morally acceptable. After demolishing hurriedly far too many buildings. As stated above breaking all the rules and guidelines the government sets down for the councils to follow. Probably happening in other towns throughout the whole of Great Britain, who are receiving this same disrespectful and unacceptable treatment.

Not forgetting the serious issue of all the properties in the near neighbourhood, all being devalued considerably between £20,000/30,000. Which is completely unacceptable, and not considered or understood or completely ignored by the planning office, as an important consideration? **Try to imagine just for one moment with this fine straightforward example, on your own it is this very same respect for the local environment that surrounds your area.**

Which is the single most important aspect surrounding you? Introduce one other person; you now have to show respect for that other person.

Likewise respect shown in return towards you, if a third person is now involved, that person should show respect for both, and this I believe is where the problem first starts to get complicated, after you add a greater amount of people like in a community where it is most important to show respect for all.

With the above example now only needs one person to show disrespect to one, or both then continued respect has proved essential. Because we all know, the result, even with a small numbers involved, when increasing the numbers the problem needs serious controlling. Addressing this problem, is however more difficult, being treated by the planners and authorities in your local council, when stating that a meeting is unnecessary and 'too time consuming.' 'For whom?'

Introducing yet another aspect of respect, with this next fine example, to explain briefly that after the birth of a baby and the child takes its first breath, from that moment on, it needs immediate attention and total respect. Unlike some animals, concerning wildlife such as the horse, sheep, Buffalo, deer, and countless others are able to stand, and have the natural instincts with survival within minutes of birth, finding the nipple of the mother and so on, soon running from any danger. Human Babies would never stand a chance of survival. Without the intervention, from other humans nearby with the respect that the Baby needs help and encouragement. That same respect returned later in life after the understanding that the baby must now show respect for others throughout his/her life, is extremely important.

Let us now continue with the Army training, when joining you have to carry out the necessary compulsory 13weeks training. Learning the ropes with having to march in time with a group of other lads, until we turn out as soldiers, is a skill on its own. Which the drill sergeant will spend hours, shouting all horrid remarks until it all comes together some weeks later. Where there was a rabble weeks before now the whole group will halt together in one sharp 'crack,' you could not believe the coming together of these individuals now with the proud feeling of wanting to perform, or the sergeant and the (RSM) will see to it that more training is necessary.

This is why approximately 13weeks training is necessary and essential, to turn a rabble of blokes into an army of lads now able also reliable, to take on any task throughout the world, asked of them anything without question?

From the photo following you can see me carrying out a dally task, of cleaning our kit ready for inspection the following morning.

We rejoin one evening while all of us are busy cleaning our kit for inspection in the morning, with an intense argument about national service against regular volunteer arrangement. I of cause supported my own self in this open discussion, stating that I would have been called up within weeks anyway, so I decided what was best for me.

Importantly it was my choice! However, several of the lads who were forced to do their two years national service, disliked and disagreed with me, with the fact of me signing up as a regular soldier. That is there opinion and they are fully entitled to share their opinion.

Me Cleaning My Kit.

My immediate answer was that, "the more senior soldiers in the army such as the corporals, sergeants and above. Are normally found to be regulars; and without them and their vast experience, the army would be very much weaker as a result. It is these men we call upon in an emergency, anywhere in the world, where action is urgently needed. Against any and all enemies, without a useful strong force, so thankfully the person who decides to sign for a number of years, like I had decided, for the next nine years shows some commitment and bottle."

Thinking I had got my point over to them, most evenings while cleaning our gear for the next day, were spent talking and discussing a whole range of interesting topics, which were found to be extremely motivating. When you appreciate that the lads were called up interrupting their carriers. Each barrack room housed approximately 20 soldiers of all occupations and trades. Starting with myself, just out of apprenticeship in engineering, deciding mainly with tool making. Just fancied a change, and was determined to sign up in the army, after several years on very low pay as an apprentice.

In our barrack room, we had such a variety of interesting mix of specialized area of business professionals, starting with two lads in the watch repair business.

One banker, three poets, one individual who was clearly 'gay' but harmless, another lad learning and training to be a jockey, a vet, also two labours, and many other trades including two lawyers.

Not forgetting, an excellent close friend of mine, Alan Quartermaine, who fancied himself as a good runner, and athlete, which admittedly he was always extremely keen to be involved with cross-country running. In front at all times, he was faster than me over long distance, but I would never admit it. Like in that 'Film called Forrest Gump' where his comrades' would call out 'run Forrest run' to encourage him on. The dell boy type, who could sell you anything on the open or black market, living years ago in The Manor area, posh part of Islington in London.

All of these very different amazing diverse characters' such as (The Elephant) Andy Gapp, also (Blossom) Flowerdew another boxer. All of whom, were drawn into the army to serve their time, and many, many more. Collectively over the next two years will be some experience for us all.

We will call upon all these skills, when leaving the army, from time to time to great use, but clearly, Respect for each other was paramount.

Before closing this book, could I invite you to complete the 'exam' set out to see how attentive you have been while reading this interesting informative book.

With the answers showing on my website when I manage to get it up and running, please visit just to see how successful you have been with your answers, good luck. They are meant to be straightforward like what colour is 'Orange' for example?

Email for now: www.actionsofafewarefeltbyall@gmail.com

Hopefully the site will be up and running soon.

While visiting the site, I would be intrigued also inquisitive to know whether you are treated appallingly in your town by the local officials; the main reason I am interested whether this treatment is replicated throughout the whole country.

Please if you have a few moments, I would be delighted to hear of your comments and feedback, to share with other visitors or (victims) to the site, possibly finding themselves in the same or similar predicament.

Thank you, I do hope this book has helped, and assists in some way to your success, now you have some of the tools to work with. Let me give you something to think about with this fascinating true summary, just before you close this book.

CHAPTER FIFTY-FOUR

*

I cannot believe it

Portrayed by a grumpy old pensioner, and inherent in most of us older people, is the most famous actor of all times Richard Wilson. Who has been a favourite of mine over the years, and I would feel this volume complete, to end this last chapter of this book, headed with a well-remembered quote of his.

I cannot believe it. With respect to all the current residents that a meeting was not held or ever considered prior to this new development.

I cannot believe it. In our local magazine, The Chronicle/summer 2010 stating on page (6) (Happy playing). Allowing the children to play in the street, as long as they use a soft ball to prevent damage to your neighbours fences, gardens, and cars.
(Should the children be advised to play in the street by the Council, or should they have small-grassed areas like 'Shortmeadow green,' which has now been snatched from the locals and built on)?

I cannot believe it. The local residents have allowed the green to be taken without considering a fight.

I cannot believe it. All but four garages out of 51 were demolished without a whimper, from the current residents who have lost any chance of a secure place locally to place their cars safely away from criminals.

I cannot believe it. The local residents have accepted a worsening parking situation throughout the local neighbourhood for the future, without shouting, and refusing the inevitable scenario.

I cannot believe it. All the residents excepting the loss of all the mature trees affecting the local environment, without standing up against this change.

I cannot believe it. That three mature 50/60ft trees can be cut down 'accidentally.' Followed soon after by the very same developers with three more trees seriously damaged and having to be removed because they were left in an unsafe situation, near to the local resident's rear gardens with no hefty fine to pay?

I cannot believe it. In addition, I feel extremely sorry for all those who have lost their vista and expanse of the green, replaced with unsightly horrendous buildings now, and being observed to the rear of their gardens, by the new resident's extremely large windows facing their homes without complaining.

I cannot believe it. The council selling the open space to the developers, then the developer selling the open space to Guinness trust housing. This was a designated play area for the children/residents to use and enjoy. **Importantly, where are the children supposed to play now?**

I cannot believe it. Seriously, how they changed the Policy background, stating that the open space would never be considered for residential housing, now changed without consultation with the local residents on this most important fundamental issue, where is democracy in this free society?

I cannot believe it. No consideration was ever given towards the effect of devaluing of each privately owned property in the local neighbourhood, with this new development taken over our green, and still nobody is up in arms and protesting against the development takeover.

I cannot believe it. With common knowledge, that any development is not discussed, and agreed with, at least two years in advanced with the developer, before public announcement. So how can it be regarded as 'unforeseen circumstances' like presented by letter, concerning the demolishing all 47 garages, by the housing manager. 'Sir Knight.'

I cannot believe it. The £millions spent on achieving this development, without serious questions as to the location, and the aftermath of placing 21 units into a small compact area, and the placement of an unacceptable **'Septic Tank'** only yards from the current neighbours rear gardens on the new site in the 21 century, without serious consequences for the future.

I cannot believe it. That it was ever agreed by the local council, to cut down our only remaining two mature Cherry trees in the close, which were situated outside the development site, without consultation with the local residents beforehand.

Lastly, I cannot believe it. That after approximately 60years claim, using the green as common play area for the local children, plus residents, is taken without consultation or debate, affecting the whole Community which seriously separated the community in half some 20 years ago, and continues dividing the whole community for the future.

Truly, how was it possible to have all of these serious issues, with regards to only one development?

So why do we have policy plus procedure in place.
To safeguard against.
'Actions of a few (councillors), affecting us all.'

'Only Two Pairs.'
If you have two pears.
You actually have four pairs.
Together adds in total to eight pairs.
Which were really only four pairs?
That started with only two pears?

As a final calculation, have you ever gone to take a short stride, then wish you had stretched just that bit further with a giant stride? This was remarkably the same, when I took on this challenge in writing this book, which started as an extended letter to my local (MP) who was ever so busy sorting out her. Parliamentary expenses?
Enjoy yourselves and smile.
As promised the exam?

Exam.

1. Locally where are the young children going to play now?
2. Objections best person to help.
3. Natural advantage in separating your objections why?
4. Guess, the best month for Councils to propose development?
5. Mention who states you will never beat the Council.
6. Essential reason why a Committee meeting is held?
7. Alas, can you ask a question at a Committee meeting?
8. Do you know what nepotism means?
9. Only developers know when a green is not a green.
10. What name was showing on the car number plate, Bandy/Bent?
11. Guess who is responsible, for losing the fight to save the green?
12. Reason why local Councillor lost her seat?
13. Exactly what holds a tree in the vertical position?
14. Example, what is a "free fall site?"
15. Now what is meant by off street parking?
16. Obviously, you cannot cut down three trees accidentally "can you?"
17. Are bats protected by law in Great Britain Yes/No?
18. Knowing what is understood by a healthy environment?
19. Firstly, who should show respect?
20. Incidentally, what is understood by loss of all creditability or respect?
21. Established, housing association hidden for 11months "who?"
22. Lesson for all, what was 'too time consuming?'
23. Did Mr. Henderson my teacher ask me to spell a word, which word?
24. State a reason why the houses were devalued?
25. Close, approximation dimension of the green in yards/meters.

Old git waiting at the bus stop.